Marx, Engels, and Marxisms

Series Editors
Marcello Musto, York University, Toronto, ON, Canada
Terrell Carver, University of Bristol, Bristol, UK

The Marx renaissance is underway on a global scale. Wherever the critique of capitalism re-emerges, there is an intellectual and political demand for new, critical engagements with Marxism. The peer-reviewed series Marx, Engels and Marxisms (edited by Marcello Musto & Terrell Carver, with Babak Amini, Francesca Antonini, Paula Rauhala & Kohei Saito as Assistant Editors) publishes monographs, edited volumes, critical editions, reprints of old texts, as well as translations of books already published in other languages. Our volumes come from a wide range of political perspectives, subject matters, academic disciplines and geographical areas, producing an eclectic and informative collection that appeals to a diverse and international audience. Our main areas of focus include: the oeuvre of Marx and Engels, Marxist authors and traditions of the 19th and 20th centuries, labour and social movements, Marxist analyses of contemporary issues, and reception of Marxism in the world.

More information about this series at
http://www.palgrave.com/gp/series/14812

Ronaldo Munck

Rethinking Development

Marxist Perspectives

palgrave
macmillan

Ronaldo Munck
Centre for Engaged Research
Dublin City University
Dublin, Ireland

ISSN 2524-7123 ISSN 2524-7131 (electronic)
Marx, Engels, and Marxisms
ISBN 978-3-030-73810-5 ISBN 978-3-030-73811-2 (eBook)
https://doi.org/10.1007/978-3-030-73811-2

Cover illustration: xenotar, Getty Images

This Palgrave Macmillan imprint is published by the registered company Springer Nature Switzerland AG
The registered company address is: Gewerbestrasse 11, 6330 Cham, Switzerland

para Ernesto

Titles Published

1. Terrell Carver & Daniel Blank, *A Political History of the Editions of Marx and Engels's "German Ideology" Manuscripts*, 2014.
2. Terrell Carver & Daniel Blank, *Marx and Engels's "German Ideology" Manuscripts: Presentation and Analysis of the "Feuerbach chapter,"* 2014.
3. Alfonso Maurizio Iacono, *The History and Theory of Fetishism*, 2015.
4. Paresh Chattopadhyay, *Marx's Associated Mode of Production: A Critique of Marxism*, 2016.
5. Domenico Losurdo, *Class Struggle: A Political and Philosophical History*, 2016.
6. Frederick Harry Pitts, *Critiquing Capitalism Today: New Ways to Read Marx*, 2017.
7. Ranabir Samaddar, *Karl Marx and the Postcolonial Age*, 2017.
8. George Comninel, *Alienation and Emancipation in the Work of Karl Marx*, 2018.
9. Jean-Numa Ducange & Razmig Keucheyan (Eds.), *The End of the Democratic State: Nicos Poulantzas, a Marxism for the 21*st *Century*, 2018.
10. Robert X. Ware, *Marx on Emancipation and Socialist Goals: Retrieving Marx for the Future*, 2018.
11. Xavier LaFrance & Charles Post (Eds.), *Case Studies in the Origins of Capitalism*, 2018.

12. John Gregson, *Marxism, Ethics, and Politics: The Work of Alasdair MacIntyre*, 2018.
13. Vladimir Puzone & Luis Felipe Miguel (Eds.), *The Brazilian Left in the 21st Century: Conflict and Conciliation in Peripheral Capitalism*, 2019.
14. James Muldoon & Gaard Kets (Eds.), *The German Revolution and Political Theory*, 2019.
15. Michael Brie, *Rediscovering Lenin: Dialectics of Revolution and Metaphysics of Domination*, 2019.
16. August H. Nimtz, *Marxism versus Liberalism: Comparative Real-Time Political Analysis*, 2019.
17. Gustavo Moura de Cavalcanti Mello and Mauricio de Souza Sabadini (Eds.), *Financial Speculation and Fictitious Profits: A Marxist Analysis*, 2019.
18. Shaibal Gupta, Marcello Musto & Babak Amini (Eds), *Karl Marx's Life, Ideas, and Influences: A Critical Examination on the Bicentenary*, 2019.
19. Igor Shoikhedbrod, *Revisiting Marx's Critique of Liberalism: Rethinking Justice, Legality, and Rights*, 2019.
20. Juan Pablo Rodríguez, *Resisting Neoliberal Capitalism in Chile: The Possibility of Social Critique*, 2019.
21. Kaan Kangal, *Friedrich Engels and the Dialectics of Nature*, 2020.
22. Victor Wallis, *Socialist Practice: Histories and Theories*, 2020.
23. Alfonso Maurizio Iacono, *The Bourgeois and the Savage: A Marxian Critique of the Image of the Isolated Individual in Defoe, Turgot and Smith*, 2020.
24. Terrell Carver, *Engels before Marx*, 2020.
25. Jean-Numa Ducange, *Jules Guesde: The Birth of Socialism and Marxism in France*, 2020.
26. Antonio Oliva, Ivan Novara & Angel Oliva (Eds.), *Marx and Contemporary Critical Theory: The Philosophy of Real Abstraction*
27. Francesco Biagi, *Henri Lefebvre's Critical Theory of Space*
28. Stefano Petrucciani, *The Ideas of Karl Marx: A Critical Introduction*
29. Terrell Carver, *The Life and Thought of Friedrich Engels, 30th Anniversary Edition*
30. Giuseppe Vacca, *Alternative Modernities: Antonio Gramsci's Twentieth Century*

31. Kevin B. Anderson, Kieran Durkin & Heather Brown (Eds.), *Raya Dunayevskaya's Intersectional Marxism: Race, Gender, and the Dialectics of Liberation*
32. Marco Di Maggio, *The Rise and Fall of Communist Parties in France and Italy*
33. Ryuji Sasaki, *A New Introduction to Karl Marx: New Materialism, Critique of Political Economy, and the Concept of Metabolism*
34. Kohei Saito (Ed.), *Reexamining Engels's Legacy in the 21st Century*
35. Paresh Chattopadhyay, *Socialism in Marx's Capital: Towards a De-alienated World*
36. Marcello Musto, *Karl Marx's Writings on Alienation*
37. Michael Brie & Jörn Schütrumpf, *Rosa Luxemburg: A Revolutionary Marxist at the Limits of Marxism*
38. Gianfranco Ragona & Monica Quirico, *Frontier Socialism: Self-organisation and Anti-capitalism*
39. Stefano Petrucciani, *Theodor W. Adorno's Philosophy, Society, and Aesthetics*
40. Miguel Vedda, *Siegfried Kracauer, or, The Allegories of Improvisation*

Titles Forthcoming

Vesa Oittinen, *Marx's Russian Moment*

Kolja Lindner, *Marx, Marxism and the Question of Eurocentrism*

Jean-Numa Ducange & Elisa Marcobelli (Eds.), *Selected Writings of Jean Jaures: On Socialism, Pacifism and Marxism*

Adriana Petra, *Intellectuals and Communist Culture: Itineraries, Problems and Debates in Post-war Argentina*

George C. Comninel, *The Feudal Foundations of Modern Europe*

James Steinhoff, *Critiquing the New Autonomy of Immaterial Labour: A Marxist Study of Work in the Artificial Intelligence Industry*

Spencer A. Leonard, *Marx, the India Question, and the Crisis of Cosmopolitanism*

Joe Collins, *Applying Marx's Capital to the 21st century*

Levy del Aguila Marchena, *Communism, Political Power and Personal Freedom in Marx*

Jeong Seongjin, *Korean Capitalism in the 21st Century: Marxist Analysis and Alternatives*

Marcello Mustè, *Marxism and Philosophy of Praxis: An Italian Perspective from Labriola to Gramsci*

Satoshi Matsui, *Normative Theories of Liberalism and Socialism: Marxist Analysis of Values*

Shannon Brincat, *Dialectical Dialogues in Contemporary World Politics: A Meeting of Traditions in Global Comparative Philosophy*
Francesca Antonini, *Reassessing Marx's Eighteenth Brumaire: Dictatorship, State, and Revolution*
Thomas Kemple, *Capital After Classical Sociology: The Faustian Lives of Social Theory*
Tsuyoshi Yuki, *Socialism, Markets and the Critique of Money: The Theory of "Labour Note"*
V Geetha, *Bhimrao Ramji Ambedkar and the Question of Socialism in India*
Xavier Vigna, *A Political History of Factories in France: The Workers' Insubordination of 1968*
Attila Melegh, *Anti-Migrant Populism in Eastern Europe and Hungary: A Marxist Analysis*
Marie-Cecile Bouju, *A Political History of the Publishing Houses of the French Communist Party*
Gustavo Moura de Cavalcanti Mello & Henrique Pereira Braga (Eds.), *Wealth and Poverty in Contemporary Brazilian Capitalism*
Peter McMylor, Graeme Kirkpatrick & Simin Fadaee (Eds.), *Marxism, Religion, and Emancipatory Politics*
Mauro Buccheri, *Radical Humanism for the Left: The Quest for Meaning in Late Capitalism*
Rémy Herrera, *Confronting Mainstream Economics to Overcome Capitalism*
Tamás Krausz, Eszter Bartha (Eds.), *Socialist Experiences in Eastern Europe: A Hungarian Perspective*
Martin Cortés, *Marxism, Time and Politics: On the Autonomy of the Political*
João Antonio de Paula, Huga da Gama Cerqueira, Eduardo da Motta e Albuquer & Leonardo de Deus, *Marxian Economics for the 21st Century: Revaluating Marx's Critique of Political Economy*
Zhi Li, *The Concept of the Individual in the Thought of Karl Marx*
Lelio Demichelis, *Marx, Alienation and Techno-capitalism*
Dong-Min Rieu, *A Mathematical Approach to Marxian Value Theory: Time, Money, and Labor Productivity*
Salvatore Prinzi, *Representation, Expression, and Institution: The Philosophy of Merleau-Ponty and Castoriadis*
Agon Hamza, *Slavoj Žižek and the Reconstruction of Marxism*
Kei Ehara (Ed.), *Japanese Discourse on the Marxian Theory of Finance*
Éric Aunoble, *French Views on the Russian Revolution*
Elisa Marcobelli, *Internationalism Toward Diplomatic Crisis: The Second International and French, German and Italian Socialists*
Paolo Favilli, *Historiography and Marxism: Innovations in Mid-Century Italy*
Terrell Carver, Smail Rapic (Eds.), *Friedrich Engels for the 21st Century: Perspectives and Problems*

Juan Dal Maso, *Hegemony and Class: Three Essays on Trotsky, Gramsci and Marxism*
Patrizia Dogliani, *A Political History of the International Union of Socialist Youth*
Alexandros Chrysis, *The Marx of Communism: Setting Limits in the Realm of Communism*
Stephen Maher, *Corporate Capitalism and the Integral State: General Electric and a Century of American Power*
Paul Raekstad, *Karl Marx's Realist Critique of Capitalism: Freedom, Alienation, and Socialism*
Alexis Cukier, *Democratic Work: Radical Democracy and the Future of Labour*
Christoph Henning, *Theories of Alienation: From Rousseau to the Present*
Daniel Egan, *Capitalism, War, and Revolution: A Marxist Analysis*
Genevieve Ritchie, Sara Carpenter & Shahrzad Mojab (Eds.), *Marxism and Migration*
Emanuela Conversano, *Capital from Afar: Anthropology and Critique of Political Economy in the Late Marx*
Marcello Musto, *Rethinking Alternatives with Marx*
Vincenzo Mele, *City and Modernity in George Simmel and Walter Benjamin: Fragments of Metropolis*
David Norman Smith, *Self-Emancipation: Marx's Unfinished Theory of the Working Class*

Preface

To rethink development is an essential task if the term is to have any meaning for us at all. As an area of study and as a policy intervention in the global South, it has taken on an absolutist, yet at the same time a somewhat vacuous, character. While the modalities and theories of development proliferate, its overall benign and beneficial nature is simply taken for granted. Even in its radical variants—such as the 'dependency' approach—we still see a reproduction (albeit in reverse) of the dominant paradigm. And when it is questioned radically, it is largely through a post or anti-development lens that simply rejects the whole problem without putting an alternative in place. It is therefore timely to engage in a thorough deconstruction of the development discourse to allow us to rethink its meaning and purpose, and to establish whether it can have a meaningful role in the twenty-first Century. The endless recycling of development discourses—and the much-discussed crisis, or impasse, in development theory and practice—calls, in my view, for a 'back to basics' approach that will allow us to better understand the nature of the development discourse(s) and its contradictions.

Development—in its dominant forms—is, in fact, a Western or Northern development discourse. It is a linear and teleological (heading towards a pre-defined end) perspective that has complete faith in the inexorability of human progress so long as that prescriptive model is followed. It simply assumes the universal benefits of the model, in a form of secular utopianism as it were, and a self-conception that it is ultimately doing good in a general way. In the 1990s this development paradigm reached its zenith with the advent of capitalist globalisation and the demise of state socialist and state capitalist alternative models. The project or utopia of globalisation did not, however, materialise. We have not witnessed the 'great convergence' of the global North and South and the eradication of poverty that was promised. Rather, we have seen a greater degree of inequality between and within nations, but also a concerted resistance to the universal development model with a resurgence of alternative development visions.

The deconstruction of the development discourse I propose here entails critically examining the binary oppositions on which it is based—such as those opposing rural/urban, Western/Oriental, North/South, developed/underdeveloped, etc—to problematise them and uncover the way in which they were constructed. Following Derrida's understanding of deconstruction, these are not taken as metaphysical oppositions but, rather, a hierarchy or order of subordination. Deconstruction thus calls for a double manoeuvre to thus allow us to carry out a general displacement of the system. While this is clearly a different approach to the Hegelian thesis, antithesis and synthesis present in much Marxist theorising, Derrida is arguably correct in asserting that deconstruction is a radical extension of Marxism, or at least 'a certain spirit' of Marxism. This is a radical programme that is not meant to be purely academic and speculative but one that engages with the world as Derrida puts it.

An (in) famous statement by Derrida and its (mis)interpretation—encapsulated in Derrida's cryptic phrase '*Il n'ya pas de hors-texte*'—has led many critics including Marxists to portray his thinking as an idealism of the text. But, in fact, if Derrida had meant to say there was nothing outside of writing he would have said '*il n'ya rien dehors du texte*'. It is more plausible and consistent with his work, that what he meant was that everything, just like text, can be interpreted in multiple ways and is never a pure signifier (ie. the material form of the sign) of the signified (ie. the mental concept associated with it). That is to say, the text does not simply reflect a pre-existing world and there is no pre-text or presence pre-existing the sign. From a deconstructionist perspective, we cannot thus appeal to a transparent 'real world' or simply oppose all 'ideologies' with our own pristine scientific perspective, as can happen in some Marxist approaches. This is important to note insofar as this text will not grant itself any special privileges in its rethinking of development from the various Marxist perspectives.

This text's engagement with—rethinking of—development hinges around the various Marxist perspectives regarding development that are often very different and even opposed to one another. This means that we cannot simply critique the ideology of development from the standpoint of a putative Marxist science. I would agree (albeit it for different reasons perhaps) with Derrida, for whom Marxism remains at once indispensable and structurally insufficient and, above all, with his call for a radical transformation and opening- up of Marxism. Certainly, Marxism's research agenda since the 1960s has greatly advanced our understanding of economics, history, politics, culture and philosophy. However, in relation to what we call 'development' in this text, it will be necessary to carry out a double deconstruction of both development and Marxist theorising in this domain if we wish to both understand and change the world. Marxism will make a better contribution to this enterprise if it is, at the same time critically interrogated and not just repeated as a holy script.

The collapse of the Soviet Union in the1990s led to the death of Marxism as a state ideology yet it also allowed Marxism to be liberated from itself, that is the externalised form in which it was alienated from itself. The dead hand of official Marxism—embodied first in German social democracy and then in Soviet communism—had emptied it of much of its radical, contestatory, critical and utopian impulses. In the mid-1990s, Derrida was to note that when the 'dogma machine' began to disappear we no longer had any excuse to not engage in a thorough deconstruction of Marxism itself, from within as it were. Derrida thus, after all of the sound and the fury of the deconstructionist vs Marxist polemics in the US academy, clearly claimed his inspiration from 'a certain spirit of Marxism' and, most especially, what he called its 'emancipatory and *messianic* affirmation', a strand within Marxism we will give full voice to below.

The Marxist engagements with the development that we pursue below—from Marx himself to the post-development approaches—show how heterogeneous the Marxist 'inheritance' for the present generation actually is. We bring to the fore some of the repressed alternatives—such as the late Marx on Russia or Rosa Luxemburg—and deconstruct the once previously received truths such as Lenin's theory of imperialism, often taken to be holy script. In fact, there is no one Marxist theory of development but, rather a cacophony of voices, often in total contradiction with one another. So, following Derrida albeit in a different context, we will find that to make sense of the engagement of the various strands of

Marxism with development we need to filter, sift, criticise and sort out the various possible paths that may coexist within the same Marxist imagination. In other words, we cannot take a single univocal or unified 'Marxism' as a privileged lens with which to observe and analyse development. We need to thus engage in a simultaneous deconstruction of development and Marxism if the dialogue between rethinking development from Marxist perspectives is to be fruitful.

Critical thinking cannot be based on pre-determined positions, an all-knowing uncontestable vantage point. Rather, we need think our critique, our deconstruction of 'development' from Marxist perspectives as a process. There is no point in reading development knowing in advance what our findings will be, as we will merely find what we expect. Taking theoretical critique as a process—and not as revealing a truth—will lead us to understand the way in which 'development' as discourse and practice, emerges and how we can construct counter-knowledges. Our critical thinking—decolonial in all senses of the word—will not seek premature closure through a high-level synthesis or resolution of the contradictions in encounters. The Marxist perspectives on development that we explore will thus necessarily be provisional, subject to critical thinking themselves and often liminal, that is existing on borders of the ossified mainstream and on the threshold of something new in the colonial knowledge–power encounter.

Derrida has shown us the pitfalls of what he calls a 'proprietorial' attitude towards Marxism, much in evidence in some attacks on the deconstructionist approach and asks himself and us what proprietary right must still be protected? Which borders must still be patrolled? To whom is 'Marxism' supposed to belong? In the chapters below as the complex engagement between Marxism and development unfolds, we do not assume any proprietorial rights. We try, insofar as possible to let the key texts speak for themselves. Nor will we seek to 'resolve' contradictions or deny the silences and *cul de sacs* in Marxism. Finally, I believe that Derrida's deconstruction of Marxist ontology and the relationship between Marx and science does not depoliticise Marx but, rather, re-politicises his inheritance and relevance today. Marxism is clearly not above deconstruction, and we cannot take it as a privileged lens of absolute truth through which to critically examine and analyse what we call development.

Dublin, Ireland Ronaldo Munck

Praise for *Rethinking Development*

"Does capitalism generate development or underdevelopment in the 'Global South'? In this excellent book Ronaldo Munck not only carefully revisits the main ideas of Karl Marx, Vladimir Lenin and Rosa Luxemburg on this topic, but also provides us a very useful guide to the contemporary theories and critiques of development. This volume is a must-read both for specialists and for a new generation approaching Marxism for the first time."

—Marcello Musto, *Professor of Sociology, York University, Canada*

"An immensely important book that deconstructs the complex history of the notion of development, providing thereby a deep contextualised, anti-teleological and non-dogmatic understanding of Marx's legacy. It is a painstakingly historical enquiry and an eye-opening must-read that critically traces Marxist contributions and debates from the nineteenth century to date, inviting us to rethink the development question from a refreshingly new perspective."

—Raúl Delgado Wise, *Professor of Development Studies, Universidad Autónoma de Zacatecas, Mexico*

"Ronaldo Munck does a thoroughly comprehensive job in reviewing the historical material on Marxism and development, but what is of particular value is that he then goes on to apply these to more contemporary issues such as post-development, globalisation and indigenism, in the process drawing out the strengths and weaknesses of Marxist approaches. This book is highly recommended."

—Ray Kiely, *Professor of Politics, Queen Mary University of London, UK*

"Ronaldo Munck's critical reassessment of Marxist thought has important and timely relevance to contemporary material relations and epistemic realities. He juggles Marxism's protean strands adeptly, summarizing principal thinkers and debates in the context of geo-political-economic relations across time and space. His ultimate methodological goal of divining the current capitalist order is especially significant for incorporating non-European thought, thereby complicating how such a world order can be analysed and progressively transformed."

—Philip McMichael, *Professor of Global Development, Cornell University, US*

"This book pairs a journey through Marxist perspectives on growth and development with international development questions. It does so with historical depth and finesse, wide engagement and crystal clear language. A formidable work that offers many fresh insights."

—Jan Nederveen Pieterse, *Global Studies, University of California Santa Barbara, US*

"Munck cogently traces the origins of dependency, post-development, indigenous development and globalisation theories to the classical Marxist thinkers and the debates they generated. By weaving together a critical and nuanced analysis of the classics and contemporary critical theories, he not only leads the reader to rethink development, but also lays the foundations fora renewed Marxist development theory. This book should become a core text in courses on critical development studies, globalization and Marxism."

—Cristóbal Kay, *Emeritus Professor, International Institute of Social Studies, Erasmus University Rotterdam, Netherlands*

"Liberal free market approaches have failed the poor and the planet, yet development theorists and practitioners struggle to articulate a radical alternative to the mainstream. In this unique account, Munck sets out to rescue the idea of 'development' from both its colonialist origins and

World Bank co-optation of apparently progressive agendas. He unpicks the thorny relationship between Marxism, modernity and development and provides a tour de force account of development theories from their origins in the Enlightenment and Marxist ideas of capitalism. The final chapters, which are absolutely outstanding, offer a bridge between Marxism and the imperative of decolonising development via Fanon, and an intriguing reading of Latin America's Buen Vivir movement through the lens of the region's twentieth century Marxist indigenista school. This is a welcome and much-needed book that seeks to provide the reader with realistic hope for transformation. One for my students and colleagues alike."

—Jean Grugel, *Director of Interdisciplinary Global Development Centre (IGDC), University of York, UK*

"The book is absolutely essential reading for scholar activists and others in the tradition of critical development studies who are concerned about capitalism as an insurmountable obstacle in the search for another world of genuine progress and the possibilities of transformative change. One way forward, Munck argues (with an extended reference to Marx, or, more precisely, to various marxisms), is to understand that capitalism is not hegemonic and that a critical analysis of its inherent contradictions provides an essential tool in the search for progressive transformative change. Another way forward, emphasised by Ronaldo Munck in this book, is to combine this theoretical awareness with a postdevelopment perspective of knowledge as power—an awareness of one's own potential power—and for people to act on this awareness. Munck's radical deconstruction of development discourse from a Marxist perspective provides a valuable theoretical tool in helping us to move beyond this theoretical impasse."

—Henry Veltmeyer, *Professor Emeritus, Development Studies, St Mary's University, Canada*

"Ronaldo Munck tackles the conceptions of development beyond the conventional approaches, through a historical and thematic approach that is at the same time both broad and detailed, but always erudite. Marx is always present but not in a dogmatic way, in dialogue with various disciplines and very much focused on the perspectives of the global South. A much needed contribution in these times of crisis and confusion."

—Eduardo Gudynas, *Latin American Center for Social Ecology (CLAES), Uruguay*

"This book is a tour de force, engaging with "inheritances" of Marxism and Development, seen as 'parallel discourses both contending with the issue of human progress'. Munck provides the reader with an extremely rich and erudite critical reflection of their relationship, revealing through his deconstruction the heterogeneity of the Marxist tradition and the binaries of conventional development discourse. He pursues the theme of 'uneven development' continuously throughout the book, whilst discussing Marxist thought ranging from Marx and Engels, Lenin and Luxemburg, Neo-Marxism and Dependency, Indigenous peoples' perspectives, to post-modern and post development theorists. His intention is to contribute to 're-politicizing' Marxism and its relevance today, in a time of increasing resistance to the universal development model and the resurgence of alternative visions. This book should be read by everyone interested in constructing new radical alternatives to the too long historically dominant discourse of 'Development'."

—Barry Gills, *Professor Global Development Studies, University of Helsinki, Finland*

"With admirable command over a vast terrain of development and Marxist theories, Munck offers a reinterpretation of both and illuminates contemporary debates in development in a new light. The book presents refreshing, new perspectives on established paradigms, bringing them into productive conversation with recent bodies of literature, such as postcolonial theory. Written with exceptional clarity and sophistication, this book will be of interest to experts and students alike."

—Nandini Gooptu, *Professor of South Asian Studies, Oxford Department of International Development, Oxford University, UK*

"Ronaldo Munck provides a truly insightful analysis of contemporary development beyond dualist reason. Deconstructing both Marxism and the developmental discourse — from Marx, Lenin and Mariategui to the politics of the Zapatistas and the Buen Vivir — this book is an important reference point to those trying not only to rethink the meaning and purpose of development, but also to break with the status quo and build new utopian futures."

—Lucia Pradella, *Senior Lecturer in International Political Economy, King's College London, UK*

"In this essential reading and ambitious synthesis, Ronaldo Munck successfully links Marxism to various understandings of development by contrasting classical and contemporary theories and ideas. This comprehensive overview of Marx's insights serves as understanding of capitalism and development in its many forms and opens up major questions in our search for a relevant developmental theory. Essential reading for scholars and students."

—Ronald H. Chilcote, *Professor Emeritus of Economics and Political Science, University of California Riverside, US*

"This book is a masterful tour de force that will be useful for scholars and activists alike. Written in accessible prose and brimming with original insights, this book helps to situate the past and contemporary debates that have raged since the mid-nineteenth century over the meaning of development and its relationship to capitalism."

—Susan Spronk, *School of International Development and Global Studies, University of Ottawa, Canada*

"Ronaldo Munck has long sought to renew Marxism through an engagement with post-modernist and post-structuralist thinking and now he brings this skill to development. Seeking to rescue it from its contemporary impasse of absolutism and ambiguity, Munck proposes to re-think the various discourses of development in a sort of Derridean deconstructive dialogue with the diverse and often conflicting currents of Marxism. The result is a 'double deconstruction' of both traditions whose more finely sorted strands then weave a distinctive new understanding."

—Radhika Desai, *University of Manitoba, Canada*

"Ronaldo Munck delivers a tour de force tracing, interrogating and assessing the relationship between Marxism and development over two and a half centuries. Written critically, yet sympathetically, he analyses the various debates, contradictions, cul-de-sacs and avenues of genuine insight and possibility that have characterised Marxist perspectives on development. If you are looking for a clear-headed, insightful and encyclopedic volume on two of the most important ideas of our time—Marxism and development—then this is it."

—Paul Bowles, *University of British Columbia, Canada*

Contents

CHAPTER 1

Definitions and Dilemmas

This introductory chapter sets out to define the broad terrains of both Marxism and development with a view to posit the main dilemmas now facing us in theory and in practice in terms of the global order and its transformation. I see Marxism and development as, to some extent, parallel discourses both contending with the issue of human progress, albeit in very different ways. What I will argue, essentially, is that Marxism can greatly contribute to our understanding of development in the twenty-first century. To pose that possibility we first need to carry out a genealogy of the two discourses, fully aware of the lacunae and contradictions in both, before we bring them into dialogue with each other. That will be the task of this opening chapter.

In the section on *Marxism* below I start with the proposition that the relatively recent publication of Marx's economic manuscripts in full poses the possibility of a 'new Marx'. I also propose—as a working hypothesis—that Marxism is, at the very least, a methodology for the study of capitalist society. Then I carry out a hugely simplified review of 'classical' Marxism, the 'neo-Marxism' that emerged in the post-war period as capitalism stabilised, and the 'post-Marxist' that emerged since 1968 and the rise of the new social movements. While cognisant, of course, of the social democratisation and Stalinisation of Marxism that emptied it of radical content I do not respond with my own version of a 'correct' Marxism.

R. Munck, *Rethinking Development*, Marx, Engels, and Marxisms,
https://doi.org/10.1007/978-3-030-73811-2_1

Instead, I seek to emulate Gramsci who used Marxist conceptual tools to develop an understanding of the new capitalist order emerging in his day.

Next, in the section on *Development* I briefly outline the problematic of development from the Enlightenment to 'post-development' today. While development is to some extent an 'open signifier' (it can be articulated with many different politics) it is inherently tied to the notion of progress, modernity and ultimately, Europe. A Europe that colonised and dominated the non—Western world in the name of progress. There is also another form of development—Development 2 I will call it—articulated in the post-war period as an instrument of domination to replace colonialism. Finally, there is what we might call a Development 3 discourse that emerges in the 1990s in the wake of the collapse of the non-capitalist development option and the consolidation of capitalist globalisation as the one true path. In this way, we show the need to break with any notion that development is a unitary and self-evident conceptual category that is timeless and see how it is situated historically.

Finally, in *This Book*, I seek to provide a road map to the unfolding of my arguments in the chapters to come. While inevitably this text coves a vast terrain and the coverage of issues is selective, I embrace complexity and contradictions to the best of my ability and do not seek closure for the sake of it. Likewise, it is important to note that throughout I emphasise the original texts of the authors and schools of thought I examine. For both Marxism and development studies there is a vast secondary literature that is sometimes useful (other times not) but which can also lead one into a maze and debates that are no longer central to our understanding of the contemporary world and how to change it. I would wish to encourage the reading of the original works more than to present a superficially polished and finalised rendering of their works.

Marxism

Marxism is an intellectual and political minefield and anyone venturing therein needs to carefully define their mission and their assumptions. Until recently it was common for those calling themselves 'Marxists' as much as for his opponents to be using only a quite restricted reading of his work. At times it sounded like debates around phrases in the Bible debated with exegetical fury but with little or no contextualisation. It is always well to remember that Marx once commented in relation to his 'followers' that 'I am not a Marxist'. Now, since the greater accessibility to his work and through proper contextualised reading of it we can start with a 'real' or 'another' Marx more fit for purpose in terms of understanding and changing the present order. As Marcello Musto has shown, we can now base ourselves on a more critical and open interpretation of his complex and evolving theoretical frame (Musto 2020).

Marx's 'ultimate purpose' in his main work *Capital*, as he put it in the Preface was to 'disclose the economic law of motion of modern society' (Marx 1976, 35). He was a theorist of modernity-conscious of both its emancipatory and exploitative nature—and thus speaks directly to what we today call 'development'. We cannot, however, 'read off' from Marx's engagement with early industrialising society what the 'law of motion' of contemporary society will be. Conscious that some Marxists will consider this too minimalist, I will, for now, adopt Lukács's 1919 argument that 'orthodox Marxism…does not imply the uncritical acceptance of the results of Marx's investigations. It is not the 'belief' in this or that thesis, nor the exegesis of a 'sacred book'. On the contrary, orthodoxy refers exclusively to ***method***. It is the scientific conviction that dialectical materialism is the road to truth and that its methods can be developed, expanded and deepened only along the lines laid down by its founders' (Lukács 1971, i). I may, for my part, reserve judgement on 'the road to truth' and might cast my net wider than 'the lines laid down by its founders' but the focus on the Marxist method will guide my approach.

To argue for a dialectical method is, of course to invite criticism and an endless debate on Hegel's influence on Marx that would be a distraction for us at the moment. But, put simply Marx's dialectic, to quote Lenin, implies 'a twofold analysis, deductive and inductive, logical and historical' (Lenin 1963, 320). Essence and appearance never coincide and thus we require research. That research implies the empirical appropriation of what we are studying, 'development' in our case. To start from the concrete and move to the abstract can only be achieved if we are able to reproduce what Lenin calls 'the unity of diverse elements present in the concrete' (Lenin 1963, 320). It is at an abstract level that we seek to discern the 'laws of motion' of capitalist development. We can then move from the abstract to the concrete, exploring the mediations between essence and appearance and 'apply' our knowledge to the infinite complexity of reality and practice, so as to then 'dialectically' interrogate further our theoretical frame.

The 'classical' Marxism I deal with below refers just to Marx (and Engels), Lenin and Rosa Luxemburg. This brutal simplification is due only to my focus on Marxism's engagement with capitalist development above all else. These thinkers were all driven by the immediacy of social revolution, and Rosa Luxemburg was murdered in pursuit of that objective. Marx has left us a rich legacy of theoretical insights into the laws of motion of capitalism that we can now appraise outside of the canonical atmosphere that has prevailed hitherto, by entering his theoretical 'workshop' so to speak. Both Lenin and Luxemburg carried out substantial (and somewhat neglected) research into capitalist development. They also both articulated a new departure from Marx with their respective theories of imperialism to explain the unfolding of capitalism (and its contradictions) on a global scale in a much more concrete way than Marx did.

After the deaths of Luxemburg (1919) and Lenin (1924) 'Western Marxism' was marked by the receding dream of imminent revolution in the West. For Perry Anderson this was 'an entirely new intellectual configuration within the development of historical materialism.... Marxism became a type of theory in certain critic respects quite distinct from anything that had preceded it' (Anderson 1976, 25). According to Sartre what happened was that 'Marxism stopped. Precisely because this philosophy wants to change the world, because its aim is "philosophy-becoming-the-world", because it is and wants to be *practical*, there arose within it a veritable schism which rejected theory on one side and *praxis* on the other' (Sartre 1968, 23). Marxism lost its overwhelming drive towards the seizure of power. Though some have contested this (e.g. Therborn 2008) Western Marxism would, indeed, seem to be characterised overall by a sense of defeat. It turned inwards, it turned away from political economy and from revolution. While it made great advances in developing a critical theory capable of understanding late capitalism, it did not turn its attention until much later (and then only on the fringes) to the issues of global development and the prospects of revolution in the world beyond Europe.

For its part, the Russian Revolution had turned to the 'East' and initiated a new chapter in the history of Marxism. The failure of the revolution in Germany in 1919, and its own location, led to this world-historic shift that culminated with the success of the Chinese Revolution in 1949. To the figures of Marx and Lenin we now could add Mao, then Cabral and Castro as emblematic of a new Tricontinental Marxism. Marxism had provided the inspiration for successful anti-colonial revolutions but the question that then emerged was whether it had been co-opted by nationalism in the process. Marxism provided a common language and political strategy across the Third World as it became known in the 1960s. However, as Therborn notes 'via Lenin and Leninism, Marxism became a global ideological current. But Marxism-Leninism turned out to be an unsustainable modernism' (Therborn 2008, 61). It did not lead to socialism—except in rhetoric—nor did it generate a general 'modernisation' and sustainable development in the European image. This hybrid Third World Marxism was, essentially, a new discourse quite removed from the theoretical frames of classical Marxism.

In the 1960s Marxism was a driving force of many national liberation struggles and a new 'Third World Marxism' emerged. Emblematic of this new hybrid that broke with Marxism as European thought system was Franz Fanon who rejected the 'civilising mission' of Marxism from a Marxist perspective. For Fanon 'when you examine at close quarters the colonial context it is evident that what parcels it out is to begin with the fact of belonging to or not to a given race, a given species….you are rich because you are white, you are white because you are rich. This is why *Marxist analysis should always be slightly stretched* every time we have to do with the colonial problem' (Fanon 1969, 3, emphasis added). Fanon 'stretched' Marxism beyond its European parameters but also in regard to its absolute priority to the proletariat in countries where the peasantry was the overwhelming majority of the subaltern classes. Above all, Fanon 'racialised' capitalist development and thus opened up a whole new area of enquiry.

Could Marxism be 'stretched' in this way to accommodate the colonial difference? Third World Marxism always seemed to be characterised by a somewhat vague attachment to Marxism in its classic guise, always mediated by the Soviet textbooks which tended to simplify (to put it mildly) and adopt new formulations about 'non-capitalist' development, etc. to keep Marxism as a frame but only in the most general terms. In more radical interpretations, such as that of Fanon, Marxism was not so much stretched but translated into a very different language where national liberation loomed large even though Fanon himself was extremely sceptical of the progressive prospects of the postcolonial regimes and, in particular about the national bourgeoisie.

In the West (soon to become the North) Marxism tended to become a neo-Marxism to match the neo-capitalism that seemed to have overcome the crisis-ridden nature of capitalism and the inevitable subjugation of the working class. The 'golden era' of capitalism seemed a new steady state with full employment, strong welfare provisions and rising wages. Capitalist planning seemed to do away with the earlier Marxist critique of capitalism as unplanned anarchy. The neo-Marxists (to give them a name) began to focus more on the 'early Marx' who wrote about the alienation of labour and the notion of capitalism irrationality through waste. As Anne Philipps notes, it also articulated a new theory of 'underdevelopment' (as against inexorable capitalist development) and 'by posing a contradiction between capitalism and development it opened up a whole new area for critique of capital and helped to fill the lacuna created by the reconciliation between capital and labour in the advanced counties' (Philipps 1997, 9). Neo-Marxist engagement with development/underdevelopment was thus, to some extent anyway, a response to the perceived futility of classic Marxism in the advanced industrial societies.

In the 1980s we saw the general 'crisis of Marxism' and the emergence of various strands of 'post-Marxism'. Behind this lay the growing contradictions within 'actually existing socialistic' countries the erosion of Marxist–Leninist discipline and the rebelliousness of the 'children of 1968'. This was part of the broader turn towards 'postmodernism' in the social sciences that questioned the empiricist, rational-logical model prevailing hitherto, and also the teleological readings of history in its critique of 'metanarratives' such as Marxism. While this is not the place to enter the fray around postmodernism it is relevant for us to discern two distinctive strands in this theoretical-political movement: one is pessimistic and gloomy in its prognosis of ever greater fragmentation and disintegration underpinned by moral relativism, while the other is more affirmative, hopeful and radical that sees a range of non-capitalist futures for society opening up 'after' modernism. A Third World postmodernism would be one variant of that second oppositional postmodernism with its rejection of Western 'logocentrism' and its claim to legitimacy by reference to universally truthful propositions. Certainly, the truth claims of modernist Marxism were being contested from many quarters.

Within Marxism there were extremely varied reactions to the emerging discourse of postmodernism. Some were extremely defensive (eg Callinicos 1990), others welcomed it with open arms (Ryan 1982) while others offered a cautious reading of a 'postmodern Marx' (Caver 1998). Since the 1960s there had in fact been several moves within Marxism (for example the Althusserian tradition) that had rejected the notion of

Marxism as a single, unified narrative. Ever since the 'crisis of Marxism' in the 1980s it had become harder to hold fast to the modernist version of Marx and the teleological view of history, as articulated by 'official' Marxism. That this might reflect a possible confluence between the critics of logocentrism and the critics of capitalism is posed by none other than Jacques Derrida for whom 'Deconstruction has never any sense or interest, in my view at least, except as a radicalization, which is to say also *in the tradition* of a certain Marxism, in a certain *spirit of Marxism*' (Derrida 1994, 92).

What remains of Marxism in the early twenty-first century? Can we go back to the 'classics' and recover tools for the analysis of the new global capitalism? After all, Marx was very clear that capitalism would not cease its expansion until it dominated the world. So now is probably time to take stock of all the various strands of Marxism without preconceptions or any vestiges of dogmatism. We will trace the various engagements between Marxism and development in the chapters below, but for now, I just wish to stress a couple of methodological points I would like to foreground, even if they are not taken for granted by all the stands of Marxist theory and practice. They centre around the concepts of 'anti-essentialism' and of 'overdetermination' that I think need to inform both our engagement with Marxism and with development theory in the stages that follow.

Essentialism implies a commitment to explaining the complexity of the real world and social processes through an appeal to a true essence lying at its core unchanging and ever-present. The long and often reductionist and simplified debate within Marxism around 'determination in the last instance' by the economy would be one example of this problem. Economism is, of course, a form of essentialism that seeks to reduce complexity to a hidden essential cause with other mechanisms of causation deemed inessential. Anti-essentialism—sometimes in the form of a constructivist epistemology—undermined traditional cause and effect arguments and thus their claims to universality were undercut. A positive manifestation of anti-essentialism has been Althusser's notion of 'overdetermination' developed by him and contemporary 'postmodern Marxism' currents (see Callari and Ruccio 1996) which played a key role in an anti-economic or non-essential Marxism. All social processes—not least capitalism development—need to be understood in terms of their multiple (and contradictory) determinations which always pushed and pulled it in different directions in a process of continuous change. As an epistemological position, the concept of overdetermination directs towards a non-reductionist theory of social causality and is thus key to understanding a concept so prone to teleology (a reason or explanation for something as a function of its end, purpose, or goal) as is development.

It is perhaps ironic that Althusser, who was responsible for an overly 'scientifistic' reading of Marx in the 1960s, was also, in his posthumous writings a precursor of the contemporary concerns of the new social movements that take Marxism out of the straightjacket of modernism. That Marxism is not a single unified narrative should be the clear conclusion of this section and will guide us in the chapters that follow. One of Althusser's interesting posthumous essays is '*Marx in his Limits*' (Althusser 2006) that lays the basis of the 'aleatory materialism' that replaced his earlier structural Marxism. Aleatory materialism stresses the contingency of the social order: what exists did not, and does not, have to be so. To craft a new society the full range of alternatives that may result from human action and the multiple possibilities for self-determination must be fully understood. There is an 'ultimate lack of guarantees' as to the path history may take. History has no pre-ordained end. The trajectory of the historical process is, then, influenced by active individuals or groups, actors or agents, which must be taken into account.

From this 'postmodern' Marxism we can take a strong focus on the anti- teleological nature of Marxism and what Althusser calls 'the necessity of contingency' such as the way in which he describes a mode of production as originating in 'an aleatory encounter of independent elements'. More generally, we can note with Althusser how 'Marx's thought contains, on the question of historical necessity, extremely original suggestions that have nothing to do with the mechanism of inevitability, or with the inevitability of destiny or the hierarchical order of the modes of production' (Althusser 2006, 93). This Marxism is better able to deal with the teleology of development theory compared to the German social democratic and Soviet Marxisms that were themselves thoroughly teleological.

Development

The overarching theme of this book is whether capitalism generates development or underdevelopment on the global periphery outside its North Atlantic heartlands. Marxism has always engaged with development, albeit in dramatically opposed ways. For some Marxists capitalist development worldwide is progressive insofar as it leads to the creation of a working class and this paves the way towards socialism. For others development as we know it, is inherently detrimental to the non-European world insofar as it only leads to 'underdevelopment'. Lenin, likewise, has an earlier positive view of the potential of capitalist development in Russia that seemingly contrasts with his well-known theory of imperialism. Today, some Marxists see globalisation as fulfilling Marx's vision of a worldwide expansion of the forces of production, whereas others support the anti-globalisation movement and oppose all aspects of neoliberal globalisation. To unravel these seemingly incompatible views we need to carry out a brief genealogy of the term 'development' itself.

Marx and Marxism are heirs of the European enlightenment. The critique of political economy was firmly within a European frame. There was a shared faith in human progress and a linear, even teleological belief in modernity as predestination. Taken out of context Karl Marx could be brought in to support this paradigm with his statement that 'The country that is more developed industrially only shows, to the less developed, the image of its future' (Marx 1976, 91). Marx's stages of historical development (primitive communism, slavery, feudalism, capitalism, socialism) could be taken at first glance to be very similar to Walt Rostow's 'anti-communist' manifesto (Rostow 1960) of the stages of modernisation issued at the launch of Development II after the Second World War and the move towards de-colonisation, providing the underpinnings for both the theory and policy of neo-colonial development. From this logic, it is a short step to Kay's statement in his Marxist analysis of development and underdevelopment that 'Capital created underdevelopment not because it exploited the underdeveloped world but because it did not exploit it enough' (Kay 1975, x). Marxism as an ideology of modernisation is thus very real, although it masks the deep contradictions around how Marxism engaged with development as we shall see.

For want of a better term, I shall call the original development theory Development I. It emerged in Europe in the nineteenth century as a means to deal with the chaos caused by urbanisation and industrialisation. It was inherently Eurocentric for the simple reason that the original transition to capitalism (with industrialisation and urbanisation) occurred in Europe. The French Revolution and the Enlightenment thinkers had effectively destroyed the certainties of the old absolutist order. There was a sense that *laissez-faire*-settings develop at their own pace—could only lead to disorder. Thus August Comte (taken to be the founder of sociology) referred to how progress had to be made compatible with order: 'Progress [is] the development of order under the influence of Love' (cited in Cowen and Shenton 1996, 34). Comte can thus be seen as the originator of the Development I paradigm, whereby social evolution is seen to have two aspects or facets, namely development and improvement.

Comte was, in fact, just one figure in a pantheon of European philosophers who fervently promoted the concept of development as a guide to social action. We can include Hegel, Saint-Simon, Spencer, Morgan and, of course, Marx in their number. While the Western notion of development had a heterogeneous history and contained contradictory strands, it had several unifying and remarkably durable themes. The theory of development was based on an even older notion of growth as a metaphor for human evolution. This had both a religious and secular character but always essentialist in its outlook. For Robert Nisbet this theory 'regarded change as natural, immanent, or preceding from forces within the entity, continuous, directional, necessary, corresponding to differentiation in society, typically moving from the homogeneous to the heterogeneous, and finally, as proceeding from uniform causes' (as cited in Nederveen Pieterse 2001, 36). The remarkably durable discourse of development would persist through the various shifts from Development I to II and III as we shall see below.

That Marx was a modernist should not come as a surprise, but it is often downplayed in Marxism's own histories and accounts of its development. For Marx and Engels, writing in 1848, 'the bourgeoisie, during its rule of scarce one hundred years has created more massive and more colossal productive forces than have all previous generation together' (Marx and Engels 1973, 72). Nature is subjected to humankind, chemistry is applied to industry and agriculture, the railway and telegraph revolutionised communications. Markets expand constantly, capitalist social relations corrode all others, productivity increases by leaps and bounds. There is an insatiable pressure for growth and progress with new human desires being continuously created. There is pitiless destruction of the traditional order in the milestones of progress and development. Where Marx differs from his fellow modernisers is in this belief that out of this process of destruction and chaos will emerge a crisis of such magnitude that it will serve as a springboard for the building of a new post-capitalist society.

After the Second World War and in the wake of the unraveling of European colonialism we saw the emergence of what we might call Development II. It was, in a sense, the United States taking on the role of the new global hegemonic power and articulating a discourse of 'development' to replace the new discredited politics of colonialism. For Arturo Escobar this new discourse of development was, like that of Orientalism, 'a mechanism for the production and management of the Third World...organizing the production of truth about the Third World' (Escobar 1992, 413). It linked forms of knowledge about the Third World with the deployment of development power that would seek to remap the Third World. It took over, and 'modernised' as it were, the nineteenth century development paradigm to produce a Development II fit for (imperial) purpose in the twentieth century. It became the main target of Marxist underdevelopment and theory from the 1960s onwards and still informs, arguably, the Development III mode with which we designate globalisation.

Modernisation theory exemplified the post-war mood in the United States as it became a hegemonic power. Rostow in his 'non-communist manifesto' of 1960 promoted economic growth as the *sine qua non* of development but went on to contextualise by declaring that' The glory of America has been not its relative material wealth but the sense of the transcendent political mission in reconciling liberty and order' (Rostow 1960, 6). Comte's thinking of 'development and order' was here matched by 'modernization and order' with support from God. The economic analysis was based on an overarching divide between tradition and modernity that could only be transcended by this new mission. Economic (and political) integration with the global economy, under the tutelage of the new imperial power and the economic power of his large corporations, was the secret to overcoming underdevelopment and aspiring to the promised land.

The neo-Marxist response to the modernisation theory underpinning Development II was, essentially, to stand it on its head. While one saw market mechanisms leading to development the other saw it as creating underdevelopment. The national bourgeoisie seen by one as the driver of development, was seen by the other as a weak dependent class. While one argued that the diffusion of innovations would lead to development the other argued that it would only deepen stagnation and backwardness... The main difference was in terms of whether integration with the world economy was positive for development or not. In the event, the neo-Marxist underdevelopment school (see Amin 1990; Frank 1998) ended up adopting some variant of autarky or delinking from the world economy as the only way to overcome underdevelopment. With globalisation this strategy was not even an option and, anyway, it had proven futile in practice wherever it was attempted.

After the collapse of communism and the rise of globalisation in the 1990s, we can detect a third distinctive variant of development we might call Development III. The internal differentiation of the Third World with the emergence of the 'East Asian Tigers' in the 1980s and the emergence of a new international division of labour, paved the way for a new hegemonic development project in the 1990s. The incorporation of the Soviet Union, the whole Soviet sphere of influence and those regions where the national development state model thrived, meant that neoliberalism was now hegemonic. A set of interlinked measures—such as liberalisation of trade, flexibilisation of labour and privatisation of state companies—were designed to increase the power of capital and colonise organised social networks. The national development model was declared deficit and a new orthodoxy of global free trade and globalisation as a whole created a new development project or paradigm we can call globalisation or Development III.

The development project or paradigm we have called Development II had offered a universal blueprint for national development. But the increase of global economic integration from the 1980s onwards and the decline of the economic power of the nation state led to a new post-development era he calls the Globalization Project (McMichael 2016, 147) and which we will call, without doing violence to it, Development III. It partly responded to the failings of the Washington Consensus development model with its imposed economic straitjacket on developing countries. It was also, in some ways, conceived of as a utopian project, based on universal marketisation after the collapse of state socialist and national developmental alternatives. Not only had we arrived at the 'end of history' (Fukuyama 1992) as there was no alternative, but we were also moving into a 'flat world' (Friedman 2005) in which international inequalities would be ironed out by the free market and by Enlightenment aspirations of Development I could finally be realised.

If this project of universal market fundamentalism could be realised it would finally disprove Marx's vision of the dynamics of capitalist development. It would have overcome its innate tendency towards crisis and its inherently uneven character. It has clearly not achieved those objectives and the rise of China as global economic power has brought to the fore Marx's analysis of primitive accumulation and the contradictions of capitalism development. But it has severely questioned the neo-Marxist analysis of underdevelopment as a natural concomitant of capitalist development. There had been over the last 25 years a huge expansion of the forces of production worldwide and the generalisation of the capital/wage–labour relation. Capitalism as a global order is what Marx predicted and a Marxist analysis should be able to contribute to our understanding of this new order.

Marxism does not have a systematic theory of development as such, but it can and does engage with Development I, II and III. The Marxist 'classics' share much of the positive view of capitalism of Development I in terms of its tendency to dissolve pre-existing traditional modes of production and oppression. A neo-Marxist school engaged closely with Development II in the post-war period and in particular its manifestation as a 'modernisation' theory. Thus, dependency theory emerged in Latin America that turned modernisation theory on its head and argued only that development (Development II) only led to underdevelopment. In relation to the new development paradigm of globalisation (Development III) we find Marxists on both sides of the fence. For some, much as was the case with Development I, it was necessary to support the historically 'progressive' elements of this paradigm shift whereas for others it was necessary to support the anti-globalisation movement and even moves to reject modernity for some more communal way of living as prevailed pre-capitalism.

Development theory cannot thus be seen as self-contained; rather it derives from various social theories; nor is it unitary insofar as it reflects complex and contradictory elements. There is no simple correlation between development and improvement of the human condition. Not least as in different perspectives this improvement has been put down to varying pre-conditions such as industrialisation, poverty alleviation, roll-back of the state, good governance or enhancement of human capacities. Post-development like postmodernism has questioned the whole enterprise of development but the issues development is focused on—poverty and inequality, uneven development, etc.—are not going to disappear through a discursive manoeuvre so we shall need to continue the dialogue with development from a Marxist perspective, conscious it does not have all the answers.

This Book

Having set the scene with overviews of Marxism and development we now need to bring those two discourses into conversation with each other. We need to bear in mind the innate complexity of discourses and not go for simplistic model-building. We cannot assume coherence and continuity in these discourses. Like all discourses they are marked by discontinuities, a characteristic that can also take the shape of internal contradictions. The discourses need to be situated in their historic context and cannot be 'read off' as it were, from some underlying spirit or set of principles. There is no hidden hand creating a unity that binds these discourses together. We do not assume any inherent superiority of any discourse as a guiding light to the truth. We do not posit science against ideology; we seek simply to offer a description of two hugely influential discourses and their complex interaction with each other. These discourses are much more than ways of thinking and producing meaning; they can gain the status of 'truth' and dominate our conception of the social world while marginalising other alternative discourses.

In Part I, we take up the *Classics* of Marxism, namely Karl Marx (and Engels), Lenin (and the Bolsheviks) and Rosa Luxemburg who dominated the early phase of the Marxist discourse under the aegis of imminent revolution.

Chapter 2 on *Marx and Capitalism* sets out the main parameters of Marx's theory of capital accumulation and the laws of motion of the capitalist mode of production. Marx is often assumed to have produced a Eurocentric and unilinear theory of development. On the basis of recent more complete versions of this work we can now present a more 'global' Marx, who was keenly aware of uneven development and did not take Britain as the model of development that would be followed everywhere. Marx was also very dialectical in his view of the impact of colonialism in India, showing that the destructive impact it had on Indian society was not matched by a 'regenerative' impact. Nevertheless, overall, Marx can be seen as the precursor of the view that capitalism is historically progressive in the sense that it sweeps aside pre-capitalist social relations of production and paves the way for capitalist development and hence for socialism. An important proviso of Marx is given in a footnote to *Capital* Vol. 1 where he says that 'in order to examine the object of our investigation in its integrity, free from all disturbing subsidiary circumstances, we must treat the whole world of trade as one nation, and assume that capitalist production is established everywhere and has taken possession of every branch of industry' (Marx 1973, 727 ft 2).

In Chapter 3 we turn to *Marx and Underdevelopment* where we discover his late break with any unilinear conception of development. His understanding of the national question in Ireland was, in a way, a hinge through which he became less convinced of capitalism's 'progressive' role. But in the last decade of his life, he engaged closely in research on the Russian peasant commune and in debates with Russia's first 'Marxists'. This led to an epistemological break—long hidden by the Soviet keepers of the archives—that saw Marx accepting that the non-capitalist commune could be a stepping stone to a post-capitalist future for Russia. Later, of course, Soviet orthodoxy would impose a rigid schema of historical stages leading mechanically from feudalism to capitalism and hence socialism. That history could 'skip stages' was a finding that would come back into Marxist theory and shape its theory of underdevelopment in the later guise of 'neo-Marxism' (Chapter 7) that came to fruition in the 1960s and 1970s.

Lenin, of course, led the first successful communist revolution in Russia, a European country that was relatively backwards and thus came at development from a different perspective to Marx. Thus it is crucial to understand how Lenin understood development in that direct and immediate context, a task we set out to do in Chapter 3 '*Lenin and Development*'. Lenin's little known early economic writings set out to analyse the development of capitalism in Russia, a pioneering undertaking, that showed a close understanding of Marx's Capital. Lenin's main political target was the Narodnik movement that supported the Russian commune as a springboard to socialism. Lenin was keen to demonstrate that capitalism would create its own home market and did not suffer from underconsumptionism. After the October 1917 Revolution, Leninism was to become virtually an ideology of developmentalism, following Lenin's striking comment that socialism meant 'Soviets + electrification'. This tendency was accentuated after his death in 1924 and the ossification of a constructed 'Marxism–Leninism' became the worldwide orthodoxy of the communist movement. Nevertheless, in the early Lenin we find a creative application of Marx to the reality of underdevelopment in a peripheral region.

Lenin was also, of course, the great populariser of a Marxist theory of imperialism in the early twentieth century, an engagement we analyse in Chapter 5 *Lenin and Imperialism*. This new focus on the global economy was prompted by the looming First World War and the increased competition between European powers over the carve-up of Africa. This new form of imperialism—as distinct from colonialism—was seen as the highest stage of capitalism (Lenin 1970). Lenin still saw the role of capitalism s progressive in the sense that it would dissolve pre-capitalist or traditional modes of production. There were, however, indications that imperialism might hinder the development of the forces of production in the non-European world. Above all the Lenin of imperialism signals an epistemological break in Marxism with his assertion that the 'division of nations into oppressor and oppressed … forms the *essence* of imperialism, and is *deceitfully* evaded by the social-chauvinists and Kautsky' who were by now settling down into acceptance of 'the philistine Utopia of peaceful competition among independent nations under capitalism' (Lenin 1974, 410). From these debates, the later neo-Marxist theory of underdevelopment would spring for which there was a direct causal connection between capitalist development at the centre and underdevelopment on the periphery. To what extent this second Lenin displaces the early Lenin of the development of capitalism is a contested point.

Rosa Luxemburg stands out among the Marxists classics as the thinker who engaged most directly with the impact of imperialism in the non-European world. Chapter 6 thus deals with *Luxemburg and Global Development* and the way in which this complex thinker-activist opened up an entirely new way of viewing the world. The underlying theme of her intellectual work was whether capitalism at the centre was obliged to expand to the periphery in search of markets. The theory of under-consumption underpinning this notion is debatable, but Luxemburg effectively 'stretches' Marxism into a theory of permanent primitive accumulation. Thus, plunder and enslavement are not just seen as a phase of capitalism's emergence but a permanent feature. This vein of enquiry has continued in contemporary studies of 'accumulation by dispossession' as a key facet of globalisation. Rosa Luxemburg is thus also a very 'contemporary' thinker (and revolutionary) representing a bridge, as it were between the classics and contemporary theories of underdevelopment we turn to in part II.

In Part II we turn to *Contemporary* theories of development from various Marxist perspectives, seeking to establish the main lines of debate, over and above the sometimes stormy polemics. We do so conscious of the enduring lessons from the classical phase of Marxism that displayed a richness not often see in the years since. The 'classics' may thus serve as an anchor our critical analysis of the very disparate engagements of Marxism and development discourses.

In Chapter 7 we turn to *Dependent Development* to take up the story of how Latin American activist researchers in the 1960s Sought to extend Lenin's theory of imperialism by looking at it from the dependent country perspective. While codified in the global North as a simple metropolis/satellite model of development, the Latin America exponents of dependency articulated a quite nuanced dialectic of the internal and external determinants of development. The problem lay in posing a 'non-dependent' development model usually seen as 'autocentric' that often ended up in advocating a form of autarchy, just as globalisation was getting into its stride. The methodological nationalism of this school was also to be an impediment as we moved into this new era when national development was becoming a chimera. We bring to bear Marx's own scattered writings on the world economy to construct plausible theory of dependent development for the present.

In Chapter 8 we introduce the theory of *Post-development* set in the context of the critique of modernism thinkers. We consider whether this approach takes us back to the romantic critique of capitalism in thenineteenth century. We also relate it to the emergence of a 'postcolonial' school of thought based originally in the realm of cultural studies. The critique of the European paradigm of rationality/modernity has contributed to a fundamental critique of development studies to which some social movements in the Global South have been most receptive. What is posed here is the need for a de-colonial perspective that radically questions the assumed universality of the West, thus returning to Marx's original dilemmas on the universality of capitalist development. The post-colonial approach is a variant that is more directly engaged particularly but also questions dominant notions of development.

The post-development strand of thinking brought to the fore the importance of indigenous knowledge that we focus on Chapter 9 on *Indigenous Development*. During the left-of-centre governments that prevailed in Latin America after 2000, we saw the rise of the philosophy of Buen Vivir (living well) that posed the need for an alternative to a development on a strong sense. It brought together pre-conquest indigenous cosmologies, environmentalism and some feminist strands. It was enthusiastically received in the global North, particularly in Germany. Another strand of Marxist indigenism was articulated by Jose Carlos Mariátegui who died in 1930. A fierce critic of the third (Communist) International he posed the need to build socialism on the Inca's primitive communism, that echoed some of Rosa Luxemburg's anthropological writings. We pose indigenous development as building on a subordinated tradition of Marxism going back to Karl Marx's writings on the Russian Commune.

Chapter 10 on *Global Development* considers the impact of globalisation as development theory and practice since 1990. We were told then that we were entering a 'flat world' and that we were witnessing 'the end of history'. If this had really been the case, Marxism would no longer have a central role in mapping capitalist development and its eventual demise. What we have seen instead is a confirmation of Marx's and Luxemburg's prediction that capitalism would inevitably spread across the world and subsume all other modes of production. The contradiction of capitalist development is most evident in China where a 'classic' Marxist development path has occurred alongside accumulation by dispossession. In terms of the prospects for global development we examine various future scenarios that assume the uneven and combined development of capitalism on an unprecedented scale.

While it appears that I am dealing with compartmentalised theoretical and political conversation there are many themes cutting across all chapters. One overarching theme is the question of whether capitalist development can/must overcome underdevelopment in the non-European world. If we read history backwards from the current era of capitalist globalisation our answer would have to be broadly in the affirmative. Yet our continuous theme of 'uneven development' throughout the book will tell us this has not been a smooth harmonious process. We have not found one particular theoretical approach—for example 'the' Marxist theory of imperialism—that could answer all our questions. Thus within the classics of Marxism we find contradictions more than continuity heading to the truth. In the contemporary critical theories of development, we find much of interest not least an upwelling of original thinking in the non-European world that was not the focus of the Marxist classics. But the early Marxists have given us theoretical tools that allow us to question some of the assumptions of these more recent radical theories of development. Approaching these themes in this book in a flexible and non-linear way will, hopefully, allow for more of these cross-sectoral, cross-temporal conversations to take place.

References

Althusser, Louis. 2006. *'Marx in His Limits' in Philosophy of the Encounter. Later Writings, 1978–87*. London and New York: Verso.

Amin, Samir. 1990. *Delinking Towards a Polycentric World*. London: Zed Books.

Anderson, Perry. 1976. *Considerations on Western Marxism*. London: New Left Books.

Callari, Antonino, and David Ruccio, eds. 1996. *Postmodern Materialism and the Future of Marxist Theory. Essays in the Althusserian Tradition*. Press Hanover and London: Wesleyan University Press.

Callinicos, Alex. 1990. *Against Postmodernism. A Marxist Critique*. Cambridge: Polity Press.

Carver, Terrell. 1998. *The Postmodern Marx*. Manchester: Manchester University Press.

Cowen, Michael, and Albert Shenton. 1996. *Doctrines of Development*. London: Routledge.

Derrida, Jacques. 1994. *Spectres of Marx the State of the Debt, the Work of Mourning and the New International*. New York and London: Routledge.

Escobar, Arturo. 1992. *Encountering Development. The Making and Unmaking of the Third World*. Princeton: Princeton University Press.

Fanon, Frantz. 1969. *The Wretched of the Earth*. Harmondsworth: Penguin Books.

Frank, Andre Gunder. 1998. *Re Orient: Global Economy in the Asian Age*. Berkley: University of California Press.

Friedman, Thomas. 2005. *The World Is Flat. A Brief History of the Twenty First Century*. New York: Farrar, Straus and Giroux.

Fukuyama, Francis. 1992. *The End of History and the Last Man*. New York: Free Press.

Kay, Geoffrey. 1975. *Development and Underdevelopment: A Marxist Analysis*. London: Palgrave Macmillan.

Lenin, Vladimir Illich. 1963. *Collected Works*, vol. 38. Philosophical Notebooks. Moscow: Foreign Languages Publishing House.

Lenin, Vladimir Illich. 1970. *"Imperialism, the Highest Stage of Capitalism" in VI Lenin. Selected Works*, vol. I. Moscow: Progress Publishers.

Lenin, Vladimir Illich. 1974. The Revolutionary Proletariat and the Right of Nations to Left Determination. In *Collected Works*, vol. 21. Moscow: Progress Publishers.

Lukács, Georg. 1971. *History and Class Consciousness. Studies in Marxist Dialectics*. London: Merlin Press.

Marx, Karl. 1976. *Capital*, vol. 1. Harmondsworth: Penguin Books.

Marx, Karl, and Frederick Engels. 1973. Manifesto of the Communist Party. In *The Revolutions of 1848*. Political Writings Volume 1. Harmondsworth: Penguin Books.

McMichael, Philip. 2016. *Development and Social Change. A Global Perspective*. California: Sage.

Musto, Marcello, ed. 2020. *The Marx Revival. Key Concepts and New Interpretations*. Cambridge: Cambridge University Press.

Nederveen Pieterse, Jan. 2001. *Development Theory. Deconstructions/Reconstructions*. London: Sage.

Philipps, Anne. 1997. The Concept of 'Development'. *Review of African Political Economy*, N° 8 (January–April: 7–20).

Rostow, Walt. 1960. *The Stages of Economic Growth: An Anti-Communist Manifesto*. Cambridge: Cambridge University Press.

Ryan, Michael. 1982. *Marxism and Deconstruction: A Critical Articulation*. Baltimore: John Hopkins University Press.

Sartre, Jean Paul. 1968. The Search for Method (1st Part). *Introduction to Critique of Dialectical Reason*. New York: Vintage Books.

Therborn, Göran. 2008. *From Marxism to Post-Marxism?* London: Verso.

PART I

Classics

CHAPTER 2

Marxism and Capitalism

Marx did not write about 'development' as currently understood in development studies for example but, rather, about the development of the capitalist *Mode of Production*, a much more specific and grounded topic. We follow in this chapter his analysis of how capitalism emerged and spread its wings across the globe, eventually dominating every sphere of human activity. There was always an element of evolutionism in this analysis, but Marx understood complexity and contradictions much better than some of his followers. Above all, Marx was imbued with the contemporary spirit of progress and modernity best captured by his phrase '*All that is ruled melts into air*' our second subtitle. Capitalism was, for Marx, extremely dynamic as a mode of production, and was inextricably bound up with modernity and modernisation. That the advanced country showed to others what their future held was a basic tenet of his thought system. Marx the 'developmentalist' to put it that way was, however, well aware of the *Contradictions* of capitalist development which we deal with next. We see how, in relation to India in particular, Marx was clear that a colonial capitalism would never result in social development and he supported calls for national independence. Capitalist development was not a smooth, unilinear process and it did not lead to a better life for all. In this chapter, we begin to establish the basis for an understanding of development as capitalist development, based on the classic Marxist

R. Munck, *Rethinking Development*, Marx, Engels, and Marxisms, https://doi.org/10.1007/978-3-030-73811-2_2

understanding of capitalism as a dynamic mode of production based on the appropriation of surplus labour.

Mode of Production

Capitalist development has always followed Karl Marx's advice: 'Accumulate, accumulate: That is Moses and the prophets…Accumulation for the sake of accumulation, production for the sake of production: this was the formula in which classical economics expressed the historical mission of the bourgeoisie in the period of its domination' (Marx 1976, 742). It is a system that is driven, it must continuously expand, reproduce itself, and sweep away all barriers to its progress. Capital is thus not a thing, it is a relation: 'the production of capitalists and wage labourers is … a chief product of capital's realization process' (Marx 1976, 512). Capitalism is only possible when the worker is separated from the means of production—doubly 'free' that is of ownership of the means of production and 'free' to work for capital. As Marx puts it in *Capital* Vol. I 'The historical conditions of its [capitalism's] existence are by no means given with the mere circulation of money and commodities. It arises only when the owner of the means of production and subsistence finds the free worker available as the seller of his own labour-power' (Marx 1976, 274). It is that relationship between the owner of the means of production and the 'free' worker that creates the social relation that is at the heart of capitalism as a mode of production.

Capitalism, for Marx, was a mode of production, that is a complex structure articulated by the forces and relations of production, containing three elements: the worker, the means of production and the non-worker. The concept of mode of production thus combines the means of production within society—be they labour power, raw materials, machines or workplaces—and the specific relations of production that are established between those who own the means of production (capitalists) and those who do not (proletariat) with history evolving through their interaction as the mode of production moves towards the realisation of its fullest productive potential. In Marx's 1859 *Preface to a Contribution to the Critique of Political Economy* he advances a somewhat basic framework along those lines:

'In the social production of their existence, men inevitably enter into definite relations which are independent of their will, namely *relations of production* – appropriate to a given class in the development of their material *forces of production*....At a certain stage of their development, the material productive forces of society come into conflict with existing relations of production... Then begins an era of social revolution' (Marx 1977, 5). The 'modes of production' thus created were for Marx discerned at this early stage of his work as, 'in broad outline, the Asiatic, ancient, feudal and modern bourgeois modes of production [which] may be designated as epochs marking progress in the economic development of society' (Marx 1977, 5).

Capitalism was thus seen to emerge out of the feudal mode of production and there has been much debate around this 'transition'. An early debate—that was followed through in contemporary theories of underdevelopment, pitted the orthodox Marxist reading of Maurice Dobb (1972) against the reading of Paul Sweezy (1970) who stressed the corrosive effect of international trade on the feudal order. The rise of a trade-based division of labour as a driver of development was in fact the interpretation advanced by Adam Smith (with his emphasis on individual self-interest) as against Marx's more structural interpretation. As Robert Brenner, who has reviewed and renewed this debate in detail, concludes that 'the rise of trade is not at the origin of a dynamic of development, trade cannot determine the transformation of class relations of production' (Brenner 1977, 138). It is the struggle between social classes that sets the parameters of development thus and not the increase of trade relations, as the 'circulationist' rather than 'productivist' school argues. That divide between an emphasis on capitalism as a mode of production and capitalism as just another trading system, would have a huge influence of subsequent debates around development.

Capitalism as a mode of production was, in its origins, restricted geographically to a small section of the world, namely North West Europe. Marx concentred on the emergence of capitalism in England (home of the original Industrial Revolution) but warned European readers of *Capital* that, while '"the locus classicus" has seen England.... the German reader prosaically shrugs his shoulders... I must plainly tell him: "*De te fabula narrator* [the tale is told of you]"' (Marx 1976, 90). What happened in England would occur in Germany and the rest of Europe for Marx. Capitalism as a mode of production was analysed by Marx in what he saw as its 'pure' form but he was well aware that reality was, in fact, 'impure'. Marx understood the phenomena of uneven development which meant his theory of capitalism was not seen as a universal blueprint for progress everywhere. Shortly after the passage quoted above

(*De te fabula narratur*) Marx lamented that 'we suffer not only from the development of capitalist production, but also from the incompleteness of that development' (Marx 1976, 91). Capitalist development entailed exploitation, but its incomplete development also created oppression and misery. That will be a constant theme for Marx when dealing with what we today call development.

Beyond its places of origin, Western Europe basically, capitalism boosted its mode of production through its interaction with pre or non-capitalist modes of production. Karl Marx was keenly aware, especially compared to other political economists of his era, that capitalism promoted accumulation on a world scale. Marx was also very cognisant that this depended on 'extra economic' coercion as he put it: 'force is the midwife of every old society which is pregnant with a new one. It is itself an economic power' (Marx 1976, 916). This brute force was most evident in the colonial system: 'the discovery of gold and silver in America the extirpation, enslavement and entombment in mines of the indigenous population of that continent, the beginning of the conquest and plunder of India, and the conversion of Africa into a preserve for the commercial hunting of black skins, are all things which characterize the dawn of the era of capitalist production' (Marx 1976, 915). To sum up, for Marx 'capital comes [into the world] dripping from head to toe, from every pore with blood and dirt' (Marx 1976, 926).

Marx did not offer a moral critique of capitalist colonialism as such, as the anti-abolitionists did of slavery around the same time (the Second Abolition of Slavery in the United Kingdom occurred in 1848 and the United States abolished slavery in 1865). While Marx stressed the element of violence and brute force in the subjugation of labour he also recognised that all the colonising powers 'employ the power of the state, the concentrated and organized force of society, to hasten, as in a hothouse, the process of transformation of the feudal mode of production into the capitalist mode, and to shorten the transition' (Marx 1976, 915–916). The state drove this process of primitive accumulation and the creation of the conditions for the emergence of capitalism. Much later in the debates around development in Russia after the revolution and across the colonial world, this role of the state, especially in conditions of economic backwardness, would come to the fore. It somewhat contradicts the image of the early industrialist/capitalist as an agent of innovation and a bold agent of development in its own right.

Marx had a clear view of 'development' as we now understand it when he was developing his Volume 1 of *Capital*, the only full critique of political economy book he actually published himself. There he states unambiguously that 'the country that is more developed industrially only shows to the less developed the image of its future' (Marx 1976, 91). This would appear to be an openly evolutionist schema but, seen in its context, this comment is clearly about Europe and Germany's ability to 'catch up' with Britain. It certainly does not apply to the colonial world and thus Marx cannot be seen as an early proponent of Walt Rostow's stages of economic development (Rostow 1960) that proposed a universal set of stages that all societies must go through to 'develop'. What Marx did foreshadow was something like the contemporary theories around an international division of labour between 'North' and 'South'. Colonialism and colonisation destroy pre-existing industries for Marx and 'A new and international division of labour springs up, one suited to the requirements of the main industrial countries, and it converts one part of the globe into a chiefly agricultural field of production for supplying the other part, which remains a pre-eminently industrial field' (Marx 1976, 580). It is in comments like this that Marx can be seen as a precursor to some themes in radical global development theories of the present era.

In recent years we have (re) discovered a 'new' Marx who was far less evolutionist in his development thinking than previously thought. That accepted understanding of Marx, even among most Marxists, would change with the resumed publication in 1998 of the Marx-Engels-Gesamtausgabe (MEGA^2), the new historical–critical edition of the complete works of Marx and Engels. And it was only in 2013 that the Part II of the MEGA^2 (*Capital* and the preliminary studies that led up to it) was finally completed. This was not an 'unknown' Marx coming forth but certainly a different one. There could no longer be facile talk about the young Marx and the mature Marx with an epistemological break in between. This was a new seamless Marx, a developing Marx and certainly a more complex Marx. This was not the mythological Marx of the Marxists but a living Marx, above all a revolutionary. Marx was able to change his views (for example, on the development of capitalism) and was not the dogmatic thinker supporters and detractors alike saw him as since his death. From that perspective we should interrogate Marx and, of course, subsequent 'Marxists' a term Karl Marx himself refused.

We need to ask, for example whether Marx operated within a national framework—e.g. German capitalism or Indian capitalism—or whether he was an early critic of what we today call methodological nationalism as an intellectual orientation and pattern in research that conceives of the nation state as the sole unit of analysis or as the self-explanatory container for all social processes. Lucia Pradella argues persuasively against the common view in the current critical analysis of the international economy that 'Marx concentrated on a self-enclosed national economy in his main work' (Pradella 2014, 2). Not only is he seen as someone who believed in the overall civilising mission of capitalism but also as someone who did not understand the uneven and combined nature of capitalism development on a global scale. We have already referred above to Marx's analysis of the new international division of labour created by colonialism. Pradella shows persuasively that there is much textual evidence in *Capital* Vol. 1 (and its unpublished supporting notebooks) to show Marx had overcome the dominant nation state centred approach—even if incompletely—and saw a world economy characterised by increasing inequality and what we today call a centre and periphery.

Our overarching theme in this section has been Marx's concept of 'modes of production' and how it might contribute to a Marxist theory of development. After Marx's death (and partly encouraged by Engels) the Second International codified this approach in a quite mechanical manner, a process which was intensified under the Third International after the death of Lenin in 1924. In one of the most comprehensive critical reviews of Marx on modes of production Jairus Banaji concludes that 'modes of production have to be constructed as objects of much greater complexity. The theory has to be *stripped of its evolutionism* and refurbished to allow for more *complex trajectories*' (Banaji 2010, 6). Most of the world did not go through stages of slavery and feudalism before arriving at capitalism. The evolutionary schema of modes of production does not particularly help us develop a robust but multilinear theory of development, though it should direct us to the realm of production rather than circulation (trade) in explaining the development of capitalism. Marx's work was left far from finished and is only now being revealed fully, but his strong sense of history and the spatial nature of capitalist development on a world scale may provide us with concepts and insights that can be useful in elaborating a contemporary theory of development on a global scale. We need to examine in a concrete way the 'laws of motion' of capital that means including the element of capitalist competition that *Capital* Vol. I abstracts from. In brief, the current relations of production on a world scale are not reducible to the relations of exploitation explored in that first volume of *Capital*. So to achieve a rounded and grounded analysis of capitalist development world-wide, we thus need much more concrete analysis and not just an 'application' of abstract schemas.

In this chapter we are reviewing Karl Marx's conception of 'capitalist development' even though this was not a term he used himself. Marx was an early, and still relevant, analyst of the rise of capitalism and its inherent contradictions. He conceived of capitalism as a mode of production that would inevitably spread across the world. Marx did not analyse the non-capitalist modes of production to the same degree, but he does offer some leads for contemporary students of development. A dominant theme of what we might call 'Manifesto Marxism' is the dynamism of capitalism and its ability, even necessity, to overcome barriers to development created by traditional pre-capitalist societies. But Marx was well aware of the contradictions of capitalist development, and how its 'progressive' nature would not lead to universal human development. Overall, we find that the 'new' Marx now emerging, as against the popularising texts we have had to date, had a far from simplistic, unilinear vision of development (a theme developed in Chapter 3).

'All That Is Solid Melts into Air'

The *Communist Manifesto* is, of course, the most famous and most read work by Karl Marx and Frederick Engels. It contains the lyrical phrase 'all that is solid melts into air' (*Alles Ständische und Stehende Verdampft* to be precise) which matches the famous Yeats phrase 'Things fall apart, the center does not hold' in its resonance. The *Manifesto* opens with a consideration of 'Bourgeois and Proletarians' where Marx and Engels present a picture of what we would now call modernisation beginning with the famous phrase 'The history of all hitherto existing society is the history of class struggles' (Marx and Engels 1973, 67). Modern industry establishes a world market in which colonialism plays a key role. All feudal and patriarchal relations are swept away by this new bourgeois order. The 'cash nexus' now dominates the relationship between people. In short 'the bourgeoisie cannot exist without constantly revolutionizing the instruments of production, and thereby the relations of production, and with them the whole relations of society' (Marx and Engels 1973, 70). This was a truly revolutionary mode of production that would advance some version of 'development' by leaps and bounds.

The proletariat is the product of the dynamic development of this new capitalist mode of production but also the agent of its eventual undoing. For Marx and Engels: 'with the development of industry, the proletariat not only increases in number; it becomes concentrated in greater masses, its strength grows, and it feels that strength more. The various interests and conditions of life within the ranks of the proletariat are more and more equalised, in proportion as machinery obliterates all distinctions of labour, and nearly everywhere reduces wages to the same low level....' (Marx and Engels 1973, 75). The increasing improvement of machinery, ever more rapidly developing, makes their livelihood more and more precarious; the collisions between individual workmen and individual bourgeois take more and more the character of collisions between two classes. Thereupon, the workers begin to form combinations (Trades' Unions) against the bourgeois; 'they club together in order to keep up the rate of wages...The real fruit of their battles lies, not in the immediate result, but in the ever expanding union of the workers'. This union is helped in this by the improved means of communication that are created by modern industry, and that place the workers of different localities in contact with one another. It was just this contact that was needed to centralise the numerous local struggles, all of the same character, into one national struggle between classes. But every class struggle is a political struggle. 'Of all the classes that stand face to face with the bourgeoisie today, the proletariat alone is a really revolutionary class. The other classes decay and finally disappear in the face of Modern Industry; *the proletariat is its special and essential product*' (Marx and Engels 1973, 87).

The creation of a working class through the unfolding of capitalist development is a key insight of Marx and Engels. We may debate today whether only the proletariat on its own is a really revolutionary class and we are much more aware of non-class contradictions, but across the global South new working classes have emerged following precisely this process as outlined by Marx and Engels. In terms of the uneven development of capitalism and the emergence of national oppressions, Marx and Engels were on less sure ground and they tended to minimise the appeal of nationalism for the working classes in the originally industrialising countries as Marx and Engels in the *Manifesto* proclaim that:

'The working men have no country. We cannot take from them what they have not got. Since the proletariat must first of all acquire political supremacy, must constitute itself the nation, it is, so far, itself national, though not in the bourgeois sense of the word. *National differences and antagonisms between peoples are vanishing gradually from day to day, owing to the development of the bourgeoisie, to freedom of commerce, to the world market, to uniformity in the mode of production and in the conditions of life corresponding thereto.* The supremacy of the proletariat will cause them to vanish still faster. United action, of the leading civilised countries at least, is one of the first conditions for the emancipation of the proletariat. In proportion as the exploitation of one individual by another is put an end to, the exploitation of one nation by another will also be put an end to. In proportion as the antagonism between classes within the nation vanishes, the hostility of one nation to another will come to an end' (Marx and Engels 1973, 85).

This vision of a post-national order has not come to pass, quite obviously, from the First World War breaking up of the Second International till today, with signal exceptional events of international and transnational solidarity. The 'nationalising' of the working class—in the sense of its national embeddedness—was not a phenomenon they foresaw and, to be fair it was not the dominant process during the formative phase of the labour movement they were engaged in. Nor do Marx and Engels show much of an intuitive grasp for movements of national liberation with some exceptions as we shall see in Chapter 3, where this questioned is examined in more detail.

We return now to that dramatic vision of capitalist development dissolving all pre-existing social relations. For Marx and Engels: 'Conservation of the old modes of production in unaltered form, was the first condition of existence for all earlier industrial classes. Constant revolutionising of production, uninterrupted disturbance of all social conditions, everlasting uncertainty and agitation distinguish the bourgeois epoch from all earlier ones. All fixed, fast-frozen relations, with their train of ancient and venerable prejudices and opinions, are swept away, all new-formed ones become antiquated before they can ossify. *All that is solid melts into air, all that is holy is profaned*, and man is at last compelled to face with sober senses his real conditions of life, and his relations with his kind. The need of a constantly expanding market for its products chases the bourgeoisie over the entire surface of the globe. It must nestle everywhere, settle everywhere, establish connexions everywhere' (Marx and Engels 1973, 70).

'The holy is profaned' is not some crass nineteenth-century anti-religious expression, but represents a deeper commitment to human liberation. And what follows is a fundamental statement of what surpassing the capitalist modes of production might mean 'When, in the course of development, class distinctions have disappeared and all production has been concentrated in the hands of a vast association of the whole nation, the public power will lose its political character. Political power, properly so called, is merely the organized power of one class for oppressing another. If the proletariat during its contest with the bourgeoisie is compelled, by the force of circumstances, to organize itself as a class, if, by means of a revolution, it makes itself the ruling class, and, as such, sweeps away by force the old conditions of production then it will, along with these conditions, have *swept away the conditions for the existence of class antagonisms*, and of classes generally, and will thereby have abolished its own supremacy as a class. In place of the old bourgeois society with its classes and class antagonisms we shall have an association in which the *free development of each is the condition for the free development of all*' (Marx and Engels 1973, 87, emphasis added). Marx is always aware of the contradictory nature of capitalist development: its positive contribution to human development is that it creates the conditions for a transition to a society free of class antagonisms. The individualism of capitalist society must give way to the universal development of individuals post-capitalism.

The *Manifesto* is, of course, a modernist statement and Marx shared, to a large extent, the aims and objectives of the modernist project. Marx was imbued by the developmental ideal of the German humanist culture of his day: Goethe, Schiller and the Romantics. The humanist idea of self-development flowed naturally for him, alongside the economic development of capitalism. But even at the high point of Marxist modernism, we find Marx and Engels entering a caveat in their 1882 Preface to the Russian edition of the *Manifesto* where they note that it 'had, as its object the proclamation of the inevitable impending dissolution of modern bourgeois property. But in Russian [where] we find…more than half the land owned in common by the peasants…must it first pass through the same process of dissolution such as constitutes the historical evolution of the West?'….and conclude that 'the present Russian common ownership of land may serve as the starting point for a communist development' (Marx and Engels 1973, 6). We have here the start of a counter-discourse within Marxism around the universality of the capitalist development process that we will explore in detail in Chapter 3 below.

To say Marx was a modernist could be an ahistorical statement to make (he could hardly be a postmodernist) but it is worth exploring. Marx and Engels put forward a modernist critique of capitalism, stressing the power of modern science and leaning heavily on the rationalist wing of modernism. They sought the scientific understanding of the 'natural laws' of capitalism. They saw, as we have, stressed above, how capitalist modernity sweeps away all forms of superstition and particularism. Yet they were neither simple positivists nor romantics. Science and technology were not self-motivated mechanisms, they were tools for human development. And their critique of the current order was not based on a return to a mythical pre-conflict past. The romantic critique of capitalism was thus stood on the head, because Marx and Engels argued consistently that only a higher form of human development could overcome the contradictions between the potential of capitalism and its reality.

For Marx modernism was revolutionary, it would transform the old world in all its facets. Capitalism, like the bourgeois, 'cannot exist without constantly revolutionising the means of production' (Marx and Engels 1973, 7). Permanent change, never-ending development, even a crisis represented an opportunity for this new mode of production. Yet as with Goethe's *Faust* and also Mary Shelley's *Frankenstein*, the human pioneers of science and rationality also unleash a demonic power beyond human control. It is the working class produced by this dynamic system that must save it from melting from its own incandescence. As Marshall Berman puts it, when the proletariat seizes control of the modern forces of production from the Faustian/Frankenstein bourgeoisie 'they will transform these volatile, explosive social forces into sources of beauty and going for all, and bring the tragic history of modernists to an end' (Berman 1983, 115). We, of course, know now that this did not happen.

Modernity as a project has today a far more menacing air to it, it is, after colonialism, marked by Auschwitz and Hiroshima. That is the reason, of course, for the emergence of a postmodern cultural trend that has to some extent sprung from Marxism and has influenced Marxism in many domains (see Lyotard 2001). However, there has also been a continuity of the modernist Marxist strands particularly in the shape of Habermas's theory that modernity is an 'unfinished project' (see Passerin d'Entreves 1997) which sought to turn back the postmodernist tide. For Habermas, the Enlightenment project of modernity has yet to be realised but that should not lead to despair or nihilism. Significantly, when asked in an interview whether this analysis has also applicable to the Third World, Habermas chose not to answer (Habermas 1979). From the perspective of our project to reconstruct the dialogue between Marxism and development, this silence and the impasse it reflects, leads us to the conclusion that a Third World perspective needs to be developed if, we are to 'provincialize Europe' (Chakrabarty 2007) and set modernity in its global context.

While accepting the great vitality of 'Manifesto Marxism' and Marx's role in the broadly modernist movement, we might also consider the take on progress/development in a later Marxist, namely Walter Benjamin. In his 1940 'Thesis on the Philosophy of History', Benjamin refers to Klee's painting 'Angelus Novus' which he leads as 'the angel of history': 'His face is turned towards the past. Where we perceive a chain of events, he sees one single catastrophe which keeps pilin up wreckage and hurls it in front of his feet. The angel would like to stay awaken the dead, and make whole what has been smashed. But a storm is blowing from Paradise; it has got caught in his wings with such violence that the angel can no longer close them. The storm irresistibly propels him into the future to which is his back is turned, while the pile of debris before him grows skyward. *This storm is what we call progress*' (Benjamin 1973, 259–260—emphasis added).

This passage is often taken as a prophetic warning of the storm to come—Auschwitz and Hiroshima—and reflects a pessimistic Marxism as against the optimistic Marxism of the *Communist Manifesto*, that Marx may well have shared in 1940. It could be seen as a lapse into political quietism or defeatism, the revolution promised in 1917–1919 was not coming and the onward march of history was not guaranteed. Dialectical materialism was no guarantee that human development would continue in a linear fashion whatever the 'vulgar Marxists' of his day may have proclaimed. Yet it is also part of a reconfiguration of Marxism as part of the rise of monopoly capitalism and consumerism. The rubble of the past exposed the shallow nature of the belief that progress was coterminous with human liberation. And yet we can, by looking at the horrors of the past maybe might find ways to correct past injustices and redeem the hopes of previous generations.

Clearly Benjamin's angel is an allegory but does it tell us something about progress/development? It certainly draws out the dark side of Manifesto Marxism where it was not exactly to the fore. For Michael Lowy, Benjamin's storm blowing from Paradise representing Progress evoked the Biblical Fall and expulsion from the Garden of Eden, which Benjamin saw as a primitive communist society (Lowy 2005, 63). Modernity, progress and development can thus be read as infernal domination which, at the very least, achieves a demystification of progress. Benjamin's messianic Marxism rejects the pitfalls of the scientific prediction of history as inevitable and irresistible process. Against all forms of positivism, we are urged to look for the unsuspected possibilities in any situation, always rich in strategic opportunities. Above all, as against any railway timetable model where the train of history advances inexorably to the next station, we are prompted to get off the train if necessary and explore other unpredictable paths. We are very far here from any conception of the unstoppable forward march of history or its inevitable evolution through various stages of development. This perspective will be reflected in the later school of post-development (Chapter 8) that to some extent revives a romantic/religious critique of modernism. For now, it may serve as a cautionary note against the notion that Marx can be reduced to a simple modernist 'Manifesto Marxism'.

Contradictions

Contrary to popular belief, Marx and Engels did not use the term 'dialectical materialism' that was coined as part of the codification of 'Marxism–Leninism' by Stalin. However, we do find the notion of dialectics and contradiction running through their thinking. I would argue that a basic understanding is essential to craft a Marxist theory of development. Marx followed Hegel in seeing the movement of modern society as a dialectical process, even though his totality was the mode of production and not the Idea as in Hegel's original use of dialectics. The notion of contradiction was a central component in Marx's dialectical analysis of capitalist development. Put simply, conflict and struggle are not seen as temporary characteristics of capitalism but, rather, inherent in it as a mode of production. Contradictions emerged in the mode of production as between the forces and relation of production—as the increased socialisation of production meets a barrier in the private ownership and control by the capitalist of the social conditions of production, and, of course, between capital and labour. As we saw above there is a contradiction between the potential of capitalism as a mode of production and its ability to deliver on that process. And it is the contradiction between capital and labour—the class struggle —that provides the motion for the development of capitalism and for its contestation.

There is some confusion in regards to the dialectical method because Engels extended after Marx's death in 1883 to encompass nature (Engels 1973) and turned what was for Marx a social scientific method into three immutable 'laws'. From a focus on the subject–object relationship in Marx, there was a turn (continued by the Soviet codifiers of 'Marxism–Leninism') to the law-like certainties of positivist science. Lenin, for his part, was one of the few Marxists, around the time of the First World War, who understood the importance of the dialectic in Marx. Marx's *Capital* could not be understood without Hegel's logic argued Lenin. And in his *Philosophical Notebooks* he referred to 'Dialectics as *living*, many sided knowledge....with and infinite number of shades of every approach and approximation to reality....to apply...to the process and development of knowledge' (Lenin 1963, 362).

It was in his engagement with British colonialism in India that Marx most clearly articulated the contradictions of the capitalist mode of production outside its original areas of dominance. Marx, in his journalistic writings of the 1850s, dedicated considerable space to India, not surprisingly given its central role in the unfolding of British imperialism. While recognising the generally 'progressive' role in transforming India, Marx was always adamant that 'The Indians will not reap the fruits of the new elements of society scattered among them by the British bourgeoisie, till in Great Britain itself the now ruling classes shall have been supplanted by the industrial proletariat, or until the Hindis themselves shall have form strong enough to throw off the British yoke altogether' (Marx and Engels 1963, 38). While his analysis is not fully rounded, Marx did break with the current opposition of 'West' and 'East', and he certainly did not support the 'imperialist mission of capitalism' (Marx and Engels 1963, 52) as later commentators suggested.

Marx wrote about India in terms echoed by the much later theory of dependency (see Chapter 7). For Marx 'it was the British intruder who broke up the Indian handloom and destroyed the spinning wheel. England began with driving the Indian cottons from the European markets; it then introduced twist into Hindustan and in the end inundated the very mother country of cotton with cottons' (Marx and Engels 1963, 36). This led to what one hundred years later would be referred to as the 'development of underdevelopment'. Capitalist expansion in the periphery led mainly to underdevelopment. For Marx 'the decline of Indian towns celebrated for their fabrics was by no means the worst consequence. British steam and science uprooted, over the whole surface of Hindustan, the union between agriculture and manufacturing industry' (Marx and Engels 1963, 36). Thus any form of the organic development of capitalism became impossible. India was not simply at a less developed stage of capitalism than Britain.

In terms of the contradictions of capitalist development from the 'outside' in India, Marx still cling to elements of Manifesto Marxism and saw capitalism as 'progressive' in terms of overcoming the old order. While Marx recognised there was a pre-existing family-based community with an integrated economy of agriculture, weaving and spinning, the advent of English steam and English free trade 'produced the greatest, and to speak the truth, the only social revolution ever heard of in Asia' (Marx and Engels 1963, 38). Basically Marx had an extremely negative to the pre-existing social order in India—'we must not forget that these idyllic village communities, inoffensive though they may appear, had always been the solid foundation of oriental despotism…making it the unresisting tool of superstition, enslaving it beneath traditional ones, depriving it of all grandeur and historical energies' (Marx and Engels 1963, 38). As against this 'barbarian egotism' as Marx called it, it was not surprising that for him 'whatever may have been the crimes of England she was the unconscious tool of history in bringing about that revolution' (Marx and Engels 1963, 39).

More broadly, we need to understand that for Marx the progress of the capitalist mode of production was not unilinear as it would be in the Soviet popularisation of Marxism. In an early article dealing with development Marx declared that 'To hold that every nation goes through this development internally would be as absurd as the idea that every nation is bound to go through the political development of France or the philosophical development of Germany' (Marx 1975, 281). So, contrary to a dominant interpretation, Lucia Pradella argues that 'in the early 1840s Marx did not have a stagiest, unilinear vision of development' (Pradella 2014, 77). Thus, for example, Germany could deploy the principles of protectionism advanced by Frederick List to protect its infant industries and catch up with England. This was an early stage of Marx's own elaboration of a theory of capitalist development and the global aspect was missing, but he did understand that the state could play a role in hastening the development of the capitalist mode of production, for example through protectionism.

The editor of Marx's *Ethnological Notebooks*, Lawrence Kader also argues, on the basis of those documents that Marx 'opposed as a groundless utopianism the doctrine of general evolutionary progress then being advanced by ethnologist' (Krader 1974, 2). As against this positivism

Marx advanced a very clear understanding of the uneven nature of capitalist development and the role of non-capitalist relations of production therein. Thus in Volume 2 of *Capital*, Marx refers at length to how 'the capitalist mode of production is conditioned by modes of production lying outside its own stage of development' (Marx 1978, 193). While capital exists in many different forms for Marx with more or less 'developed' modalities there was an overarching tendency for capital to expand: 'As long as capital is weak, it still relies on the crutches of past modes of production, or those which will pass with its rise. As soon as it feels strong, it throws away the crutches, and moves in accordance with its own laws' (Marx 1973, 6) as he puts it in the *Grundrisse*.

The difference between the capitalist mode of production when coexisting with other modes of production and when it gains hegemony lies, or is reflected, in the way labour was organised. Where capitalism coexists with earlier modes of production, we see what Marx calls the 'formal' subsumption of labour whereby the pre-existing labour process is subsumed under capital but does not change its nature. Marx even refers at one point to how the plantation owners in America *are* capitalists, even though they are 'anomalies within a world market based on free labour' (Marx 1973, 513). The direction of travel of capital accumulation on a world scale for Marx is quite clear and it hinges around the 'real' subsumption of labour: 'it therefore requires a specifically capitalist mode of production, a mode of production what, along with methods, means and conditions, arises and develops spontaneously on the basis of the formal subsumption of labour under capital. This formal subsumption is then replaced by a real subsumption' (Marx 1973, 645) in which capital acquires direct control over the labour process.

This distinction between the formal and the real subsumption of labour, allows us to distinguish phases of capitalist development without the need to seek an 'articulation' with other modes of production. Thus, under the formal subsumption of labour there is a technological continuity with previous modes of production in the way that labour is deployed. Yet, as Marx puts it, 'the process of production has become the process of capital itself' (Banaji 2010, 280). While the labour process remains external to the movement of capital but comes under its sway. The priority given to the extraction of absolute surplus value would still be a major feature across global capitalism, and it should not be viewed as a mere historical curiosity. Certainly, then, capitalist development, in the sense used by Marx, would entail the real subsumption of labour, the prevalence of relative surplus value extraction (through technological advances) and the supersession of previously dominant labour processes. That this has not happened is due to the law of uneven but combined development that allows for, and even rewards, capital's reproduction of 'archaic' relations of production, as in the commodity chains of the transnational garment industry that reaches back into household economies and practices extra-economic coercion as part of normal business.

Marx leaves us a well-grounded and theorised account of the emergence of capitalism and its development on a global scale. Over and beyond the nuances that can be added by subsequent historiographical research, there is a cogent theory of development implicit here. Primitive accumulation, as Marx calls it, is about the accumulation of the necessary assets in the hands of the capitalist and the creation of free' wage labour to put them to work. Marx notes 'the first sporadic traces of capitalist production as early as the fourteenth and fifteenth centuries in certain towns of the Mediterranean [but] the capitalist era dates from the sixteenth century' (Marx 1976, 876). The contradiction engendered by capital development in a non-capitalist milieu led to an epoch making revolution according to Marx for whom 'so-called primitive accumulation, ...is nothing else than the historical process of divorcing the producers from the means of production. It appears as 'primitive' because it forms the pre-history of capital, and of the mode of production corresponding to capital' (Marx 1976, 875).

In his chapter on 'The Modern Theory of Colonization' in *Capital* Vol. I, Marx focuses on the obscure account by E.G. Wakefield of a Mr Peel who went to the Swan River district of West Australia with 'means of subsistence and production to the amount of £50.000....[and] 3.000 persons of the working class, men women and children' (Marx 1976, 933). But no one would make his bed or fetch his water when he arrived. 'Unhappy Mr Peel [says Marx] who provided for everything except the export of English relation of production to Swan River!' (Marx 1976, 933). So, while the plunder of the resources and the labour of the non-European world provided the conditions for the emergence of a global capitalist mode of production its essential moment is the creation of 'free labour': 'The capital-relation presupposes a complete separation between the workers and of the ownership of the conditions for the realization of their labour. As soon as capitalist production stands on its own feet, it not only maintains the separation, but reproduces it on a continually expanding scale' (Marx 1976, 874). This primitive accumulation of the proletariat is the counterpart to the primitive accumulation of capital. The condition of a 'doubly free' proletariat was never totally achieved even in the capitalist heartlands, not to mention the non-European world where something like the heterogeneous nineteenth-century proletariat prevails to this day, and modern factory workers are a minority. As Max Henninger puts it 'Marx is not to be criticised for placing labour issues at the centre of his theory, but rather for systematically reducing labour to doubly-free wage labour and refusing to see in the various forms of unfree and self-employed labour anything other than contingent exceptions to the rule or moribund residues of pre-capitalist relations' (Henninger 2014, 294).

References

Banaji, Jairus. 2010. *Theory as History. Essays on Modes of Production and Exploitation*. Chicago: Haymarket Books.

Benjamin, Walter. 1973. *"Theses on the Philosophy of History" in Illuminations*. London: Fontana.

Berman, Marshall. 1983. *All That Is Solid Melts into Air: The Experience of Modernity*. London: Verso.

Brenner, Robert. 1977. The Origins of Capitalist Development of Critique of Neo-Smithian Marxism. *New Left Review* I/104 (July–August).

Chakrabarty, Dipesh. 2007. *Provincializing Europe: Postcolonial Thought and Historical Difference*. Princeton: Princeton University Press.

Dobb, Maurice. 1972. *Studies in the Development of Capitalism*. London: Routledge and Kegan Paul.

Engels, Frederick. 1973. *Dialectics of Nature*. Moscow: Progress Publishers.

Habermas, Jürgen. 1979. On Philosophy and Politics. *New Left Review* I/51 (May–June).

Henninger, Max. 2014. Poverty, Labour, Development: Towards a Critique of Marx's Conceptualizations. In *Beyond Marx. Theorising the Global Labour Relations of the Twenty-First Century*, ed. Marcel van der Linden and Karl Heinz Ruth. Chicago: Haymarket Books.

Krader, Lawrence, ed. 1974. *The Ethnological Notebooks of Karl Marx*. Assen: Van Gorcum & Company.

Lenin, Vladimir Illich. 1963. *V I Lenin Collected Works*, vol. 38. Philosophical Notebooks. Moscow: Progress Publishers.

Lowy, Michael. 2005. *Fire Alarm. Reading Walter Benjamin's, 'On the Concept of History'*. London: Verso.

Lyotard, Jean-François. 2001. *The Postmodern Condition: A Report on Knowledge*. Manchester: Manchester University Press.

Marx, Karl, 1973. *Grundrisse. Foundations of the Critique of Political Economy* (Rough Draft). London: Penguin.
Marx, Karl. 1976. *Capital*, vol. 1. Harmondsworth: Penguin Books.
Marx, Karl. 1977. *A Contribution to the Critique of Political Economy*. Moscow: Progress Publishers.
Marx, Karl. 1978. *Capital*, vol. 2. London: Penguin Books.
Marx, Karl, and Frederick Engels. 1963. *On Colonialism*. Moscow: Foreign Languages Publishing House.
Marx, Karl, and Frederick Engels. 1973. *"Manifesto of the Communist Party" in The Revolutions of 1848*. Political Writings Volume 1. Harmondsworth: Penguin.
Marx, Karl, and Frederick Engels. 1975. *Collected Works*, vol. 4. London: Lawrence and Wishart.
Marx, Karl, and Frederick Engels. 2001. *1882 Preface to Russian edition of the Communist Manifesto*, pp. 281–304.
Passerin d'Entrèves, Maurizio. 1997. *Habermas and the Unfinished Project of Modernity*. New York: MIT Press.
Pradella, Lucia. 2014. *Globalization and the Critique of Political Economy*. London: Routledge.
Rostow, Walt. 1960. *The Stages of Economic Growth: An Anti-communist Manifesto*. Cambridge: Cambridge University Press.
Sweezy, Paul. 1970. *The Theory of Capitalist Development*. New York: Monthly Review Press.

CHAPTER 3

Marx and Underdevelopment

Whereas in Chapter 2 we presented a Marx for whom 'the country that is more developed industrially only shows, to the less developed, the image of its own future' here we examine a 'late Marx' who begins to engage with what we now call underdevelopment. In the section *Beyond Stages* we show how Marx, in the last decade of his life, engaged closely with events in Russia and broke with his earlier sometimes schematic vision of unilinear development. Marx now fully accepted that there was no unilinear path of human development and that the stages of development could be 'skipped' so to speak thus opening the way to a multilinear conception of capitalist development. Overall, we find that it is a question of *Politics in Command* when Marx and Engels deal with the world beyond Europe, for example in relation to Ireland and Latin America, where political criteria prevail in the way in which they analyse development prospects. The criteria for supporting or not national development paths is still, to a degree bound up with the Hegelian concept of historic and non-historic peoples that Engels, in particular, took up and accepted. Finally, we turn to the way in which Marx sought to account for the dynamics of the global economy, conscious of the fact that he never wrote the planned volume on the World Economy. We thus explore the issue of '*Unequal Exchange*' between the various regions of the world, developed and underdeveloped as we would say today. We see here a line of continuity between Marx's incipient theory of the global economy and the

R. Munck, *Rethinking Development*, Marx, Engels, and Marxisms,
https://doi.org/10.1007/978-3-030-73811-2_3

contemporary theory of dependency that posits a structural condition of international domination. Marx is thus very relevant for contemporary Marxist engagements with development and underdevelopment.

Beyond Stages

In his last decade Marx went beyond any lingering commitment to a stages theory of economic development. In the early 1870s Marx taught himself Russian so that he could engage with the emerging revolutionary situation. He followed the work of the populist (*narodnik*) political current that found its most dramatic expression in the People's Will (*Narodnaya Volya*) party. The Russian populists connected the Slavophil belief in the specificity of Russia and the liberal belief that Russia would follow the Western European development pattern. They understood the dominant role of the state in Russia's development promoting economic growth, the formation of a bourgeoisie and the expansion of the working class. Some of its thinkers even articulated an early version of 'uneven development' theory that would place Russia in a subordinate international position but would also encourage a revolution that would 'skip stages' and move straight to socialism. It was into this debate that Marx was to intervene at the request of some of its participants.

Marx left an ambiguous legacy in terms of the theory of the stages of capitalist development. In the 1850s and 1860s he articulated that would today be called a 'stages' theory of development within an evolutionist frame. Engagement with the Russian debates in the 1870s led a certain paradigm shift. There was no obligation for Russia to follow the path of Western Europe he would now argue. The Preface to the 1882 Russian edition of the *Communist Manifesto* could not be more clear: 'Can the Russian *obschina* [peasant commune] pass directly into the higher, communist form of communal ownership? Or must it first go through the same process of dissolution which marks the West's historical development? Today there is only one possible answer, if the Russian revolution becomes the signal for proletarian revolution in the West… then Russia's peasant communal land-ownership may serve as the point of departure for a communist development' (Marx and Engels 1973, 139). Marx went on to engage closely with the debates in Russia through various correspondents where he explored at length the nature of the Russian landholding system and the possibility that it could act as springboard for a transition to socialism.

Marx first wrote a 'Letter to the Editor of Otechestvennye Zapiski' in response to an 1877 article entitled 'Karl Marx before the Tribunal of Mr Zhukovskii' that questioned the applicability of Marx's theory of capitalist development in Russia. The author Mikhailovskii had mistakenly assumed that in section of *Capital* Vol. I dealing with 'the so-called primitive accumulation' Marx had actually been expanding a 'historico-philosophical theory of Universal Progress' (Shanin 1983, 57). Marx in responding was very clear that this chapter 'claims no more than to trace the path by which, in Western Europe, the capitalist economic order emerged from the womb of the feudal economic order' (Shanin 1983, 135). Marx's 'historical sketch' of capitalist development in Western Europe could not be misinterpreted as a 'historico-philosophical theory of the general course [of development] fatally imposed on all peoples whatever the historical circumstances they find themselves placed' (Shanin 1983, 136). Thus, for Marx the historical patterns of development of the modes of production is an empirical question and not a logical one, and there is no supra historical model of universal progress according to some overarching development theory.

A further and more sustained engagement by Marx with Russian development issues can be found in his letter to Vera Zasulich in response to a request to answer his critics in Russia who asked 'how many decades it will take for the Russian peasant's land to pass into the hands of the bourgeoisie, and how many centuries it will take for capitalism in Russia to reach something like the level of development already attained in Western Europe' (Shanin 1983, 98). Marx had already begun to think through his understanding of backward or peripheral capitalism in his letter to a Russian follower Danielson in 1879 where he discussed the corrosive effects of the railway on the pre-existing mode of production but did not address the nature of the peasant commune in particular. In response to Zasulich, Marx directly addressed the ongoing Russian debate around the question of whether Russia had the foundations for capitalist development and whether it could 'skip stages' and transition directly to socialism via the peasant commune.

Marx was obviously troubled by this request as his letter to Zasulich went through at least four drafts. Marx first made clear (again) that his discussion of primitive accumulation in *Capital* was not meant to be applicable to Russia. As to the Russian commune and its alternative paths of development he thought it could go either in the direction of individualism or collectivism dependent entirely on the 'historical environment in which the commune finds itself' (Shanin 1983, 138). While, in his final letter Marx prefers to be non-committal and says simply that 'the analysis on *Capital* therefore provides no reasons either for or against the vitality of the Russian commune' (Shanin 1983, 140) this may well have been due to political consideration in terms of supporting the populists against the 'Marxists' in Russia or simply reflected his innate carefulness about drawing hasty conclusions. Nevertheless, elsewhere in his manuscripts he declared unambiguously that 'if the revolution [in Russia] occurs in time, if it concentrates all its forces….to ensure the full flowering of the rural commune, then the latter will develop itself before long as an element in the regeneration of Russian society, as point of advantage when compared to the nations enslaved by the capitalist system' (Shanin 1983, 139).

Meanwhile, in Russia itself various followers of Marxism continued to debate these issues after his death in 1883 and that of Engels in 1895. They built on an understanding of the revolutionary Narodniks in the works of Chernyshevsky (whom Marx read) that 'the development of certain social phenomena in backward nations, thanks to the influence of the advance nation, skips an intermediary stage and jumps directly to a higher stage' (Day and Gaido 2011, 27). After the death of Karl Marx, Engels tended to move back to a more mechanical view of development declaring in one letter that the *obschina* (commune) was a 'dream of the past' that must give way in future to 'a capitalist Russia' (Day and Gaido 2011, 29). In this he sided more with the Russian leading 'Marxist' Plekhanov for whom serious revolutionaries should forsake the villages to concentrate on urban workers: capitalism was inevitable, it was historically necessary, it would create and industrial proletariat with 'the process of Russian social development creating new social formations by destroying the age-old forms of peasant's relation to the land and to one another' (Day and Gaido 2011, 29). With Plekhanov we see the emergence of a strand of Marxism called 'orthdodox' but which really simplified Marx's quite nuanced and developing views of the nature of capitalism's unfolding in different parts of the world and seemed to retreat from his incipient break with a stagiest view of development.

While Plekhanov returned to a one-sided Marx who advocated universal laws of history, other Russian Marxists at the turn of century saw Russia as 'exceptional'. Thus David Ryazanov in 1902 in developing the programme of Russia's social democrats, stressed that Russia was an 'exception' to the development pattern of Western Europe. In an analysis that prefigured Trotsky's theory of 'permanent revolution', Ryazanov argued that 'late' Russian industrialization brought with it the latest technology from abroad, had strengthened the proletariat and placed the bourgeoisie in a position of vulnerability. For him Russian capitalism was not 'at the same stage of development as capitalism in Western Europe' and, more generally, 'what we find are different stages of capitalism, which develops in each country according to specific circumstances. All that is common are the characteristic features of capitalism and the tendencies of its development' (Day and Gaido 2011, 79). He argued that 'Marx and Engels overestimated the progressive character of the German bourgeoisie' (Day and Gaido 2011, 91) and urged Russian revolutionaries not to make the same mistake and assume they would pursue the democratic revolution or the necessary tasks of development in Russia. Soviet Marxist orthodoxy was, by contrast, to create a model of development for the non-European world that depended on the democratic and developmentalist ethos of a mythical 'national bourgeoisie'. The reality is that these early Russian debates within Marxism have only recently been recovered (see Day and Gaido 2011) and show an openness to different interpretations of Marx in a way that would be later disallowed and deemed heretical.

While the Russian breakthrough, if we can call it that, took the Marxist problematic beyond the stages theory of development, it was not at all complete or ready for deployment as an alternative, guide to action. For some commentators on the Russian engagement by Marx these letters and notes 'suggest that Marx was beginning to perceive the structure unique to backward capitalism' (Wada 1983, 63). This is seen as change of course with regard to *Capital*, a radical departure, even an epistemological break. It would mean that Marx was breaking from all his previous theorising. But others suggest that 'the drafts of Marx's letter to Zasulich show no glimpse of the dramatic break with his former positions that some scholars have detected' (Musto 2020, 69). There seems no doubt that this long unavailable material does show Marx in a new light and that his thinking was continually evolving. It also shows Marx engaging with a non-Western society in a non- Eurocentric way. But it was, in a way, a quite specific rural social structure that Marx engaged with it and does not justify the emergence of a 'Third Worldist' Marx (cf. Melotti 1977) as some would claim in the 1970s. I would, in conclusion, concur with Musto that despite its limited nature this late turn in Marx does demonstrate 'an ever greater theoretical openness, which enabled him to consider other possible roads to socialism that he had never before taken seriously or had regarded as unattainable' (Musto 2020, 69).

The general framework of Marx's thinking remained firmly centred around the category of mode of production. While in the *Grundrisse* notes Marx developed this understanding of pre-capitalist forms of production the basic underlying model was still that outlined in the *German Ideology*: 'The various stages of development in the division of labour are just so many different forms of ownership, i.e. the existing stage in the division of labour determines also the relations of individuals to one another with reference to the material, instrument, and product of labour.' (Marx and Engels 2011, 9). There is more than a whiff of technological determinism here and the whole tone is different from Marx's notes and letters on Russia. As Jairus Banaji argues 'it would be foolish to deny that Marx's handing of these categories was far from finished. He never left us with a developed or mature theory of modes of production' (Banaji 2010, 213). A mode of production cannot be reduced to relations of exploitation if they are to have any purchase in understanding complex historical development. To understand the laws of motion of the world economy we need more than a static ladder like model of development that does not recognise complexity or the inter-relationship between parts of the world economy and how the 'development' of one region can lead to the 'under-development' of another.

One of the reasons why there is still a lingering 'stageism' in the Marxist thinking around development is because of the way the modes of production debate played out in the 1970s (see Foster-Carter 1978) under the sway of Althusser and Balibar's version of 'scientific Marxism' (Althusser et al. 2015) and the emergence of a Marxist school of anthropology (see Terray 1972). The modes of production were given a life of their own in a model-building exercise that far outstripped our knowledge of their history. Instead of complexity there was a formalistic combinatory (or articulation) of abstract modes of production that sought to explain history. The essentialist reading of modes of production was criticised eventually by Etienne Balibar himself who had launched the most ambitious attempt to create a systematic theory (Balibar 2015). Within Marxist anthropology it carried on for a while (see Meilassoux 1981; Rey 1973) but it was never systematically integrated into a Marxist theory of capitalist development. While the debates could, indeed, be theological at times, an opportunity was lost in not integrating the modes of production approach with the emerging dependency problematic (see Munck 1981), whose main writers tended to dismiss it without too much thought.

Overall, the emerging capitalist world economy was seen as an articulation with, for example, the feudal mode of production. But, as Banaji stresses 'historical materialism needs to move beyond this motionless paradigm to a construction of the more complex ways capitalism works' (Banaji 2010, 359). The forms that capitalism takes are extremely varied, and it has the ability to subsume other relations of production and forms of labour exploitation under its aegis until the catalyst mode of production itself prevails worldwide.

It might help us move forward if we distinguish between capitalism—that Marx detects in the fourteenth and fifteenth centuries and the capitalist mode of production that he associates with the industrial revolution. Thus, merchant capitalism helped create a new order from the Middle Ages onwards. As Marx put it 'at the initial stages of bourgeois production, trade dominated industry' (Marx 1987, 233). Put simply, the expansion of capital did not mean the capitalist mode of production prevailed as yet. The idea that the global economy emerging in the mercantilist era responded to the requirements of the reproduction of capital is purely an abstraction. Thus, for example, in relation to a debate we return to in Chapter 7, namely the colonisation of Latin America in the sixteenth and seventeenth centuries was not, strictly speaking, part of the expansion of the capitalist mode of production. As Pierre Vilar once put it, Spanish imperialism can best be characterised as 'the highest stage of feudalism' (Vilar 1971, 19) that would obviously not be creating a capitalist society in Latin America as such.

Politics in Command

We have noted in Chapter 2 how Marx articulated a dialectical view of development, conscious of its positive and negative dynamics, its destruction of previous modes of production and its construction of a new one. The emphasis in general and in relation to India in particular, was on the historically 'progressive' role of capitalist development despite its destructive consequences. The term progressive can be taken to mean the development of the forces of production, although Marx also means the development of society, that was shaken from its traditional shackles. We have seen in this chapter how late in life Marx engaged with the emerging Russian revolution and took a position that was less universal or unilinear.

What we need to do now is move beyond a purely economic leading to place Marx and Engels in their political context. It is in relation to Ireland that they moved closest to what today would be called a dependent development position (see Chapter 7). We also consider their far more troubled relationship to Latin America and Engels's theory of non-historic peoples that coloured his understanding of development outside its Western European core.

For Marx and Engels, Ireland was a central element of their political engagement that is not surprising give the significance of the Irish national question in British politics.

Engels had a long-standing engagement with Ireland and Marx also began to make systematic comment on Irish politics when he moved to London in 1849. Ireland was a significant element in *Capital*, not least because of its role in primitive accumulation in Britain. Thus, in *Capital* Vol. I Marx writes that 'England, a pre-eminently industrial country with fully developed capitalist production, would have bled to death under such a population drain as Ireland has suffered [during the Great Famine of 1845–1848]. But Ireland is at present merely an agricultural district of England which happens to be divided by a wide stretch of water from the country for which it provides corn, wool, castle and industrial and military recruits' (Marx 1976, 860). This reflects what Marx was writing about in terms of the international division of labour between industrialised and agriculture- based countries at the time, while also prefiguring much later theories of underdevelopment which showed development has as its inevitable counterpart the underdevelopment of others.

In 1853 Marx wrote about how British policy had created the conditions for 'underdevelopment' in Ireland: 'England has subverted the conditions of Irish society. At first it confiscated the land, then it suppressed the industry by 'Parliamentary enactments', and lastly, it broke the active energy by armed force. And thus, England created those abominable 'conditions of society' which enable a small caste of rapacious lordlings to hold the land and to live upon it. Too weak yet for revolutionising those 'social conditions', the people appeal to Parliament, demanding at least their mitigation and regulation'. (Marx and Engels 1971, 159). Of course, given the situation of colonialism in Ireland, Marx could say that England created the conditions that led to underdevelopment.

Marx began to engage most seriously with what was then called the 'Irish question' by the First International in 1867. In a letter to Engels at the end of 1869 he refers to a debate on the Central Council (of the International) giving his thoughts thus: 'For a long time I believed that it would be possible to overthrow the Irish regime by English working class will *never accomplish anything* until it has got rid of Ireland. The lever must be applied in Ireland. That is why the Irish Question is so important for the movement in general' (Marx and Engels 1971, 232). What we see clearly here, in a similar way to the earlier analysis of India, that the liberation of a colonialised people is seen as coming from the central working class socialist movement. The concept of a national right to self-determination was not applied universally and in relation to Ireland it was only applied because of its positive impact on 'the movement in general,' in other words it was a 'particular' question. Nevertheless, Ireland represents a turning point for Marx that takes him away from his earlier total emphasis on the development of an industrial working class. He now accepted that Irish nationalism, its republican strand in particular with its support amongst the rural poor, could play a pivotal role in the emergence of revolution in the 'British Isles'.

In terms of his overall view of Ireland, Marx was always perfectly clear. As he wrote to Engels in 1869 'what Ireland needed' was: '(1) self-government and independence from England. (2) An agrarian-revolution. (3) Protective tariffs against England.' (Marx and Engels 1971, 385). This would be achieved through a war of national liberation led by Irish republicanism, even if the more conservative wing won out in the civil war which ensued. Protectionism in regard to building industrial production had become was common wisdom in the 1930s for most of the developing world. So, Marx's general support for free trade found an exception in regard to Ireland. This was in essence what the dependency theorists in the 1960s (see Chapter 7) were advocating when they referred to 'delinking' (see Amin 1990). It is not that Marx through there was a 'dependent mode of production' where the laws of motion of capital did not apply, but he did recognise very explicitly, the impact of force, violence and national domination in the creation of a global capitalist order.

The point to remember, though, is that Marx and Engels engaged with Ireland primarily through politics and their support for the cause of national independence, possibly primarily for its impact on the revolution in Britain. In that political calculation they may have overestimated the impact of Irish national independence on the class struggle in Britain, but the political economy of Ireland they conducted is of great interest from the perspective of development theory and it has been largely neglected for some reason.

In their writing on Latin America Marx and Engels did not display such a sure footing and it is not only because they were less well informed. While their approach has been deemed Eurocentric the problem goes deeper than that (see Aricó 2014). Nor was it that Latin America that peripheral to their concerns or their writings particularly scarce. It is more about Latin America being different/eccentric to Marx's understanding of what the relationship between the state and civil society should be. Not only did he reject Hegel's prioritising of the state, he also did not grasp the particularity of Latin America's state led development model. It was the paradigm of the French Revolution which dominated his thinking on Latin America's politics. Thus Latin America's main leader of the anti-colonial struggle, Simón Bolivar became, for Marx a caricature and insulting version of France's Napoleon III. The liberator Bolivar became, for Marx, a typical Bonapartist dictator portrayed in the most derogatory way. This political prejudice seemed to colour the whole perception Marx and Engels had of Latin America.

The advance of capitalism was inevitably seen as progressive by Marx and Engels. On the occasion of the US invasion and dismemberment of Mexico in 1847, Engels wrote: 'We have witnessed the conquest of Mexico and have rejoiced at it.... It is to the interest of its own development that Mexico will in the future be placed under the tutelage of the United States' (Marx and Engels 1976, 527). There was none of the dialectical interpretation seen in the contemporaneous reading of British colonialism in India, deemed both progressive and extremely damaging to society at the same time. The United States was viewed as a vanguard of capitalist development and its imperial ambitions were not only tolerated but, even, encouraged. Engels went to criticise Bakunin who condemned the US 'war of conquest' and asked rhetorically: 'Or is it perhaps unfortunate that splendid California has been taken away from the lazy Mexicans, who could not do anything with it?....The independence of a few Spanish Californians and Texans may suffer because of it....but what does that matter compared to such facts of world-historic significance' (Marx and Engels 1977, 365) referring to the expected development of capitalism in the conquered zones.

Marx himself wrote an entry on Simón Bolivar in The New American Cyclopaedia in 1858 which concentrated on his authoritarianism rather than his role on the national independence movement. Bolívar's penchant for pomp and ceremony and his incipient personality cult led Marx to call him 'the most cowardly, mean and wretched scoundrel….a true Soulouque' [a Haitian emperor's name Marx used when referring to Napoleon III] (Marx and Engels 1972, 54). It is not his sources that are to blame for this thoroughly 'non Marxist' lack of understanding of Bolivar's role in terms of the indigenous peoples and the role of various social classes in the independence struggle. Marx had understood the role of the state in Russian development but seemed unable to grasp the way the nation-state in Latin America was constructed via the state. Likewise, his rejection of Hegel and total commitment to the French Revolution meant he would always give primacy to the social over the political when confronted with the state. However, if civil society was not present (it had to be constructed in the national independence process) then Marx was left without an interlocutor. This bias lies at the root of the ongoing divorce between Marxism and actually existing 'populist' revolts in Latin America.

There is also a lingering sense that Latin America was viewed in a similar way to the Slav peoples alleged subordination to Tsarism during the 1848 revolutions which led to them being dubbed 'non-historic' peoples following Hegel. For Marx and Engels neither a common language and traditions nor geographical and historical coordinates constitute a nation. Rather, a certain level of economic and social development was required, with priority being given to larger units. The right of nations to self-determination was also replaced by the right of 'civilisation' against barbarism in the US-Mexico case citied above. Engels also expressed his displeasure again, referring to the Swiss as 'most servile, bowing and scraping to the repellent narrow-mindedness of a small nation, which in addition to its smallness is split and immeasurably puffed up—a nation of antediluvian Alpine herdsmen, hidebound peasants and disgusting philistines' (Marx and Engels 1977, 246). Such extreme thoughts are due to politics always being in command for Marx and Engels, especially in regard to the 1848 revolution and the influence of Hegel's theory of historic and non-historic peoples.

In Hegel's theory of history he presented a view of world history based on 'the dialectic of several national minds' where each is appointed to one grade only but only a 'world-historic national mind' was allotted this task and not all nations (see Hegel 1975). Only peoples who were deemed bearers of 'historical progress' could aspire to that role, the rest were deemed 'non-historic', they had lost or would lose their sate and become subjects of another nation. This was Hegel's view on human history as a developmental process and it influenced Marx and (particularly) Engels (see Rosdolsky 1986). While in general the historical materialist theory of history developed by Marx and Engels had supersede such notions as 'national minds', in the particular crucible of the 1848 revolution, the German left in particular fell back on these Hegelian concepts to justify the thoroughly idealist notion that entire peoples could be part of its forward march of history and civilization whereas others were condemned to a counter-revolutionary and 'non-historic' role.

The more immediate background to Marx's and Engel's position on nationalism and development springs from the 1848 revolutions across Europe. The new ideas of liberalism, democracy, socialism and nationalism burst into the scene simultaneously. Popular uprisings in Paris spread to Vienna, then to Berlin, Prague and Budapest. The great Habsburg Empire seemed on the verge of collapse as the Italians and Hungarians pressed their claims for national independence. Elsewhere Slav national aspirations clashed with the 'revolutionary' nations such as the Germans and the Magyars (Hungarians). The 'great historic nation' of Germany, Poland, Hungary and Italy fulfilled the criteria for viable national states. Less dynamic or 'non-historic' nations did not, for Engels in particular, deserve that support: 'these relics of nation mercilessly trampled underfoot in the course of history, as Hegel says, these *residual fragments of peoples* always become jaundiced standard bearers of counter-revolution and remain so until their compete extirpation' (Marx and Engels 1977, 234). As always the position Marx and Engels adopted towards a given issue was over-determined politically and was thus shaped by their overall understanding of revolutionary progress across Europe.

With Engels we see a more systematic clinging to the concept of non-historic nation seemingly motivated by his conviction around the imminent demise of the Austrian Slavs, even when the era of Slav national rebirth began in the 1870s. The same as in 1848, Engels continued to believe Germany would have to be at the centre of a Central European revolution with the same allies (Hungary and Poland) and the same enemies, the 'non historic' Slavs supported by the Tsar. In the event, as Rosdolsky notes, 'Engels held fast to his previous interpretation of the nationality problem and continued to make the distinction between great, historically progressive nations and unviable 'non historic ruins of peoples' the central point of his politics on the national question (Rosdolsky 1986,

13). We would have to wait until Lenin to see a consistent Marxist position on the rights of nations to self-determination.

Unequal Exchange

Marx, as we have seen above, wrote about an 'international division of labour' between primarily industrialised and mainly agricultural nations in terms that prefigured the 1970s neo-Marxist preoccupation with the 'new international division of labour (see Fröbel et al. 1980). Also, in relation to Ireland he was to declare categorically that 'the nation that enslaves another cannot itself be free' (Marx and Engels 1971, 303) in terms that we would next see in the Third Worldism of the 1960s. A few scattered statements by Marx like these allowed for his appropriation by the emerging Third World Marxism of the 1960s which latched on to these statements and systemised them. Yet there was no indication by Marx that he in any way shifted towards what we would later call Third worldism that argued for a shift in the main motor of revolution from the industrial working class to the peasantry, from the North to the South in today's terms. Melotti, captured this mood in his *Marx and the Third World* where he argued that 'In the modern world, [the so-called underdeveloped countries] could build socialism, without going through capitalism, bureaucratic collectivism, or some similar form of antagonistic society…This applies particularly to Africa, where there are still important communal structures which in a different world could expect a great future…The same argument applies, all over the world, as it does to the one advanced by Marx last century in regard to Russia' (Melotti 1977, 12).

While Marx was not a Thirdworldist before his time, in his preparatory notes for *Capital*, he sketched out what would become the contemporary notion of 'unequal exchange' between nations. What Marx wrote in his unpublished preparatory work that would become *Capital* was as follows: 'From the fact that the profit may be *less* than the surplus value, and hence that a capital [may] exchange at a profit without being valorised in the strict sense, it follows that not only individual. Capitalists, but nations too may continuously exchange with one another, and continuously repeat the exchange without gaining equally thereby. One nation may continuously appropriate part of the surplus labour of the other and give nothing in exchange for it, except that here the measure is not as in the exchange between capitalist and worker' (Marx 1987, 244). The nation was being given here a clear epistemological status in the Marxist framework that shows his statements on Ireland were not just political as it were.

So, while Ricardo advanced a theory of 'comparative advantage' in the exchange between nations—entailing mutually shared gains from specialisation and trade involved in complementary structures of comparative advantage- Marx put forward a theory of 'unequal exchange': 'nations may continuously exchange with one another….without gaining equally thereby' (Marx 1987, 260). That Marx never wrote the promised book on world trade meant that this insight in his notes was never followed through on. The level of abstraction that *Capital*, Vol. I operated on meant it could never be dealt with at that level. We would need to introduce competition between capitals to make sense of the statement above.

Capitalist nations exist in a relationship of *competition* between one another, historically and today even in the era of globalisation that does not do away with inter-capitalist competition. Labour, on the other hand, exists in a relationship of *exploitation* with capital. These two relationships are not mutually exclusive and, in fact, reinforce each other. The reason why Marx does not develop a theory of international competition in *Capital* Vol. I is that here he was operating at a level of abstraction 'capital in general' as it were. So, as Enrique Dussel explains, based on a close reading of Marx's economic manuscripts, 'Dependency is a moment in the competition of capital…The workings of competition (and therefore of dependency) are one *real* existing moment of the mere possibility of crisis' (Dussel 2001, 214, 5). Competition is the way in which capital can realise itself and there is thus no real manifestation of the concept of a single world capital.

The 1960s debate around dependency and unequal exchange operated without, seemingly, a close understanding in 1930s debates within Marxism around this problematic. So, for example, Roman Rosdolsky (cited above in relation to Engels and the non-historic peoples) wrote in his excellent analysis of Marx's *Grundrisse* that 'within a single country, the difference of intensity and productivity of labour balance out to constitute an average level. But the same does not happen in the world market… The result is that between various nations there takes place an unequal exchange so that…the poor country…. must continuously hand over part of its national labour' (Rosdolsky 1980, 310). In a similar way Henryk Grossman wrote that 'in international trade there is not an exchange of equivalents, because, just as in the domestic market, there is a tendency towards equalisation of profit rates....In this manner *transfers of surplus value* produced in the less developed country take place within the sphere of circulation in the world market' (Grossman 1979, 278). That Grossman and Rozdolsky are not well known is due entirely to the blanket of silence, fear and conformity brought down on Marxist thinking after the death of Lenin in 1924.

We now have a better understanding I hope of how Marx distinguished between capital in general, 'total world capital', and capital specifically in the shape of 'total national capital'. Competition between these national capitals plays a key role in levelling the distribution of surplus value produced by workers worldwide. Non-economic factors clearly intervene in setting the level of wages worldwide and state intervention also pays an important role. In other words, this is not a purely market mechanism at play. Above all, we need to place this element of unequal exchange at the level of circulation within the wider picture of capital accumulation on a world scale. As Enrique Dussel puts it 'the "essence" of dependency' is about the 'transfer of surplus value as a result of international social relations' (Dussel 2001, 219). In following through on this theme, we are not just 'applying' Marx to the non-European world but remaking his concepts to fit the historical global economy as it developed.

The debate on 'unequal exchange was reopened in the 1960s by Arghiri Emmanuel (1972). His basic assumption is that capital is mobile at a global scale while workers are not (presumably international labour migration is not of sufficient scale to disrupt the thesis). Wages are seen as an independent variable and the starting point (before international trade) is that wages in the North are high and wages in the South are low (by a difference of × 20 or × 30). The free movement of capital is sufficient to equalise international profit rates and to lessen national differences. Given that Southern workers cannot move *en masse* to where wages are higher, when global surplus value is shared out according to the distribution of capital, then Southern capital areas lose out due to higher wages and exploitation (in the Marxist sense) in the North. Or, as Emmanuel puts it 'one country can only gain something at the expense of another by taking more goods than it produces or by buying the good it obtains too cheaply and selling those it provides at too high a price' (Emmanuel 1975, 56).

It was not long before Emmanuel's seemingly novel thesis was criticised by those closer to Marx's original writings. Thus, Charles Bettelheim (1972) in a Conceptual Comment within Emmanuel's book itself, explained clearly its flaws, in terms of Marx's categories. Firstly, we cannot really deploy the notion of 'independent variables' within Marx's complex structure of the laws of motion of capital where all elements are interrelated. Emmanuel's model, according to Bettelheim 'also conceals a point of essential significance, namely the ***inequality of organic composition*** [of capital, that is the capital/labour ratio]' (Bettleheim 1972, 285). Thus, Emmanuel reduces a complex structure to a simple wage differential, which is assumed and not explained. The unevenness of the development of the productive forces on a global scale can only be explained historically and cannot really be discussed without taking colonialism and imperialism into account. The world domination of the capitalist mode of production can only be understood in terms of that history and its economic political and ideological ramifications.

The subtitle of Emmanuel's book is 'a study of the imperialism of trade'. That is to say, he is seeing a form of 'commercial exploitation' before imperialist exploitation is brought into the equation. This is deemed to be one of the imminent laws of the capitalist world market. It is easy to see how this thesis would provide theoretical back-up for Third worldism in the 1960s and the notion of 'proletarian nations'. But there is little in Marx's *Capital* to support such a view in practice. In Chapter 22 of *Capital* Vol. I Marx addresses the National Differences in Wages in an abstract way and states that 'In comparing wages in different nations, we must .... Take into account all the factors that determine changes in the amount of the value of labour power' (Marx 1976, 701) and he goes on to list them. His basic conclusion, congruent with the broad thrust of 'unequal exchange' theory, is that 'on the world market....the more intense national labour....as compared to the less intense produces in the same time more value, which expresses itself in more money' (Marx 1976, 701).

That the notion of unequal exchange has solid roots in Marx is important in my view as it helps underpin the later theory of dependent development too often dismissed as mere economic nationalism by its critics (see Chapter 7). However, I would agree with Robert Brenner for whom 'in the final analysis, however, the whole discussion of unequal exchange leading to the transfer of surplus must be assigned a subordinated place in relationship to the question of the rise of development and underdevelopment' (Brenner 1977, 66). In other words, unequal exchange at the level of circulation cannot explain the development/underdevelopment dialectic in and of itself. Primitive accumulation for Marx—i.e. the 'previous accumulation' of Adam Smith—'precedes capitalist accumulation; an accumulation which is not the result of the capitalist mode of production but its point of departure' (Marx 1976, 873). From then on, unequal exchange can play a subsidiary role in the process of capital accumulation on a global scale but cannot explain its dynamic.

One way a Marxist dependency approach could have been built on Marx's theorising would have been to combine it with a modes of production perspectives and move towards a synthesis (see Munck 1981). The market-focused empiricism of the world systems approach that grew out of the dependency paradigm one hand, was matched by the theoretical inflation of the concept of mode of production by others, resulting in such confusing categories as "colonial mode of production", which conflated two distinct levels of analysis, the society or social formation and the mode of production. Following Laclau, "Marxist thought in Latin America has found considerable difficulty in moving simultaneously at the level of modes of production and that of economic systems [as he called the social formation], and that its most frequent mistakes derive from a unilateral use of one or other of the two levels' (Laclau, 1977, 42). This still leaves us, however, at the level of a prescriptive statement. The missing link, I believe, is the basic Marxist concept of reproduction. At the same time as it produces, every social formation must reproduce the conditions of its production, namely the productive forces and the existing relations of production. Marx's reproduction schemes in *Volume* 2 of *Capital* had a more restricted purpose, but the method is still valid. There Marx showed how 'Capital, as self-valorizing value... is a movement, a circulatory process through different stages... hence it can only be grasped as a movement, and not as a static thing' (Marx, 1976, 185). The function of Marx's reproduction schemes is to show how it is possible for the capitalist mode of production to survive. Does the expanded reproduction of capitalism in general, however, mean that dependent capitalism can function in the same way, and according to the same laws of motion? There have, in fact, been a number of attempts to elaborate the concept of dependent reproduction, which break decisively with some of the rather static elements in the dependency approach. One systematic theoretical attempt was made by Salomón Kalmanovitz (1980) to elaborate a theory of dependent reproduction. Marx's reproduction schemes were modified to take into account the opening of the dependent economy to international capital and commerce, insofar as this is basic to the dynamic of dependent capitalism. As against the reproduction schema of a mature capitalist economy as studied by Marx, dependent reproduction is marked by a division of labour between sectors with different relations of production. This and the fact that it relies on the foreign market for the realisation of most commodities means that the peripheral economy does not have a self-centred circuit of capital accumulation. A key element in this model would be the reproduction of social classes through the class struggle of dependent capitalism, and in the first instance, the formation and reproduction of the working class which is the essence of the capital relation and the basis of its undoing.

In this chapter we have brought to light a Marx who was at odds with many Marxists of his day/including Engels to some extent) and the Soviet popularisers of Marxism-Leninism. His engagement with Russian revolutionaries in the 1870's allowed him to move beyond the stage theories of development he had previously proposed in some popular texts. We have seen, for example, in relation to his engagement with developments in Ireland, how politics was always in command against any economic determinism. We should not be surprised that Marx sometimes got it wrong, for example in relation to Latin America which he read through a European 'Hegelian' lens. Finally, to help set the scene for subsequent chapters on capital accumulation on a world scale we show how Marx was an early proponent of the theory of 'unequal exchange' at an international level.

References

Althusser, Louis, et al. 2015. *Reading Capital*. London: Verso.

Amin, Samir. 1990. *Delinking: Towards a Polycentric World*. London: Zed Books.

Aricó, José. 2014. *Marx and Latin America*. Leiden: Brill.

Balibar, Étienne. 2015. On the Basic Concepts of Historical Materialism. In Louis Althusser et al. *Reading Capital*.

Banaji, Jairus. 2010. *Theory as History. Essays on Modes of Production and Exploitation*. Chicago: Haymarket Books.

Bettelheim, Charles. 1972. Theoretical Comments. In Emmanuel, Arghiri *Unequal Exchange*.

Brenner, Robert. 1977. The Origins of Capitalist Development: A Critique of Neo-Smithian Marxism. *New Left Review* I/104 (July–August).

Day, Richard, and Daniel Gaido, eds. 2011. *Witnesses to Permanent Revolution. The Documentary Record*. Chicago: Haymarket Books.

Dussel, Enrique. 2001. *Towards an Unknown Marx. A Commentary on the Manuscripts of 1861–63*. London and New York: Routledge.

Emmanuel, Arrighi. 1972. *Unequal Exchange. A Study of the Imperialism of Trade*. London: New Left Books.

Emmanuel, Arrighi. 1975. *Unequal Exchange Revisited*. Sussex: Institute of Development Studies.

Foster-Carter, Aidan. 1978. The Modes of Production Controversy. *New Left Review* I/107 (January–February): 44–77.

Fröbel, Folker, Jürgen. Heinrichs, and Otto Kreye. 1980. *The New International Division of Labour*. Cambridge: Cambridge University Press.

Grossman, Henryk. 1979. *The Law of Accumulation and Breakdown of the Capitalist System. Being Also a Theory of Crisis*. London: Pluto Press.

Hegel, Friedrich. 1975. *Lectures on the Philosophy of World History*. New York: Cambridge University Press.

Kalmanovitz, Salomón. 1980. *Ensayos sobre el desarrollo del Capitalismo Dependiente*. Bogotá: La Oveja Negra.

Laclau, Ernesto. 1977. *Politics and Ideology in Marxist Theory*. London: Verso.

Marx, Karl. 1976. *Capital*, vol. I. London: Penguin Books.

Marx, Karl. 1987. *Economic Manuscripts of 1857–58*, p. 233.

Marx, Karl, and Frederick Engels. 1971. *Ireland and the Irish Question*. Moscow: Progress Publishers.

Marx, Karl, and Frederick Engels. 1972. *Materiales para la historia de América Latina*. Buenos Aires: Siglo XXI.

Marx, Karl, and Frederick Engels. 1973. Manifesto of the Communist Party. In *The Revolutions of 1848*. Political Writings Volume 1. Harmondsworth: Penguin.

Marx, Karl, and Frederick Engels. 1976. *Collected Works*, vol. 7. London: Lawrence and Wishart.

Marx, Karl, and Frederick Engels. 1977. *Collected Works*, Vol. 8 (1848–1849). London: Lawrence and Wishart.

Marx, Karl, and Frederick Engels. 1987. *Collected Works*, vol. 29. New York: International Publishers.

Marx, Karl, and Frederick Engels. 2011. *The German Ideology*. Connecticut: Mansfield Centre.

Meillassoux, Claude. 1981. *Maidens, Meal and Money: Capitalism and the Domestic Economy*. Cambridge: Cambridge University Press.

Melotti, Umberto. 1977. *Marx and The Third World*. London: Palgrave Macmillan.

Munck, Ronaldo. 1981. Imperialism and Dependency: Recent Debates and Dead Ends. *Latin American Perspectives* VIII/3/4: 162–179.

Musto, Marcello. 2020. *The Last Years of Karl Marx, 1881–1983. An Intellectual Biography*. Stanford: Stanford University Press.

Rey, Pierre Philippe. 1973. *Les alliances de classes*. Paris: Maspero.
Rosdolsky, Roman. 1980. *The Making of Marx's Capital*. London: Pluto Press.
Rosdolsky, Roman. 1986. *Engels and the "Nonhistoric" Peoples: The National Question in the Revolution of 1848*. Glasgow: Critique Books.
Shanin, Teodor, ed. 1983. *Late Marx and the Russian Road. Marx and 'The Peripheries of Capitalism.'* London: Routledge & Kegan Paul.
Terray, Emmanuel. 1972. *Marxism and "Primitive" Societies*. New York: Monthly Review Press.
Vilar, Pierre. 1971. The Age of Don Quixote. *New Left Review* I/68 (July–August).
Wada, Haruki. 1983. *Marx and Revolutionary Russia*, ed. Teodor Shanin. Late Marx and Russian Road.

CHAPTER 4

Lenin and Development

Lenin put Marxism into practice, leading the Russian revolutions in 1905, July 1917 and, finally, October 1917. Lenin was also a close student of development and our first section below deals with his neglected classic *The Development of Capitalism in Russia* published in 1889. Interestingly, he took a considerably more negative view of the prospects for the Russian commune than Marx did in the late writings on Russia (Chapter 3). The various Russian revolutions occurred in conditions we might call today semi-development rather than underdevelopment. As Lenin put it 'Russia is a capitalist country …[but] … Russia is still very backward, as compared with other capitalist countries, in her economic development' (Lenin 1967, 503). For Lenin, thus, socialism would necessarily be built through *Soviets plus Electrification* as his slogan of the time dramatically put it. There were others in the Bolshevik leadership, who took different views of the development process, arguing for a more balanced strategy between agriculture and industry in an interesting debate which still repays attention. Lenin himself, in his last writings became very conscious of the limitations of the way they were building socialism in conditions of underdevelopment. However, in *Leninism as Development Ideology* we see how, after Lenin's death in 1924, his successor, Stalin, created an 'official' Leninism where all his hesitations, doubts and contradictions were ironed out, and it became an arm of the Soviet state as it expanded in the development world. This was a discourse that was no longer contestatory

R. Munck, *Rethinking Development*, Marx, Engels, and Marxisms,
https://doi.org/10.1007/978-3-030-73811-2_4

and reflected the interests of a Soviet state pledged to the building of 'socialism in one country' that was inimical to Marx's view of capitalist development as an integrated global system. With Lenin, the Marxist engagement with development was no longer theoretical and entered, brutally, into the realm of political practice.

Development of Capitalism in Russia

While Marx was resisting any attempt to 'metamorphose my outline of the genesis of capitalism in Western Europe into a historic-philosophical theory of *la marche générale*, fatally incumbent on all peoples, whatever their historical circumstances' (Marx and Engels 1965, 312) his comrade Engels was arguing (in relation to Russia) that 'only when the social forces of production have reached a very high degree of development does it become possible to increase production to such an extent that the abolition of classes represents a real and durable progress without causing stagnation, or even a regression in the mode of social production'. This has only been reached by the productive forces when in the hands of the *bourgeoisie*. Consequently, the existence of the *bourgeoisie* is from this point of *view also as necessary a condition for the Socialist revolution as the proletariat*. A person who maintains that this revolution could be carried out more easily in his country because it neither has proletariat nor bourgeoisie, proves by his statement that he has understood nothing of Socialism (Engels cited in Norman 1955, 89). And, far from being open to the potential of the Russian commune as Marx was in his letter to Vera Zasulich, Engels was writing in 1893 to Marx's anointed Russian disciple, Nicolai Danielson on the political necessity of 'a very respectable *grande industrie*' (Marx and Engels 1965, 464). There was, once again, only one road to socialism, via the development of capitalism. Marxism was advocating a natural or mechanical unfolding of the development process with clear stages to be followed in a unilinear manner. A bourgeois revolution and the development of industrialisation seemed to clearly be prerequisites for the socialism to be possible.

In Russia itself, it was George Plekhanov who articulated most clearly and in fully 'orthodox' manner what the development of capitalism in Russia would entail. When he was a Narodnik, he had seen the peasant commune, with its redistribution of land according to need, as a harbinger of socialism. By the 1880s he was articulating a very different view in the debate around the development of capitalism and the socialist revolution in Russia. The industrial revolution would tear workers away from their supposed indifference to the universal interests of humanity. The uprooting of the peasantry was essential if they were to join the world historical class of the proletariat in the onward and progressive march of capitalism. As to the Russian commune he had once pinned this hopes on, his judgement was now categorical: 'All the principles of modern economy. All the springs of modern economic life are irreconcilably hostile to the village community. Consequentially to hope for its further independent "development" is as strange as to hope for long life and further development of a fish that has been landed on the bank' (Plekhanov 1974, 45). Russia was not 'exceptional' argued Plekhanov but would follow what he saw as the universal laws of history discovered by Marx, conveniently burying his correspondence with the Russian Populists.

It was in this context that the emerging Russian social-democrat thinker Vladimir Ilyich Ulyanov (Lenin) carried out his research into the development of capitalism in Russia. His interlocutors in this debate around the development of capitalism in Russia were the Narodniks whom he critiqued fiercely in two 1897 articles 'The Heritage We Renounce' and 'A Characterisation of Economic Romanticism' (Lenin 1972a). He answered in the negative what he saw as their primary research question: 'Does the home market shrink because of the ruination of the small producers?' (Lenin 1972a, 135). For Lenin 'it goes without saying.... that the development of capitalism in general, and of capitalist farming in particular, does not restrict the home market, but *creates* it' (Lenin 1972a, 139). Lenin goes on to argue that the Narodniks were not only romanticists but also reactionaries because 'The romanticist tries to base himself upon the *undeveloped state* of the contradictions of the existing system, upon the *backwardness* of the country' (Lenin 1972a, 246). This was seen as a backward-looking discourse that was inimical to the progressive outlook of Marxism which saw the path to the promised land passing through the development of capitalism without any short cuts being possible.

Lenin went on to write a full-length book in 1899 '*The Development of Capitalism in Russia*' described by one of his biographers as 'the fullest, best-documented and best-argued examination of the crucial period of the evolution of capitalism out of feudalism in the literature of Marxism' (Harding 1980, 107). Lenin improved on previous accounts of development in Russia (for example by Plekhanov) insofar as his treatise was guided broadly by Marx's Volumes II and III of *Capital* which was not usually the case for Marxists of that era who took the more 'popular' texts of Marx as their basis for interpreting his thought. Essentially Lenin was contesting the Populist argument about the impossibility of an adequate home market developing in Russia that could absorb the produce of capitalist industry given the impoverishment of the masses of the people. Lenin, to be clear, was also seeking theoretical justification for his political position that only the proletariat could articulate the grievances of all the exploited because they were 'the sole and natural representative of Russia's entire working and exploited population' (Lenin 1972a, 203). The emphasis on the development of capitalism in Russia thus had a directly political counterpart, namely the belief in the leading role of the industrial proletariat in the revolution Marxists saw as inevitable. This despite the very small numerical size of this class in pre-revolutionary Russia.

It is worth noting at this stage that Lenin's early work, in the first three volumes of his collected works (Lenin 1967, 1972a, b) made an important contribution to the Marxist theory of modes of production and social (or socio-economic) formations that was later taken up by the Althusserian school in the 1960s (see Althusser and Balibar 1970). What is particularly interesting in Lenin's analysis of the development of capitalism in Russia is how he started with Marx's *Capital* Vol. 2 that was not part of the repertoire of most Marxists at the time and where Marx discusses the way in which capitalism develops and, in particular, the way in which capitalism subsumes other modes of production under its sway. Lenin recovers Marx's dynamic concept of socio-economic formation that was not taken up at all by Engels after his death nor by German social democracy. The erasure of the concept of socio-economic formation lay at the heart of social democracy's theoretical reductionism and the emergence of a positivist and teleological concept of development. By focusing on the development of a 'pure' capitalist mode of production, rather than on the concrete socio-economic formation that could consist of various modes of production, social democracy sought to apply the rules of the natural sciences of the time to the social world in an evolutionist way. This organicist approach to development created the belief that socialism was inevitable, something that was totally inimical to Lenin the organiser.

In his *What the Friends of the People Are* of 1894 Lenin articulated the concept of socio-economic formation very clearly. Marx, he argued 'took one of the social-economic formations—the system of commodity production—and on the basis of a vast mass of data (which he studied for not less than twenty-five years) gave a most detailed analysis of the laws governing the functioning of this formation and its development. This analysis is confined exclusively to production relations between members of society: without ever resorting to features outside the sphere of these production relations for an explanation' (Lenin 1972a, 200). To be very clear, 'Marx speaks of one 'economic formation of society' only, the capitalist formation, that is, he says that he investigated the law of development of this formation only and of no other' (Lenin 1972a, 220). For Lenin, Marx developed the 'skeleton' of capitalist development and the creation of social classes. But this was no ordinary 'economic theory' and the development of a given formation of society could not be read solely through its production relations. To leave our analysis at the level of abstraction of the mode of production would be to invite the mechanical evolutionism that social democracy ended up with. Only at the more concrete level of the socio-economic formation can we, for example, pose the national and colonial questions that were, of course, the great advances generated by Lenin and his comrades.

More concretely, *The Development of Capitalism in Russia* makes a number of clear arguments based on a close reading of existing agricultural census data. The erosion of the natural economy by capitalism was a classic Marxist theme and Lenin argued that it had already 'disintegrated' the Russian peasantry into rich, middle and poor strata. The increasing commercialisation and diversification of Russian agriculture in the 1860s and the dissolution of serfdom is analysed in great detail. Lenin articulated a quite minimalist definition of capitalism where human labour power is a commodity and hence he was prone to exaggerate its dominance in pre-revolutionary Russia. His main point, though, was to refute the under-consumptionist views of the Narodniks by showing how capitalism (and the machine industry in particular) creates its own market. Lenin's understanding of uneven development is undoubted and he recognised the persistence of the 'pre-capitalist village' and how peasant subjection 'inevitably acquires the form of bondage' (Lenin 1967, 388).

Taken overall, Lenin stresses the 'progressive' nature of capitalist development with few of Marx's reservations (e.g. in relation to India, see Chapter 2 above): 'Capitalism draws these [local] markets together, combines them into a big national market, then into a world market destroys the primitive forms of bondage and personal dependence, develops in depth and in breadth the contradictions which in a rudimentary form are also to be observed aiming to community peasantry—and thus paves the way for their resolution' (Lenin 1967, 388). Lenin's opponents, the Narodniks or 'Populists' as they incorrectly became known as, had a different vision of the development of capitalism in Russia. Their leader, Victor Chernov, was committed to a form of highly decentralised village communism as the main driver of socio-economic and political progress in Russia. Against any notion of forced collectivization this movement was committed to voluntary cooperation and the free association of fundamentally autonomous households. The movement was based on the political philosophy of Alexander Herzen who emerged in the 1850s as one of the main champions of peasant liberation. For Herzen 'The idea of social revolution is European [but] That doesn't mean that the people most capable of its realization are those of the West' (cited Bideleux 1985, 31) going on to argue that 'Slavophiles have a true sense of the people's living soul, a "glimpse of the future"' (cited Bideleux 1985, 31). This sensitivity to 'national particularities' and opposition to what he saw as Marx's unilinear concept of development did not prevent Herzen becoming a social democrat.

A major theorist to emerge from the Russian agrarian debates was Alexander Chayanov who still plays a pivotal role in international peasant studies today (see Chayanov 1966). Chayanov started from the distinction made by Marx between capitalism and single (or petty) commodity production where self-employment and family labour prevailed. His emphasis on the family form and explanation of its durability is part of the underlying political philosophy of international peasant movements that defy in practice the orthodox Marxist predictions on the 'death of the peasantry'. Chayanov hoped the Russian revolution would develop a decentralised, pluralist and egalitarian society that could accommodate the family farm and the commune system. He opposed while all collectivisation and state control over agriculture and though he recanted these heretical views he still ended up—along with many other independent minded radicals—in Stalin's labour where he perished in the 1930s.

By 1907, Lenin himself was realising that his early analysis of the 'peasant question' was flawed. He now admitted in *The Agrarian Question and Social Democracy* (Lenin 1978) that his earlier works had contributed to 'an *overestimation* of the *degree* of capitalist development in Russian agriculture The survivals of serfdom appeared to us then to be a minor detail, whereas capitalist agriculture on the peasant allotments and on the landlords' estates seemed to be quite mature and well-established ' (Lenin 1978, 292). His revised agrarian programme now postulated two 'paths' for Russian agriculture: a 'Prussian' path where the feudal economy gradually becomes capitalist and the 'American' path where the landlord economy is broken up and the farmer becomes a capitalist. Lenin was beginning to realise the innate revolutionary potential of the Russian peasantry give its strong desire to break up the landlord system. Harnessing this peasant energy for the proletarian revolution was now his priority. Large-scale industrialization was still, for Lenin, the pathway to socialism in Russia and the role of the peasants never more than a support role.

Ultimately, the Lenin/Narodnik fierce debate on the development of capitalism in Russia needs to be evaluated in political terms. Politics flowed from the economic analysis and, ultimately, the goal was state power. It is worth remembering that in its only democratic elections held in revolutionary Russia the Constituent Assembly elections of November 1917, the Socialist Revolutionaries (SR's) obtained 38% of the vote, wheals the Bolsheviks itself obtained 23% of the popular vote. Lenin's following of one Marx-that of the Communist Manifesto—and ignoring of his late engagement with the Russian commune had its price. What can only be called a theological belief in the destiny of a minuscule industrial proletariat (soon to be decoded by the civil war) in a predominately peasant country meant that, inevitably, there would be a confrontation with those who here expedited to feed the cites and subordinate their natural economy to the needs of Engels's '*grande industrie*'.

The importance of this debate reverberates down to the present-day with the accusation of 'populism' and 'romantic' views of the peasantry being bandied about freely by those who cling to a 'stages' view of capitalist development. Any policy that deviates from a strict evolutionary view of capitalist development is dismissed as 'romantic'. Any sympathetic appraisal of non-capitalist modes of production is seen as reactionary and backward looking. Yet the left Socialist revolutionary (SR) agrarian programme in Russia was not starry-eyed or romantic wishful thinking. A counterfactual history of Russian revolution could easily imagine a less confrontational approach to the 'rural question' than that adopted by the Bolsheviks guided by a very particular interpretation of Marxist orthodoxy and the one true path to socialism via industrialization.

We see this debate play out today in the confrontation of 'peasantist' and 'proletarianist' readings of rural transformation. For the first current there is a stress on the durability of peasant farming as a form of petty commodity production that can effectively compete with capitalist agriculture. Peasants are not seen as 'about to become' or disguised proletarians. Nor do they see a generalisation of the wage relation that would spell the death of the peasantry that many Marxists have forecast over the years. This current often references the classic work of Chayanov. The 'proletarianist' current of interpretation, in contrast, stresses the impact of social differentiation in the countryside that will have the effect of turning most peasants into proletarians. Peasant farmers cannot compete with capitalist farmers. It argues that the peasant form of production is not viable ultimately and that the petty commodity mode of production will disappear with the development of capitalism. This strand of thinking would still, albeit it indirectly, be inspired by the work of Lenin and, in particular, Kautsky's classic *The Agrarian Question* (Kautsky 1988) that extended and generalised Lenin's early analysis of Russian agriculture.

There has been much debate around what some have called 'agrarian Marxism' (Levien et al. 2018) that takes up the classic concern with the 'agrarian question' problematised by Kautsky in particular. Overall, there appears to be an impasse between the two currents identified above, namely the orthodox Marxist/proletarianist and the Populist/peasantist discourses. As Levien et al. note 'agrarian studies is marked by durable—and enduring—tensions and even polarities in theoretical approach. While Marxists have long criticised 'populists' for ignoring capitalism and class, populists have charged Marxists with an obsessive concern with accumulation and class, an insensitivity to the contingencies of history and various blindspots regarding gender and identity' (Levien et al. 2018, 853–854). But in practice we see some degree of convergence with Marxists becoming more concerned with social reproduction and the gendered division of labour and more accepting of peasant identity and political agency. The linear Eurocentric conception of history and the structuralism of the modes of production debate have been largely superseded. What was once called the neo-populist current is now focused on issues such as food sovereignty and land grabs for example that, of necessity, brings to bear Marxist insights around the dynamics of capitalist development and class struggle. The one-time stark divide between class and 'non class' factors now seems largely overcome. Issues such as organic food and the question of genetically modified produce, for example, cannot be studied without bearing in mind the increasing financialization and corporate control over agriculture where classic Marxist approaches still have something useful to say. It is just that they cannot tell the whole story on their own.

Soviets Plus Electrification

The full expression of this well-known phrase was '*Communism is Soviet power plus the electrification of the whole country*' (Lenin 1971a, 519). This was not just a turn of phrase as contemporary readers in the global North might think. The imperatives of development were very real, and the new Soviet government needed to answer the needs of the population. There was a clear and present danger that capitalism could return to Russia, Lenin argued because 'while we live in a small-peasant country, there is a firmer economic basis for capitalism in Russia than for communism' (Lenin 1971a, 518). In the Russian countryside 'the internal enemy' lay in wait in the small-scale production sector, and the only way it could be undermined was to place the whole country, 'including agriculture, on a new technical basis, that of modern large-scale production: Only electricity provides that basis' (Lenin 1971a, 518). So only the development of capitalism in agriculture could prevent the restoration of capitalism in Russia, a strange, productivist and evolutionary logic that made little sense. This was a form of evolutionist Marxism in practice as it navigated a way forward in uncharted waters given this was the first socialist experience in conditions of lesser development, hardly the socialisation of plenty.

Lenin—as much as anyone else at the time—was well aware that the Russian Revolution did not occur as the *Communist Manifesto* predicted, namely that socialism would emerge from the most advanced capitalist conditions as its contradictions were burst asunder. Antonio Gramsci, the Italian communist leader famously called the Russian revolution a 'Revolution Against Capital' by which he meant it went against the mechanical reading of development according to dogmatic readings of Marx's *Capital*: 'It's a revolution against Karl Marx's Capital. In Russia, Marx's Capital was the book of the bourgeoisie, more than of the proletariat. It was the crucial proof needed to show that, in Russia, there had to be a bourgeoisie, there had to be a capitalist era, there had to be a Western-style of progression, before the proletariat could even think about making a comeback, about their class demands, about revolution. Events overcame ideology. Events have blown out of the water all critical notions which stated Russia would have to develop according to the laws of historical materialism. The Bolsheviks renounce Karl Marx and they assert, through their clear statement of action, through what they have achieved, that the laws of historical materialism are not as set in stone, as one may think, or one may have thought previously' (Gramsci 1977, 34).

Lenin did not go as far as Gramsci, but he fully acknowledged in 1920 'the general truth that it was easy for Russia, in the specific and historically unique situation of 1917, to *start* the socialist revolution, but it will be more difficult for Russia than for the European countries to *continue* the revolution and bring it to its consummation' (Lenin 1971b, 384). While we could never really say it was 'easy' to mount a successful revolution it is certainly true that maintaining power and building socialism in conditions of underdevelopment is extremely problematic.

As the Russian Revolution overcame an invasion by the Western powers and a bitter civil war between the Red and White armies Lenin would survey the situation in *Better Fewer. But Better* written in 1923, only months before his death in 1924. He argued on the one had that 'in the last analysis, the outcome of the struggle will be determined by the fact that Russia, India, China, etc., account for the overwhelming majority of the population of the globe' but, on the other hand, he argued that to win the next inevitable conflict between 'the counter-revolutionary imperialist West and the revolutionary and nationalist East, between the most civilised countries of the world and its Orientally backward countries….the majority must become civilised' (Lenin 1965, 787). In terms that sound wrong today about 'civilisation' and 'backwardness', Lenin seems to recognise just how hard it was to build socialism in Russia: 'We, too, lack enough civilisation to enable us to pass straight to socialism, although we do have the political prerequisites for it' (Lenin 1965, 789). It was in this political arena that a great debate on development took place in the first country that sought to apply Marx's theory of development and socialism in practice.

In the 1920s the economic strategy debate in Russia broke new grounds as various Marxist approaches to development in a non-capitalist context were put forward. We consider here, in a slightly simplified way the cautious and balanced approach of Bukharin, the super-industrializer vision of Preobrazhensky and the ultimately victorious strategy of 'socialism in one country' put forward by Stalin who succeeded Lenin on his death in 1924.

Nikolai Bukharin had always been on the left of the Bolshevik party but he began to articulate what might be called a moderate development path to socialism from the mid 1920s onwards (Bukharin 1979). He advocated a balanced and integrated relationship between small-holder agriculture and light industry. The town-country relationship would not be placed under strain and it would be underpinned by steadily rising consumption levels. Against Lenin he argued that the New Economic Programme (that slowed down the transition to socialism) would induce the peasants to become more amenable to socialism.

Whereas with Lenin the retreat represented by the New Economic Policy (NEP) did not change his views on the Russian peasantry, with Bukharin it led to a veritable paradigm shift. He argued for a more open and trusting attitude towards the peasantry who were not just seeking to become capitalists but would be open to a cooperative model of development. The NEP and the co-operative path to socialism was seen by Bukharin as a more evolutionary as against revolutionary path. What Bukharin envisaged was a development strategy that would create the framework for industrialization, along with rural development and a decline of coercion. Bukharin distinguished between the way in which 'revolutionary violence must destroy the fetters on the development of society' (Bukharin 1979, 158) through the revolution but now, after it, coercion, in any form whatsoever will disappear once and for all' (Bukharin 1979, 166). It would be wrong to see this as simply a 'right wing' development strategy given the history of 'actually existing socialism' subsequently.

Evgeny Preobrazhensky is usually seen as the 'left' of the development debate and advocate of forced industrialisation against the consumerist fantasies of the NEP. In his book, *The New Economics* (Preobrazhensky 1965), he advocated that the new Soviet would need to prioritise forced state-funded industrial development. Preobrazhensky was going for the most advanced capital-intensive model of Development-Fordism as a means of labour control included—with financing to come from various sources but including a squeeze on the peasant sector and private profit more generally. The gradualist model of accumulation versus this forced industrialisation paradigm had various middle ground positions—Trotsky, Kondratiev, and many others articulated 'least cost' industrialization strategies often based on international economic relations—but it effectively encapsulated the two main articulating models in play. They are debates that also played out in many 'non-capitalist' development debates across the once colonised world became independent from the 1950s onwards.

Preobrazhensky added to the classic Marxist study of primitive accumulation by advancing a new 'law of primitive socialist accumulation.' This law, an analogy with its capitalist equivalent 'means accumulation in the hands of the state of material resources mainly or partly from sources lying outside the complex of state economy' (Preobrazhensky 1965, 841). This accumulation plays an extremely important role in 'a backward peasant country' and is designed to hasten the 'technical and scientific' reconstruction of the state economy that can then go in to demonstrate its 'purely economic superiority over capitalism' (Preobrazhensky 1965, 84). Of course, this approach, based on the assumed necessity of heavy industry as driver of development would undermine market relations and exacerbate town-country contradiction. This vision of forced development has echoes in subsequent 'development' debates. Preobrazhensky himself, shortly after Bukharin, would be murdered by Stalin in the 'great purges' of 1926–1927.

It is sometimes assumed that Stalin had no political or economic strategy of its own. In fact, he articulated a middle path between the 'right' and 'left' represented schematically by Bukharin and Preobrazhensky. The conventional account is that he adopted Bukharin's position in 1924–1927 to help defeat Trotsky and then adopted 'Trotskyist' positions to get rid of Bukharin. In fact, following Lenin's death in 1924, Stalin began to forge a coherent plan in his *Foundations of Leninism* (Stalin 1950) that sought theoretical justification for an enforced development strategy of self-reliance. Whereas the previously held consensus across the party has that socialism in Russia could not be built without a revolution in the West, Stalin now put forth a vision of 'socialism in one country' for which he sought justification in a self-interested simplification of Lenin's thinking and practice.

In his report to the 1925 party Congress, Stalin articulated this position clearly. Russia had to become 'an economically self –reliant, independent country based on the home market' (Stalin 1925, 350). Socialism in one country was an inevitable option for Stalin as was his conclusion that 'we must build our economy in such a way as to prevent our country from becoming an appendage of the world capitalist system' (Stalin 1925, 354). Instead of the international working class being the focus of the revolution, from now on the Soviet Union for Stalin 'would serve as a centre of attraction for all other countries that little by little drop out of capitalism and enter into the general channel of socialist development' (Stalin 1925, 374). This state driven national development model—and its international dissemination-would, of course, represent a clear breath with Marx's vision and even of Lenin's although he shared some of the self-reliance instincts.

The less developed economy of Russia would find it very hard, if not impossible, to escape Marx's law of value under which capitalism as a mode of production operated. The idea was that the state would control the means of production and distribution sufficiently to act as a countervailing power to the law of the market. In practice this plan did not succeed, and the international capitalist market proved totally corrosive of any national attempt to control the levers of economic power. Above all, Russia as a resource-constrained economy existed more in the 'realm of necessity' than in the 'realm of freedom' as Marx had hoped for. The legacy of underdevelopment constrained all decision-making and there was no 'socialisation of plenty'. As US radical economist Paul Baran once put it 'Socialism in backward and underdeveloped countries has a powerful tendency to become a backward and underdeveloped socialism' (Baran 1968, vcci). This clear statement was not one that was easily accepted by many Third World Marxists at the time, who often thought the power of the will would prevail.

Underdevelopment of the forces of production also means underdevelopment of the working class, the agent of transformation in the classic Marxist schema. It is possible to detect a working class role in socialist revolutions usually deemed peasant-based, such as that in China. More often the 'workers' party' has substituted for the actual participation of workers *en masse* in the revolutionary struggles. The main point remains that it is hard to conceive of socialism developing in the context of what were often pre-capitalist social and economic conditions. Socialisation of the means of production was often replaced by a socialisation of misery. It may be the case that the best that socialism, in conditions of underdevelopment, can achieve is (was) the development of capitalism under slightly more democratic conditions. Even this is unlikely, however, given the prevailing international political context in which the socialist revolutions occurred. To the legacy of underdevelopment one must add the hostile international environment which socialist regimes faced from 1917 onwards. Being a 'weak link' in an imperialist chain may have facilitated a socialist revolution but, for sure, imperialist aggression would ensue. This was the case for Russia, Cuba, Vietnam and Angola. Revolutionary, nationalist self-determination had its place in the imperialist system. Wars, boycotts, external aggression and blockades have been a fact of most successful revolutions. The transition to socialism has thus been 'over-determined' by the conditions prevailing in the international political system. This situation can only exacerbate the already difficult internal conditions for democratic, let alone socialist, development. The internal balance of forces between democratic transformation and restoration are, inevitably, tilted towards the latter. While in the short term, external aggression may hasten the transformation of social relations after the revolution, in the longer term it needs only to be maintained to fatally weaken the transformation project or turn it in an authoritarian militarist direction, as happened in Nicaragua.

The twin constraints of economic underdevelopment and external aggression pointed many victorious revolutions towards self-reliance, if not outright autarky. The radical dependency theory of development, which built on Lenin's concept of imperialism, advocated some form of 'de-linking' from the world economy as the remedy for underdevelopment. National liberation, however defined, became a central goal of socialist movements and regimes. This is understandable, but it does not lead to socialism in the way Marx understood it. Nor do we need to look beyond the experience of Burma or Kampuchea to see the terrible cost of autarky as a substitute for socialism. It is clear by now, that the socialist regimes of the twentieth century existed more in the 'realm of necessity' than in the promised 'realm of freedom'. underdevelopment. In this scenario, it is inevitable that there will be distributional conflicts between industry and agriculture, investment and consumption, or military and civilian expenditure, for example. There was no abundance to be socialised, no irrationality to be ironed out to everyone's benefit, no benign or virtuous circle waiting to be activated. It is certainly easy to see how, from the very start, there would be a tendency towards full reintegration into the world market in a bid to escape the critical resource constraints which the new socialist economies faced. The resource-constrained economy finds it very difficult to escape the capitalist 'law of value' and launch the system of planning deemed essential for a transition to socialism. The idea was that the state would control the means of production and distribution sufficiently to act as a countervailing power to the law of the market. Central planning was seen as a key element in gaining social control over the economy. E. V. K. Fitzgerald even argued, with Nicaragua in mind, that 'The advance towards the effective socialisation of the enterprise sector of the economy through subordination to the plan may … be more rapid than in a larger, more developed economy' (Fitzgerald 1986, 44). The idea was that prices could be set through economic calculus by a central decision-making power without recourse to internal market forces. In practice, this model did not succeed, and the international capitalist market proved totally corrosive of any national attempt at control over the levers of economic power. Thus, central planning proved to be as much chimera as self-reliance. The fragmentation of the post-revolutionary state and the 'dollarization' of the economy was the seemingly inevitable result imposed by a hostile capitalist world. Faced with the inevitable contradiction engendered by state socialist economic policies, economic reform was inherently unlikely to achieve its objectives.

Leninism as Development Ideology

Leninism, as codified by Stalin, began to take on a life of its own after 1924. It is not too exaggerated, to argue, with David Lane that 'Leninism provided an ideological stimulus for and legitimation to the formation of a large-scale industrial system' (Lane 1974, 25). And while Lenin had many facets, including a quasi-anarchist grass-roots belief at times it is also important to recognise for our purposes here that 'Lenin was a passionate advocate of what was once fashionable called 'modernization' for underdeveloped counters' (Lane 1974, 26). This is in keeping, of course with what we have called Manifesto Marxism (see Chapter 2) above. Of course, this modernisation or developmentalist ideology was set in the context of the class struggle. Lenin imagined that spreading up capitalist development would help usher in the era of socialism and the satisfaction of social needs.

Leninism (not Lenin) coined the term 'non-capitalist mode of development' that would be led by the working class in the colonial and semi-colonial countries. Socialism thus became redefined in theory and practice to signal the wielding of political power to achieve the industrial development of the economy. The social downside of capitalism in terms of oppression, degradation and exploitation would no longer apply and large-scale industrial production would benefit the whole of society because it was led by the proletariat or their political expression. As Clive Thomas puts it, in a sympathetic review in 1978: 'the theory of the non-capitalist path to socialism is based on the revolutionary potentialities among the petty-bourgeois leadership usually found in [Third World] countries, in alliance with the peasantry, proletarian and semi-proletarian classes and "progressive" sectors of the emerging national bourgeoisie' (Thomas 1978, 11). In practice, it was this progressive national bourgeoisie which would lead the struggle for 'socialism' and not the proletariat.

Leninism as development ideology is related, of course, to the politics of the Russian Revolution and the so-called 'turn to the East' after the failure of the German Revolution in 1919. The Soviet Union was, of course, a multinational entity and thus there was an 'internal' element to this turn beyond the proletariat in the Russian urban centres. The minority ethnic workforce of this largely Muslim population suffered from the impact of uneven development. Many joined the anti-Bolshevik White forces who mounted a civil war that continued until 1920. Hanafi Muzaffar, who contested that allegiance in 1922 explained that 'the essential point for us is the survival of our nation and even more broadly, the survival of all Muslim peoples and all colonial peoples who are oppressed and threatened by European imperialism….It would be a great mistake for us peoples who are oppressed by Europe to fail to recognise that Marxism is fighting imperialism' (cited in Post 1997, 29).

This perspective paved the way for the doctrine of 'socialism on one country' and the stages theory of development to socialism. With the shift to the East as epicentre of the world revolution the Marxist theory of global development had to be altered. On Lenin's death in 1924 Stalin moved decisively on two ideological fronts: the 'law of uneven development' was reinterpreted to mean the 'non-skipping of stages' and the Soviet Union was declared ready to start organising a socialist economy. Against all previous understandings of the global nature of the struggle against capitalism 'socialism in one country' was now deemed not just possible but necessary. In the developing world this new socialist state would act as a bulwark against capitalist imperialism and as a guarantor of 'national democracy' and 'non-capitalist development' under the aegis of a 'patriotic national bourgeoisie.

This reorientation of official Marxism-Leninism was to have a very real effect. When the Soviet Union collapsed in 1989-not least from its internal contradictions as a development model-it not only meant the end of a great, yet tragic, experiment but also the end of the 'non-capitalist' road in the Third World. The globalisation revolution of the 1990s (see Chapter 10) thus incorporated the whole once socialist world under its aegis but also the national developmentalist states that sought some level of national autonomy within the global capitalist system. This was to have a huge impact on development theory insofar as only the market was deemed central and all forms of state intervention were condemned as counter-productive. This brutal and comprehensive setback for the model that prevailed between 1919 and 1989 does not mean, of course, that we can simply return to the classic debates on 1917–1919 and choose the other side now.

'Soviets plus electrification' was an attractive vision for development in the 1950s. Leninism as development ideology became an attractive legitimising discourse in the Soviet sphere of influence in the Third World. The ideology of proletarian revolution in the West became the ideology of peasant mobilisation in the East and then the ideology of modernising elites in the South. David Lane puts it bluntly but not inaccurately: 'Leninism is the developmental ethic of Marxism' (Lane 1974, 31). Of course, we could argue that this judgement is one-sided but it does capture the trajectory of the state-sanctioned version of Leninism. This Leninism was very close to what the 'modernisation' theory was postulating in the United States in the 1950s. This productivist—economistic—developmentalist vision of Marxism was articulated clearly by Stalin for whom 'socialist industrialisation is the development of large-scale industry and primarily heavy industry….it ensures the victory of socialism and strengthens the country's technical and economic independence and defence capacity in the face of the capitalist world' (Stalin 1950, 351).

Underlying this industrialising bias was the strategy of delinking from the global economy and at the extreme the notion of autarchy and self-sufficiency. In the Soviet sphere of influence this meant, inevitably, an economic dependence on the Soviet Union. Subsidised Soviet fuel. Raw materials, technical know-how soft credit and preferential access to Soviet markets was attractive to a Third World developing country, but also, of course, deepened dependence. As Bideleux writes 'the autarkic, import-substituting policies of industrialising communist states are commonly defended on the grounds that, in the long run, they promote greater national independence, learning-by-doing, industrial technological capabilities and self-reliance' (Bideleux 1985, 152). Yet because of the new dependency on the Soviet Union that it created this was not the case in practice. Even as an objective national independence and self-reliance are not the same as socialism as envisaged by Marx.

Soviet foreign policy dominated 'Marxist-Leninist' thinking and activism through the communist parties and its own state actions. Thus, its attitude towards the colonial revolution was coloured by the needs of the Soviet state and not those of a putative 'world revolution'. The Congresses of the Communist International (until its dissolution in 1943) were a good barometer of that policy. The rationalisation of the 'world revolution' and Soviet state interests emerged most clearly at the Third Congress of the Comintern (Communist International) in 1921. The Fourth Congress in 1922 took a somewhat critical alliance towards the 'national bourgeoisie' but this was reversed at the 1924 Fifth Congress that took a much more conciliatory line insofar as bourgeois governments in semi-colonial countries were seen as potential allies against Anglo-French imperialism. A major change occurred at the 1928 Sixth Congress which stated bluntly that imperialism retarded industrialization and the development of the forces of production and thus 'anti-imperialism' began to take over from socialism as the mission of all communists. For a whole historical period both Marxism and 'Leninism' had argued that capitalist development was generally progressive when it expanded into the non-European world. From the *Communist Manifesto* to Lenin's *Development of Capitalism in Russia* it had always been explicitly argued that capitalism corroded and dissolved archaic modes of production and exploitation.

The balance sheet of socialism and underdevelopment or underdeveloped socialism is, inevitably, a mixed one. Certainly, the grossest forms of inequality and health were addressed and a country like Cuba stands out for its education and health capacity and commitment. But one could question whether, for example, that showcase for Third World socialism, Cuba, has really done all that better than it would have done under dependent capitalist development (see Farber 2011). Cuba on the eve of the revolution was among the better off Latin American countries not just in terms of per capita income but also according to health indicators, for example. There are limits, of course, to the usefulness of this type of counterfactual exercise, but it is still the case that Cuba has failed to provide an alternative development model as originally hoped for by dependency theory. Socialism was once seen as the best means to 'catch up' with advanced Western capitalist societies. In 1936, Jawaharlal Nehru spoke for many Third World nationalist leaders when he declared: 'I see no way of ending the poverty, the vast unemployment, the degradation and the subjection of the Indian people, except through socialism' (Nehru 1977, 180). Some years after that Nikita Khrushchev could still, with some credibility, talk about 'catching up' with the West, as Sputnik reached for the stars and the combine harvesters reaped bumper crops. Yet fifty years after Nehru's desperate leap of faith, it was abundantly clear that 'socialist development' was just a pale imitation of its capitalist progenitor, with its own undesirable features and inefficiencies thrown in.

References

Althusser, Louis, and Étienne Balibar. 1970. *Reading Capital*. London: New Left Books.

Baran, Paul. 1968. *The Political Economy of Growth*. New York: Monthly Review Press.

Bideleux, Robert. 1985. *Communism and Development*. London: Methuen.

Bukharin, Nicolai. 1979. *Economies of the Transition Period*. London: Routledge Kegan Paul.

Chayanov, Alexander. 1966. *The Theory of Peasant Economy*. Homewood, IL: Irwin.

Farber, Samuel. 2011. *Cuba Since 1959: A Critical Assessment*. New York: Haymarket Books.

Fitzgerald, Valpy. 1986. Notes on the Analysis of the Small Underdeveloped Economy in Transition. In *Transition and Development, Problems of Third World Socialism*, ed. Richard Fagan, Carmen Deere, and Louis Coraggio. New York: Monthly Review Press.

Gramsci, Antonio. 1977. The Revolution Against 'Capital'. In *A. Gramsci Selections from Political Writings 1910–1920*. London: Lawrence and Wishart.

Harding, Neil. 1980. *Lenin's Political Thought*. London: Macmillan.

Kautsky, Karl. 1988. *The Agrarian Question*, 2 vols. Michigan: Zwan Publications.

Lane, David. 1974. Leninism as an Ideology of Soviet Development. In *Sociology and Development*, ed. Emanuel De Kadt and Gavin Williams, 23–30. London: Tavistock Publishing.

Lenin, Vladimir Illich. 1963. *Collected Works*, vol. 38. Philosophical Notebooks. Moscow: Progress Publishers.

Lenin, Vladimir Illich. 1967. *The Development of Capitalism in Russia*. Moscow: Progress Publishers.

Lenin, Vladimir Illich. 1971a. Eight All-Russia Congress of Soviets. In *Lenin Selected Works*, vol. 3. Moscow: Progress Publishers.

Lenin, Vladimir Illich. 1971b. 'Left Wing' Communism: An Infantile Disorder. In *Lenin Selected Works*, vol. 3. Moscow: Progress Publishers.

Lenin, Vladimir Illich. 1972a. *Collected Works*, vol. 1.

Lenin, Vladimir Illich. 1972b. *Collected Works*, vol. 2.

Lenin, Vladimir Illich. 1978. The Agrarian Question and Social Democracy. In *Collected Works*, vol. 13. Moscow: Progress Publishers.

Lenin, Vladimir Illich. 1965. Better Fewer But Better. In *Lenin Collected Works*, vol. 33. Moscow: Progress Publishers

Levien, Michael, Michael Watts, and Yan Hairong. 2018. Agrarian Marxism. *Journal of Peasant Studies* 45 (5–6): 853–883.

Marx, Karl, and Frederick Engels. 1965. *Selected Correspondence*. Moscow: Progress Publishers.

Nehru, Jawaharlal. 1977. The Presidential Address. in *Selected Works*, ed. Sarvepalli Gopal, vol. 7. Delhi.

Norman, Daniel. 1955. *Marx and Soviet Reality*. London: Batchworth Press.

Plekhanov, Georgi. 1974. Our Differences. In *Selected Philosophical Works*, vol. 1. Moscow: Progress Publishers.

Post, Ken. 1997. *Revolution's Other World. Communism and the Periphery, 1917–39*. Basingstoke: Macmillan.

Preobrazhensky, Evgeny. 1965. *The New Economics*. Oxford: Oxford University Press.

Stalin, Joseph. 1925. *"Political Report to Fourteen Party Congress" in Leninism*. London: Allen and Unwin.

Stalin, Joseph. 1950. *Foundations of Leninism*. Moscow: Foreign Languages Publishing House.

Thomas, Clive. 1978. The Non-Capitalist Path" As Theory and Practice of Decolonization and Socialist Transformation. *Latin American Perspectives* 5 (2): 10–28.

CHAPTER 5

Lenin and Imperialism

Lenin's early work on the development capitalism in Russia took a dramatic turn during the First World War when he articulated an influential theory of international political economy. Based largely on the work of other Marxists (Hilferding and Bukharin) and liberal writers (Hobson) Lenin argued that imperialism was the *Highest Stage of Capitalism.* The theory or theories of imperialism have continued to have an impact till the present-day both in Marxist and liberal circles. After evaluating that work in the context of its own period, we turn to the broader issues of *Imperialism and Development* to examine how most Marxists began to turn away from the notion that capitalism was broadly progressive in the non-capitalist world towards a belief that it actually caused underdevelopment. That view coloured nearly all subsequent Marxist engagements with development and underdevelopment. Finally, we turn to one of the most productive early Marxist approaches to development in the world system, namely the theory of *Uneven and Combined Development* and the associated notion of 'permanent revolution'. This represents a signal contribution from a Marxist perspective to our critical understanding of capitalist development. Currently, it is enjoying somewhat of a revival albeit in the academic milieu of international relations. Overall, the Lenin 2 that we examine in this chapter is a very different theorist of development than the pre 1917 revolution Lenin 1 we examined in Chapter 4.

R. Munck, *Rethinking Development*, Marx, Engels, and Marxisms,
https://doi.org/10.1007/978-3-030-73811-2_5

Highest Stage of Capitalism

Against those who focused on imperialism as a state policy-basically colonialism-Lenin stressed that it was a stage of capitalism, the most advanced. The 'old type of capitalism' was based on 'free competitions' while in the 'new capitalism' by contrast 'monopoly reigns' (Lenin 1970, 697). The economic building blocks of this new world order were clearly articulated by Lenin as: '1) the concentration of production and capital has developed to such a high stage that it has created monopolies which play a decisive role in economic life. 2) the merging of bank capital with industrial capital, and the creation on the basis of this 'finance capital' of a financial oligarchy; 3) the export of capital as distinguished from the export of commodities acquires exceptional importance; 4) the formation of international monopolist capitalist associations which share the world amongst themselves, and 5). The territorial division of the world among the big capitalist powers in completed' (Lenin 1970, 737). Each of those tendencies have been questioned, as we shall see below, and their inter-linkages are never made explicit by Lenin but his work, nevertheless, had a huge impact.

Lenin's 'pamphlet' as he called it was based on extensive research (see his extensive *Notebooks on Imperialism*, Lenin 1968) and especially on the work of Rudolf Hilferding that still stands out as an original Marxist treatment of imperialism. Rudolf Hilferding wrote his *Finance Capital: A Study of the latest phase of Capitalist Development* in 1905 but it was not published until 1910 (Hilferding 1981). He was explicitly 'updating' Marx and his work has a depth of analysis missing in Lenin's short work. Whereas Marx analysed capital in terms of industrial, financial and commercial capital, Hilferding argued that in the era of monopoly capitalism it was not possible to separate industrial and financial capitalism, thus 'finance capital' is the product of the fusion of industrial and financial capital. In Hilferding's words 'the previously separate spheres....are now brought under the direction of high finance, in which the masters of industry and the banks are united in close personal association. The basis of this association is the elimination of free competition among individual capitalists by the large monopolistic combines. This naturally involves at the same time a change in the relation of the capitalist class to state power' (Hilferding 1981, 301). As the monopolies of the early twentieth century were not yet in a position to dominate the world market, they sought to protect their markets through protectionist tariffs and 'the drive for colonial acquisitions [which] thus leads to a steadily growing conflict among the large economic territories and has mayor repercussions upon the relations between individual states in Europe' (Hilferding 1981, 328). This is the first explicit Marxist theory of imperialism as a natural outgrowth of capitalist development.

Nicolai Bukharin's *Imperialism and World Economy* was written in 1915 but not published until 1927 with a Preface by Lenin (Bukharin 1976). Unlike Hilferding, who saw it as a phase of capitalist development, Bukharin saw imperialism as a policy: 'We speak of imperialism as a policy of finance captal….one may also speak of imperialism as an ideology. In a similar way liberalism is at the one hand a policy of industrial capitalism (free trade, etc.) and on the other it denotes as whole ideology (personal liberty, etc.)' (Bukharin 1976, 110). This is, in a way reminiscent of contemporary denunciations of 'imperialism' as a form of international aggression. Bukharin analysed the rise of 'world capitalism' dominated by 'the great civilised powers' with 'a periphery of underdeveloped countries with a semi-agrarian or agrarian system' (Bukharin 1976, 73). We see here, to some extent the roots of a post-Marxist underdevelopment theory with the world divided into a core and a periphery. Also, very influential in terms of later orthodox communist party strategies (e.g. 'state monopoly capitalism') was his notion of the transformation of the national economy 'into *one gigantic combined enterprise under the tutelage of the financial kings and the capitalist states, an enterprise that monopolises the national market*' (Bukharin 1976, 74).

While Hilferding and Bukharin provided much conceptual input for Lenin's endeavour, he leant politically even more on the writings of an English liberal anti-imperialist propagandist. His 1902 book *Imperialism* (Hobson 1988) was based on the view that capital export from Britain could provide an outlet for excess savings and thus crated pressure for the annexation of overseas territories. To stave off depression and unemployment, imperialism was neither necessary or desirable and Hobson called for 'social reform' and income distribution instead. So, Lenin decided to use Hobson against Kautsky—the 'Pope' of Marxism at the time—who had developed a theory of ultra-imperialism (Kautsky 1970)—the idea that the mayor powers would agree peacefully to an 'ultra imperialism' rather than indulge in inter-imperialist rivalry. In his *Notebooks on Imperialism* Lenin declares that 'Hobson's book on imperialism is useful in general, and especially useful because it helps to reveal the basic falsity of Kautsky on this subject' (Lenin 1968, 116). Kautsky was, for Lenin, looking for a 'healthy', 'peaceful' capitalism based on 'peaceful relations' (the First World War was then brewing). This declared Lenin was 'petty bourgeois reformism: *in favour of* a cleanish, sleek, moderate and genteel capitalism" (Lenin 1970, 116).

Georg Lukács in his 1924 study on the unity of Lenin's thought remarks on 'his superiority—and this is an unparalleled theoretical achievement—consists in his *concrete articulation of the economic theory of imperialism with every political problem of the present epoch*, thereby making the economics of the new phase a guide-line for all concrete action in the resultant decisive conjuncture' (Lukács 1970, 41). Lenin was interpellating the leaders of European social democracy, the direct descendants of Marx and particularly of Engels. They were seen to be colluding in inter-imperialist carnage in Europe as German and French Second International leaders rallied to the flag. Lenin was also clearly labelling the 'revisionism' (to put it mildly) of those such as Eduard Bernstein (2012) who had begun a decisive turn towards open reformism after the death of Engels in 1895. Bernstein literally sought to 'revise' Marxism, doing away with the labour theory of value and the centrality of class struggle on the basis that the development of capitalism in Germany had 'disproven' Marx's predictions. Capitalism was not on the brink of collapse, capital was not being concentrated in fewer hands, the middle class was not disappearing and the working class was not afflicted by increasing immiseration. When he was joined in 1914 by Kautsky (2009a), who had hitherto maintained a 'centrist' position, Lenin knew a clean break needed to be made and the path to the formation of a new Third or Communist International in 1919 was now clear.

Lenin's work on imperialism has, not surprisingly, come in for a lot of criticism including from Bill Warren who claims an orthodox Marxist authority. Warren thus refers to 'a number of dramatic, economic criticisms of Lenin's theory [that] may validly be advanced: the non-domination of the imperialist economies by monopolistic firms the fact that a number of challenging imperialist powers were themselves not capital importers between 1870 and 1914; the fact that capital export was *always* a significant feature of industrial capitalism, showed no sudden acceleration in the late nineteenth century, and cannot be related to a specific period of maturity' (Warren 1980, 67). Some of these criticisms are more or less valid than others, for example Lenin explicitly recognised that most capital export occurred within the advanced industrial societies.

However, there is inevitably a sketchy side to Lenin's 'tendencies' that did not necessarily occur in the way he outlined.

Where I think that Lenin was wrong is in his assumption—perhaps understandable in the midst of the First World War—that imperialism was the product of a senile and decaying capitalism forced to invest abroad the capital it was not vigorous enough to absorb at home. We do not, in fact, observe any correlation between territorial acquisition and a supposed 'superabundance' of capital. Lenin seemed to take from the liberal Hobson the notion that Europe was heading towards becoming a gigantic rentier state, the class of all stake holders or 'coupon-clippers' dominant. Parasitism and decay were becoming endemic as monopoly capitalism sought to rig prices and ring-fence patents. The working class would be 'bought off' by the colonial profits and sink into opportunism and social chauvinism. Of course, there were pressing political reasons for this analysis, but Lenin was losing his earlier understanding that capitalism was inherently renewable and even revolutionary in its dynamism.

Despite these weaknesses, there is still great value in the classic Marxist theory of imperialism if we take Bukharin, Hilferding and Lenin as a unified problematic. They continue the analysis by Marx on the internationalisation of the capitalist relations of production (see Chapter 2). They were among the first to analyse the apparent fusion between industrial and financial capital and the emergence of a new 'finance capital' that came into its own later in the twentieth century. They showed how competition now became primarily a struggle military and political rivalry of the big powers. They signalled the emergence of a working class. They understood that the export of capital to the colonial and semi-colonial world would lead to capitalist development, albeit with contradiction and all three came close to a dependency framework (see Chapter 7) at times. Above all, they showed how inter-imperialist rivalry led to inter-imperialist war. The history of global capitalism since shows that much of this analysis was along the right lines even if in particulars it would need to be 'revised' but not in the way in which the German revisionists suggested that simply jettisoned Marx's frame of reference.

It is only in Lenin, however, that we get a sense of the dialectical method, insofar as Bukharin in particular, but also Hilferding, were quite mechanical in their thought processes. Lenin, for his part, was working on his philosophical notebooks at the same time as the notebooks on imperialism. There he referred to 'the recognition (discovery) of the contradictory, *mutually exclusive*, opposite tendencies of *all* phenomena and processes of nature / *including* mind and society' (Lenin 1963b, 359–360). Development, for Lenin, is the 'struggle' and 'unity' of opposites. We need to seek the source of self-movement and not invoke a hidden external hand. This is the only way, against 'lifeless pale and grey' approaches to understand the destruction of the old and the emergence of the new (Lenin 1963b, 360). Thus the emergence of monopolies does not do away with competition but transforms it. The notion of 'ultra-imperialism' ignores the 'very profound and fundamental contradictions of imperialism' (Lenin 1963b, 151) and, to end this section, we might remember with Lenin that 'pure imperialism without the fundamental basis of capitalism has never existed does not exist anywhere, and never will exist' (Lenin 1963a, 151).

There is, of course, a vast literature on Marxism and imperialism that questions, corrects and develops Lenin's original insights (see Brewer 1990). It is not necessary to review it here (even if that were possible) as we are simply trying to establish the building blocks for a robust contemporary Marxist framework for the study of development. I only wish to refer to Giovanni Arrighi's powerful distinction between 'the capitalist (economic) and territorial logics of power and state formation that have not operated in isolation form one another but in relation to one another, within a given spatio-temporal context' (Arrighi 2009, 34). Imperialism, in the traditional Leninist sense tends to conflate both logics and maybe it will be useful to (re) introduce this distinction. As Arrighi points out 'Nowhere, except in Europe, did these elements of capitalism [trade, enterprise, techniques, merchant capital, etc.] coalesce into the powerful mix that propelled European states towards the territorial conquest of the world and the formation of an all-powerful and truly global capitalist world-economy' (Arrighi 2009, 11). That understanding is useful not least as it allows us to 'provincialise' Europe as the postcolonial theorists argue we must do (see Chapter 8) rather than assume it is a universal model.

With the demise of the socialist/developmental state alternatives and the consolidation of capitalist globalisation there was a flourishing interest in the theory of imperialism. From the conservative shores there was a straight-forward apologia for imperialism and a justification of its civilising role in the non-Western world (see Cooper 2002; Ferguson 2003). From Marxist writers we saw also the emergence of a 'new imperialism' school of thought. So, for example Ellen Wood advanced the notion that 'the relationship between imperial masters and colonial subjects' has been replaced by 'a complex interaction between more-or-less sovereign states'. (Wood 2003, 7). That 'complex interaction' seemed to replace the clear hierarchical and oppositional scheme of classic imperialism theories. Indeed, it seemed similar to the mainstream theory of 'inter-dependence' between 'more or less sovereign states' designed to fundamentally rebut the radical dependency theory of the 1970s (See Chapter 7). William Robinson, who has promoted a theory of a new 'transnational capitalist state' thesis, exemplifies goes a step further and argues that 'global class formation involves the increasing division of the world into a global bourgeoisie and a global proletariat, even though global labour remains highly stratified along old and new social hierarchies that cut across national boundaries'. (Robinson and Harris 2000, 13). The international division of labour and its hierarchies is replaced by a 'pure' contraction between a 'global bourgeoisie' and a 'global proletariat'. Quite how these are manifest at a concrete level through empirical analysis is not entirely clear and the thesis of a 'transnational capitalist class' remains sketchy at best. Underlying this new imperialism thesis is the notion that the uneven development of capitalism has been surpassed by the globalisation of capitalism that gradually equalises the conditions of accumulation. Here we find a paradigm that is quite close to that of the globalisation enthusiasts who have argued that we have moved since 2000 into a smooth or flat world where hierarchies will disappear.

A basic thesis of the new imperialism paradigm that is of particular interest for this text is the notion that, as Robinson puts it 'globalization [is] the near culmination of a centuries-long process of the spread of capitalist production around the world and its displacement of all precapitalist relations' (Robinson 2004, 6). However, there is no indication that uneven development has ceased to operate as a general 'law', nor that non- capitalist relations of production are being wiped out by the capitalist juggernaut. It follows logically from the 'new' imperialism thesis that the primary contradiction of global capitalism now lies within the metropolitan countries. That is why Harvey can advance a thesis in his book on *The New Imperialism* that has not aged well which foresaw a return to ' a more benevolent 'New Deal' imperialism, preferably arrived at through the sort of coalition of capitalist powers that Kautsky long ago envisaged [...] The construction of a new 'New Deal' led by the United States and Europe, both domestically and internationally, in the face of the overwhelming class forces and special interests ranged against it, is surely enough to fight for in the present conjuncture' (Harvey 2003, 209–211).

For Callinicos (2009), in a similar vein, imperialism denoted primarily the way in which changes in the structure of capitalism had given rise to intensified economic and strategic rivalries among the great powers. The theory of imperialism is thus seen as a way of understanding capitalism at its 'core' in the advanced industrial societies. Callinicos attempts to establish a continuity between classical theories of imperialism and his theory of global political economy that relegates 'North/South relations' to a peripheral role (Callinicos 2009). But does his characterisation of the 'original theorists' of imperialism correspond to the ideas of the foremost among them, Lenin, who concluded that the 'division of nations into oppressor and oppressed forms the essence of imperialism?' or to Rosa Luxemburg, who gave such attention to Europe's depredations in Africa and elsewhere? Callinicos argues that, for Lenin and other Marxist theoreticians of imperialism, capitalism was catapulted to the beginning of its imperialist stage of development by 'structural changes' in its heartlands. He does not specify which structural changes he is referring to, but we can presume they include the enormous concentration of capital and the rise of monopolies, the emergence of finance capital). Yet, even if it is true that capitalism became imperialism as a result of its own internal contradictions—of the falling rate of profit at home, of the increasing need to make concessions to the proletariat home in order to co-opt and corrupt its privileged layers—this does not at all mean that the oppression and exploitation of southern nations was not an integral element of imperialist capitalism. For Callinicos, imperialism is essentially about competition and rivalry between 'core' nations and southern nations are primarily involved in this not as victims of imperialism but as competitors. We could say that this is a form of metropolitan Marxism that is simply the reverse of the Third World Marxism of the 1970s that posited the notion of 'proletarian nations' against the First World, including its workers.

Imperialism and Development

In Lenin's *Imperialism* we find a constant commitment to the classic Marxist view of capitalism development as progressive in historical terms. Lenin notes that 'the export of capital influences and greatly accelerates the development of capitalism in those countries to which it is exported.... expanding and deepening the further development of capitalism throughout the world' (Lenin 1970, 718). He notes elsewhere that 'capitalism is growing with the greatest rapidity in the colonies and overseas countries' (Lenin 1970, 744). Where Lenin was incorrect was in his focus on 'the *tendency to stagnation and decay*; which is characteristic of monopoly" in the originally industrialising counties. Parasitism and the decay of capitalism were not in fact the outcome of imperialism but, rather, the start of a new dynamic phase for world capitalism. But outside of Europe, Lenin maintained correctly that 'capitalism itself gradually provides the subjugated with the means and resources for their emancipation' (Lenin 1970, 762) a cause that would be taken up by the Third International.

Nevertheless, Lenin's *Imperialism* commenced a trend in Marxism away from the notion that capitalism was historically progressive. A radical theory of underdevelopment would emerge that saw development and underdevelopment as two sides of the same coin. The underlying question as put by Anne Phillips was 'Can capital promote development, or does it necessarily produce underdevelopment?' (Phillips 1977, 9). This question emerged in the 1960s in part as a response to the long post-war boom of the advanced industrial societies. To some extent, based on Lenin's comments on an 'aristocracy of labour' in the centre being 'bought off' by imperialism, many Marxists shifted attention to the Third World or what we would today call the global south. If capitalism as a mode of production was stabilising and the capital-labour conflict was attenuated by economic prosperity and a welfare state, maybe a new contradiction could be discerned between capitalism and development on a global scale.

The epistemological turn towards a new understanding of capitalist development in official Marxism, if we can call it that, occurred at the 4th Congress of the Comintern in 1928 in the theses on the colonial question where we read that 'Capitalist exploitation in every imperialist country has proceeded by way of the development of productive forces. The *specific colonial forms of capitalist exploitation,* put into operation by the same British, French or any other bourgeoisie, in the final analysis hinder the development of the productive forces of the colonies concerned' (Comintern 1928, 5, emphasis added). We thus see, for the first time, the notion that capitalist development in the periphery would follow a different route than that of the originally industrialising countries and that this was a 'specific' ie different mode of production. The Comintern theses go on to argue, more broadly, that 'the most characteristic side of the decay of imperialism, its *essential feature of usury and parasitism*, is especially clearly revealed in its colonial economy. The endeavour of the great imperialist powers to adapt to an ever increasing degree the exclusive monopolisation of the colonies to the needs of the capitalist industry of the metropolis, not only leads to the destruction of the traditional economic structure of the indigenous colonial population, but, side by side with this, leads to the destruction of the equilibrium between separate branches of production; and, in the final analysis, leads, to *an artificial retardation of the development of the productive forces in the colonies*' (Comintern 1928, 6, emphasis added). Imperialism is seen as a sign of capitalism in decay, its main feature being a form of parasitism, and in the colonial world it imposes an 'artificial retardation' of capitalist development. In its most clear-cut statement the Comintern declares that 'the entire economic policy of imperialism in relation to the colonies is determined by its endeavour to preserve and increase their dependence, to deepen their exploitation and, as far as possible, to impede their independent development' (Comintern 1928, 6). We see now a clear language of 'dependency' (see Chapter 7) and the *raison d'etre* of imperialism being to impede the independent capitalist development of the periphery.

It is Bill Warren with his *Imperialism: Pioneer of Capitalism* (Warren 1980) who sought to turn Lenin on his head as it were. Warren admits that Lenin did not actually argue that imperialism would create underdevelopment, that turn would only come in 1928 sometime after Lenin's death. What Warren argued was that 'the general twist of his argument-that monopoly capitalism was parasitic, decadent and stagnant compared to competitive capitalism—*was bound to give the impression* that the relationship between imperialism countries and colonies was one of simple robbery ("booty") rather than a dynamic process of two-sided capitalist development' (Warren 1980, 82, emphasis added). Hilferding did, in fact, articulate sentiments very like dependency or underdevelopment theory: 'The state ensures that human labour in the colonies is available on terms which make possible extra profits. In many cases it also guaranties the gross profit. The natural wealth of the colonies likewise becomes a source of extra profits by lowering the price of raw materials and so reducing the cost price of industrial products' (Hilferding 1981, 328) but it was Lenin's Imperialism, against what it actually said but, because of its global political reach, that began the process of Marxism's turn against Marx's original view of capitalism as dynamic mode of production.

The critique of Marxist underdevelopment theory by Bill Warren leaves a mixed balance sheet. It was never going to be sufficient to introduce an 'optimistic' reading of capitalist development in the periphery to counteract the 'pessimism' of the Marxist underdevelopment approach. Capitalism and democracy have not been 'Siamese twins' as Warren claimed (Warren 1980). Not would many liberals—let done Marxists—subscribe to this statement that 'Imperialism was the means through which the techniques, culture and institutions that have evolved in Western Europe over several centuries.....sowed their revolutionary seeds in the rest of the world' (Warren 198, 136). Nevertheless, in retrospect Warren's 'bending the stick the other way', as Lenin often spoke of doing, did have the salutary effect of breaking the consensus around the emerging Marxist or post-Marxist paradigm of underdevelopment.

After Warren's death it was John Sender, who had organised his book from his notes, who took up the Warrenite critiques in relation to development in Africa in particular. His analysis of development issues was often quite nuanced despite his continuous obsession with 'mechanical marxological simplicities' (Sender 1985, 136). Writing about the Berg Report in the 1980's he referred to how the analysis was flawed by Berg's assumption that 'the more you exaggerated the disastrous performance of capitalism in SSA [Sub-Saharan Africa] the stronger will be the case for accepting the pro-aid argument' (Sender 1985, 137). Likewise, he found Berg sharing the left-dependency argument (or assumption) that import-substitution—industrialisation in the periphery would be exhausted once the 'easy' phase was over. In brief, the radical underdevelopment theory, and its wider influence, was making it impossible to understand how capitalism could, actually, develop on the periphery with all its inherent contradictions.

This is not the place to carry out an empirical validation of Bill Warren's critique of the new Marxist underdevelopment theory. Most of the responses from Marxist development theorists were profoundly critical, he was allowing for a capitalist road to development. Much of what Warren had to say was, of course, congruent with what mainstream development economists were saying. Political independence did, indeed, represent a fundamental change in the development potential of once colonial countries. There is nothing inherent in imperialism as a global mode of capitalist development that prevents industrialisation on the periphery. Impediments to development are to be found within the dependent country as much as the constraints of the global economy. What Warren lacks, however, is in any sense of the dialectic and the way

Marx, for example in relation to India, analysed the continuous contradictions between capitalist development as solvent of pre-existing modes of production and creator of a new society.

Ultimately what was at stake in Warren's attempt to turn Marx against Lenin's *Imperialism* brought into question what development meant. Our original question 'Can capitalism promote development?' only makes sense if we agree on what development means. In the 1970s there was a continuous tendency to contest capitalism on 'development' given its apparent or relative success in incorporating the working class in the advanced industrial societies. The turn to the South, as Russia once turned to the East, meant that colonial, semi-colonial countries were being given a major role in contesting 'imperialism', now not defined in Leninist terms, but in a broader sense of political domination. The notion of development as the development of capitalist social relations under the capitalist mode of production was replaced by a more diffuse notion increasingly shared by liberals and Marxists alike.

Development became something quite different from what Marx or Engels understood. Samir Amin would be representative of this new Marxist approach to development which asked essentially why accumulation on the periphery had not yet led to the development of a completely auto-centric capitalism (Amin 2011). Thus, capitalist development was redefined as a process that would be 'autocentric', leading to the even development of capitalism and the meeting of all social needs. From that basis it was inevitable that when capitalist development on the periphery was measured it would be found wanting. What emerges, writes Anne Philipps, 'is an ideal type of "normal capitalist development" which serves as a measure by means of which we can recognise underdevelopment' (Philipps 1977, 11). This view came to prevail, at least partly, via the national question and thus it was not surprising that imperialism became equated with rule by foreigners who were determined to prevent indigenous national development.

It is important, finally, to place these debates around imperialism and development/underdevelopment in the context of the 'crisis of Marxism' in the 1980s. David Booth has written about the clash between underdevelopment/dependency perspective and the 'classical' Marxism of Bill Warren in terms of 'the impasse in Marxist-influenced development sociology [that] was indeed a general one: not the product of the weaknesses of one particular perspective….. but the result of a generalized theoretical disorientation' (Booth 1985, 5). The Marxist presence in developmental studies was truly in an impasse, and not only because of the general crisis of Marxism, as we moved towards the 1990s. Key concepts deployed a such as that of 'modes of production' were proving inadequate in terms of providing analytical insights, political analysis was becoming reductionist (as in the slogan 'development of underdevelopment') and there was a failure to engage with the policy issues that exercised development practitioner.

The underlying issue was, arguably, the 'false necessitarianism' (see Unger 2004) that permeated Marxist development sociology. Things were as they were because of ineluctable necessity. Development necessarily created underdevelopment and the best the non-European world could expect was the 'development of underdevelopment'. Politics could be 'read off' from the laws of motion of dependent capitalism. Bill Warren came into this picture with a seemingly orthodox reading of Marx but which was actually very partial and where the contradictions of colonialism in India and the epistemological breaks around Ireland and Russia (see Chapter 3) were simply set aside. This was a dialogue of the deaf that did not greatly advance Marxism's engagement with development. To start or (re) start that mission we need to go back to the first Russian Revolution of 1905 when Trotsky and many other Marxists of the time articulated a theory of uneven and combined development that may still provide a useful framework.

Uneven and Combined Development

While Lenin constantly referred to the uneven development of capitalism it was Leon Trotsky who most systematically elaborated a theory of uneven (and combined) development that can still prove useful for the contemporary study of development and underdevelopment. This was not some abstract study, but one conducted in the turbulent period between the 1905 and 1917 revolutions in Russia, and designed to produce a guide to action. This approach is most clearly articulated and contextualised in Trotsky's *History of the Russian Revolution* (Trotsky 1965). There Trotsky refers, against all 'pedantic schematism' to 'unevenness, the most general law of the historic process [that reveals itself most sharply and complexly in the destiny of the backward countries' (Trotsky 1965, 23). By the 'whip of external necessity' these countries are 'compelled to make leaps'. Trotsky goes on to argue that 'from the universal law of unevenness thus derives another law which, for the lack of a better name, we may call the law of combined development' (Trotsky 1965, 23) which combines or amalgamates the old and the new, the traditional and the modern.

In an analysis that is highly relevant to development theory, Trotsky also refers to 'the privilege of historical backwardness....[which] permits, or rather compels, the adoption of whatever is ready...skipping a whole series of intermediate stages' (Trotsky 1965, 22). That is to say, 'a backward country assimilates the material and intellectual conquests of the advanced countries' (Trotsky 1965, 22). Development, in a global perspective, is not only uneven but also 'combined' or integrated in a complex manner. Development thus loses its mechanical and linear characteristics—as with Plekhanov for example—and becomes interactive and multilinear in its 'laws of motion. The universal imperatives of capital accumulation do not lead this to a 'smooth' spread of capitalist relations of production across the globe. It does not lead to homogeneity or equalisation within countries or between them, rather the 'skipping' of stages leads to an instable amalgam of pre-capitalist and capitalist dynamics.

The political implications of this development theory would be what Trotsky (following Marx and Engels in 1848) called 'permanent revolution'. The unique correlation of forces in Russia and the 'privilege of backwardness' meant that the proletariat was relatively advanced compared to the bourgeoisie that did not exercise state power. So, the 'orthodox' question of whether Russia was 'ripe for socialism' was suspended because it needed to be set in the context of the global uneven and combined development of capitalism. The notion of 'permanent revolution' was simply the widely accepted notion around 1905 that the upcoming revolution would not be constrained in its tasks. As Trotsky would recount much later, in 1924, when the attack on 'Trotskyism' began that in 1905 it was widely accepted that the revolution 'first of all would have to carry through the agrarian revolution and the democratic reconstruction of the state. … But the matter would not rest there. Having reached power the proletariat would be compelled to encroach even more deeply upon the relationships of private property in general, that is to take the road of socialist measures' (Trotsky 1965, 129). There is nothing in Trotsky's work that would indicate a belief in the world revolution as a simple cataclysmic event even though the notion of 'permanent revolution' has been caricaturised as such. Trotsky was very aware (as was Lenin) that a victorious revolution in conditions of backwardness could not build a socialist classless society.

What is sometimes forgotten, due to the construction of 'Trotskyism' as a distinct ideology, is that this thinking was very much part of the common sense of early twentieth century Marxism. In fact, it was David Ryazanov who in 1902 first articulated a theory of 'permanent revolution' and not Trotsky. Whereas Plekhanov (supported by Engels) inserted on an evolutionist reading of Marx on development, Ryazanov (followed later by Trotsky) argued that the rise of capitalism in Russia was 'exceptional', being financed from abroad and incorporating the latest technologies. Against what he called the 'pure' Marxists, Ryazanov argued that 'Russia is developing in a very unique way. The activity of our party can only be effective *in historical terms* if, while following the general principles of scientific socialism, we also begin with an accurate analysis of all the peculiarities of Russia's historical development' (Ryazanoz 2009, 85). It is due to these 'specific features'—encapsulated in the notion of uneven and combined development- that it would not pass mechanically through the same development phases as Western Europe.

Perhaps more surprising is the view taken by Karl Kautsky on permanent revolution before he succumbed to 'revisionism' and reformism. Following the 1905 Russian Revolution Kautsky wrote a series of articles in *Die Nieu Zeit* that repeatedly referred to 'permanent revolution'. He also—as the then 'Pope' of Marxism –wrote a response to Plekhanov's query on the nature of the Russian Revolution that Trotsky took as an endorsement of his theory of 'permanent revolution' while Lenin read it as his then policy of a 'democrat, dictatorship' of the proletariat and peasantry. For Kautsky 'the strengthening of the working class, and its elevation to a position that would enable it to conquer and retain political power, can no longer be expected from a bourgeois revolution that, in *becoming permanent*, grows beyond its limits and develops out of itself a proletarian revolution' (Kautsky 2009b, 179, emphasis added). If that was not clear enough, in 'updating' the Communist Manifesto, Kautsky declared categorically that 'a *revolutionary bourgeoisie* no longer exists' (Kautsky 2009b, 181).

The theory of uneven and combined development entered the development mainstream through the work of Alexander Gershenkron (1962) who in the US during the Mc Carthyite era tried, understandably, to hide his own Marxist roots (see van der Linden 2012). Basically, it was an extension of the argument that one of the 'advantages of backwardness' was the possibility to 'skip stages' in the development process.

Gershenkron's interlocutor in the US academy was Walt Rostow's five-stage modernisation approach that postulated a ladder going from traditional society, establishing the preconditions form 'take off' the 'take off' of phase, as drive to maturity and its culmination in the age of mass consumption (Rostow 1960). He was also, naturally, sceptical of the unilinear Marx who stated that 'the industrially, more developed countries presents to the less developed country a picture of latter's future". Against both modernisation and mechanical Marxist theories of development Gershenkron presented a more dialectal and less linear perspective.

Like Trotsky, Gershenkron promoted the possibilities of late development: 'Industrialization always seemed the more promising the greater the backlog of technological innovations which the backward country could take over from the more advanced country'. Borrowed technology was one of the primary factors assuring a high spread of development in a backward county entering a stage of industrialization (Gershenkron 1962, 8). The dramatic economic growth of the East Asian 'tigers' in the 1970s would be a clear example of how this thesis operates in practice. Gershenkron went beyond this point to show the important role of institutions in realising the advantages of the development latecomer. Gershenkron also sought to analyse the differential impact on the choices faced by the late industrializer which in turn impacted on the social structure of each country undergoing industrialization. In brief for Gershenkron there was no universal pattern of development based on the British model (a certain reading of Marx) or the US model (as promoted by Rostow and the modernisation school).

More recently the theory of uneven and combined development has been part of a debate within Marxist international relations specialists. In doing so they built on the landmark study of 'uneven development' by Neil Smith (1984) who referred to how 'the contradictory tendencies towards differentiation and equalisation determined the capitalist production of space. In action, this contradiction emerging from the core of the capitalist mode of production inscribes itself in the landscape as the extant of uneven development' (Smith 1984, 133). Capitalism is seen as the driver of uneven development insofar as it represents as contradictory unity of 'equalization' and 'differentiation' within the social and spatial dynamics of the world order. It is clear that the nation-state system is itself dependent on the process of uneven and combined development that crates geological competition between states and as Trotsky put it 'sets one country against another and one branch of industry against another, developing some parts of the world economy while hampering and throwing back the development of others' (Trotsky 1965, 19).

Trotsky's original theorising of uneven and combined development had two basic lessons for a Marxist theory of capitalist development: the first was related to 'the whip of external necessity' and the second was encapsulated in the phrase about the 'advantages of backwardness'. The external constraints were taken up by the dependency tradition in Latin America (and elsewhere in the Third World) and, in different guise in the critical theories of globalisation. It centres our attention on the constraints posed by external factors, the world economy, on national development prospects. It sits, apparently uneasily, with the second watchword about the 'advantages' of backwardness. This points to the way in which the hybrid or uneven nature of capitalist development means a given country can 'skip' development stages insofar as it is integrated into a world system. It leads to a clean break with the more mechanical Marxism that posited a sequence of modes of production that would have to be followed as capitalism developed. In its broadest sense then the notion of uneven and (yet) combined nature of capitalist development on a global scale is a necessary building block for a critical contemporary theory of capitalist development.

More recently there been an attempt to broaden this original concept and give it a greater explanatory role. Given that classical social theory has tended to view social development in the singular it tends to rely on untheorized exogenous factors to explain concrete historical development and the emergence of inter-state rivalry in particular. Thus, in response from the realist tradition Callinicos (2009) seeks to open up a new meta-theoretical space which incorporates the relative autonomy of the state within a global historical materialist frame. Thus, economic competition and geopolitical rivalries (traditionally seen as part of the theory of imperialism) can be integrated within a foundational theory of uneven and combined development. We are dealing in a sense with a theory of national uneven and combined development and an international theory of uneven and combined development. But in reality, here is no explanatory mechanism to explain why competition between states is inevitably more important than cooperation. This new approach reaches its ultimate apex with Rosenberg (2009), for whom the solution to this dual problem facing social and IR theory, and expressed in the tensions of Callinicos's account, is to reconceptualize social development in general as uneven and combined.

While not wishing to close the door on this extension of Trotsky's theory of uneven and development we do need to register certain risks. Thus, Kiely explain that 'we cannot 'fit' contemporary capitalist geopolitics into an a priori theory of uneven and combined development, and jump from the origins of political multiplicity to claims made for the international state system in the capitalist era' (Kiely 2015, 234). There is no simple or obvious way in which the uneven and combined development lens can explain geopolitical conflict in the current late capitalist phase. To do this we need to bring in many more concrete levels of analysis that could mediate between an abstract development theory and the dramatic early twenty-first century geopolitics. In a similar vein Allinson and Anievas alert us to the dangers of overextension of the original theory of uneven and combined development that cannot act as a general transhistorical abstraction, without taking on board the distinct set of determinants of international state systems and specifically that 'the 'logic of geopolitical competition' is irreducible to any logic of capital accumulation and class conflict' (Allinson and Anievas 2009, 53).

When applied in the largely asocial and ahistorical field of international relations, the theory of uneven and combed development had a salutary effect. The debate opened with Justin Rosenberg's extension of Trotsky's theory arguing that it provides an innovation in social and political theory in its incorporation of 'the international into a theory of history' (Rosenberg 2009). If social development to reconceptualised as uneven and combined then we are led to understand that 'societies' are not ready-make entities that then interact in the international arena. The ontological distinction between 'internal' and 'external' thus fades, an insight that will become used when we deal with the Marxist dependency theory (see Chapter 7). As a methodological step this innovative extension of Trotsky's insights is welcome in developing our understanding of Marxism and development even though it is, as yet, at a rather high level of abstraction and needs more concrete studies of concrete situations.

We could argue, finally, that the uneven and combined development paradigm brings Lenin's theories of capitalist development and of imperialism together in a coherent paradigm. The contradictory dynamics of catalyst development is brought to the fore with a clear dialectical understanding of its universalising and differentiating tendencies. Capitalism has an inherent tendency towards a global spread as Marx showed but there are, of course, winners and losers in this process (see Chapter 10 for contemporary examples). Where the concept also breaks new ground aid may be relevant in the current era is in refusing a total separation between the national and international domains, that Trotsky always saw as interpenetrated and fluid. However, we should be very cognisant that uneven and combined development is an abstract paradigm and cannot really be deemed a 'universal law' as some of its proponents have called it: it needs to be grounded and historicized and taken form the abstract to the concrete in each development situations.

References

Allinson, Jamie C, and Alexander Anievas. 2009. The uses and misuses of uneven and combined development: an anatomy of a concept. *Cambridge Review of International Affairs* 22 (1): 47–67.

Amin, Samir. 2011. *Maldevelopmnet: Anatomy of a Global Failure*. Oxford: Pambazuca Press.

Arrighi, Giovanni. 2009. *The Long Twentieth Century: Money, Power and the Origins of our Time*. London: Verso.

Arrighi, Giovanni. 1983. *The Geometry of Imperialism: The Limits of Hobson's paradigm*. London: Verso.

Bernstein, Eduard. 2012. *The Preconditions of Capitalism*. Cambridge: Cambridge University Press.

Booth, David. 1985. Marxism and Development Sociology: Interpreting the Impasse. *World Development* 13 (7).

Brewer, Anthony. 1990. *Marxist Theories of Imperialism: A Critical Survey*. London: Routledge.

Bukharin, Nikolai. 1976. *Imperialism and the World Economy*. London: Merlin Press.

Callinicos, Alex. 2009. *Imperialism and Globe Political Economy*. Cambridge: Policy Press.

Comintern. 1928. *Theses on the Revolutionary Movement in the Colonial and Semi-Colonial Countries*. Moscow.

Cooper, Robert. 2002. Why We Still Need Empires. *The Observer*, April 7th.

Ferguson, Neil. 2003. *Empire*. London: Penguin.

Gershenkron, Alexander. 1962. *Economic Backwardness in Historical Perspective*. Cambridge, MA: Belknap Press.

Harvey, David. 2003. *The New Imperialism*. London: Verso.

Hilferding, Rudolf. 1981. *Finance Capital. A Study of the Latest Phase of Capitalist Development*. London: Routledge.

Kautsky, Karl. 1970. Ultra-imperialism. *New Review* I (59): 41–46.

Kautsky, Karl. 2009a. To What Extent Is the Communist Manifesto Obsolete? In *Witnesses to Permanent Revolution*, ed. Richard Day and Daniel Gaido.

Kautsky, Karl. 2009b. The Social Revolution: Reform and Revolution. The Day After the Revolution. Berlin: Kessinger Press.

Kiel, Ray. 2010. *Rethinking Imperialism*. London: Palgrave Macmillan.

Kiely, Ray. 2015. Spatial Hierarchy and/or Contemporary Geopolitics: What Can and Can't Uneven and Combined Development Explain. *Cambridge Review of International Affairs* 25 (2) (June): 231–248.

Lenin, Vladimir Illich. 1963a. *V. I. Lenin Eighth Congress of the R.C.P.(B.)*. (March): 18–23, 1919.

Lenin, Vladimir Illich. 1963b. *Collected Works*, vol. 39. Notebooks on Philosophy. Moscow: Progress Publishers.

Lenin, Vladimir Illich. 1968. *Collected Works*, vol. 39. Notebooks on Imperialism. Moscow: Progress Publishers.

Lenin, Vladimir Illich. 1970. Imperialism: The Highest Stage of Capitalism. In *Selected Works*, vol. I. Moscow: Progress Publishers.

Lukács, George. 1970. *Lenin*. London: New Left Books.

Phillips, Anne. 1977. The Concept of Development. *Review of African Political Economy* 4 (7). 4th Congress of Comintern.

Robinson, William, and Richard Harris. 2000. Towards a Global Ruling Class? Globalization and the Transnational Capitalist Class. *Science and Society* 64 (1): 11–54.

Robinson, William. 2004. *A Theory of Global Capitalism*. Baltimore: John Hopkins University.

Rosenberg, Justin. 2009. Basic problems in the theory of uneven and combined development: a reply to the CRIA forum. *Cambridge Review of International Affairs* 22 (1): 107–110.

Rostow, Walt. 1960. *The Stages of Economic Growth*. Cambridge: Cambridge University Press.

Ryazanov, David. 2009. The Draft Programme of 'Iskra' and the Tasks of Russia Social Democrats. In *Witnesses to Permanent Revolution*, ed. Richard Day and Daniel Gaido. Chicago: Haymarket Books.

Sender, John, and Sally Smith. 1985. What's Right and What's Wrong with the Berg Report and What's Left of the Crisis. *Capital and Class* 24: 125–146.

Smith, Neil. 1984. *Uneven Development: Nature, Capital and the Production of Space*. London and New York: The University of Georgia Press.

Trotsky, Leon. 1965. *History of the Russian Revolution*, vol. 1. London: Sphere Books.

Unger, Roberto Mangabeira. 2004. *False Necessity: Anti-necessitarian Social Theory in the Service of Radical Democracy*. London: Verso.

Van der Linden, Marcel. 2012. Gershenkron's Secret: A Research Note. *Critique: A Journal of Socialist Theory* 40 (4): 553–562.

Warren, Bill. 1980. *Imperialism: Pioneer of Capitalism*. London: Verso.

Wood, Ellen Meiksins. 2003. *Empire of Capital*. London: Verso.

CHAPTER 6

Luxemburg and Global Development

Rosa Luxemburg was, above all, a fierce critic of the lack of socialist democracy in post-revolutionary Russia. She was also a pioneer in the development of a Marxist theory of imperialism in a way which was quite distinct from the dominant Marxist model of Hilferding/Bukharin/Lenin (Chapter 5). Essentially, it prioritised the impact of imperialism on the non-European world in a way that was practically unique at the time and also acts as a bridge to the Third Worldist and 'dependentista' positions of the 1960 and 1970's (see Chapter 7). We start in this chapter with Luxemburg's *Critique of Marx* insofar as her pioneering 1916 work on '*The Accumulation of Capital*' (Luxemburg 2003) was based around a critique of Marx's reproduction schemes in *Capital* Vol. 2. Luxemburg argued that Marx had failed to recognise the inherent necessity of the capitalist mode of production to find external markets and thus exploit the non-capitalist world on an ongoing basis. This leads us on to a consideration of Luxemburg's understanding of *Permanent Primitive Accumulation* that she sees as structural and not just a feature of its original formation as Marx according to her saw it. This points towards a Marxist engagement with the 'developing world' that is quite distinctive, and sets it apart from the metropolitan focus of Western Marxism. Finally, we turn to a contemporary rendering of this debate and the emergence of the concept of *Accumulation by Dispossession* that seeks to account for

R. Munck, *Rethinking Development*, Marx, Engels, and Marxisms, https://doi.org/10.1007/978-3-030-73811-2_6

present-day features of capitalist development based on force and dispossession. While Luxemburg's original thinking is not always acknowledged in this emerging paradigm, it is a certain 'spirit of Luxemburg' speaking to us and renewing our link to the period of classical Marxism.

Critique of Marx

Rosa Luxemburg carried out her PhD research in Switzerland which resulted in the 1897 text *The Industrial Development of Poland* (Luxemburg 2014) that is not particularly well known or commented on. Luxemburg went on to teach economics at the German Social Democratic Party (SPD) school, the results of which are only recently available in English. In her thesis Luxemburg took Poland to be part of a global economy and rejected the call for national independence. This would, of course, put her at odds with Lenin's consistent call for the right of nations to self-determination and is one of the most famous controversies she is known for. The fact that Poland was occupied by Russia was not, for Luxemburg, an issue insofar as 'the tendencies arising from the general internal nature of large-scale capital production itself are binding Poland much more strongly to Russia with every year' (Luxemburg 2014, 73). The basic thesis was that capitalist development in Poland and Russia was leading to the disappearance of their previously self-contained nature. They were 'economically dependent' on each other and thus political separation made no sense. Clearly, this position was at some distance from Marx's stance on Ireland that was equally integrated into Britain yet he unequivocally supported national independence for Ireland. The notion that national independence for Poland was in some way impractical was proven wrong with independence in 1917 (along with Finland) and subsequent history.

Notwithstanding that fundamental political issue, Luxemburg's study of capitalist development was extremely original, especially when compared with Lenin's contemporaneous '*The Development of Capitalism in Russia*' (see Chapter 4) that focused on the development of capitalism in Russia in conventional Marxist terms. In the conclusion to her thesis, she notes that 'It is an inherent law of the capitalist methods of production that it strives to materially bind together the most distant places, little by little, to make them economically dependent on each other, and eventually transform the entire world into one firmly joined productive mechanism' (Luxemburg 2014, 73). This foresight in relation to what we now call globalisation is truly remarkable and to some extent overshadows her theory of imperialism which, in essence, argued that 'imperialism is the political expression of the accumulation of capital in the competitive struggle for what remains of the non-capitalist environment' (Luxemburg 2014, 426). This is a theme we will return to in detail, but for now we might signal Luxemburg as a precursor of the theory of globalization alongside the theory of imperialism as 'political expression' of capitalist competition.

It was Luxemburg's 1913 study of imperialism—*The Accumulation of Capital* (Luxemburg 2003)—that put her firmly on the map, not least because she openly criticised Marx, something that was not common among Marxists of that era. Luxemburg thought she had detected a logical flaw in Marx's analysis of expanded reproduction in *Capital* Vol. 2. The logical inquiry, at a very high level of abstraction, in *Capital* Vol. 2 seemed to suggest that in its 'pure' form capitalism could not secure buyers for their products since workers lacked the means to purchase them. An external market was needed, and thus capitalist circulation could only be ensured from 'outside' or external co capitalist relations of production. Capitalism is thus obliged to conquer the non-capitalist world to ensure its own survival, even if this in the longer term hastens its own demise. This necessitarian logic was flawed insofar as the reproduction schema in *Capital* Vol. 2 dealt with 'capital in general' not the real unfolding of the capitalist mode of production, the story of which only really begins in *Capital* Vol. 3.

Even if capitalism in theory did not need to expand into non-capitalist areas, in practice it did and here Luxemburg analysis stands in a category of its own. Unlike the Hilferding/Bukharin/Lenin approach to imperialism from the perspective of its impact in Europe her focus was squarely on its impact in the colonial world. Luxemburg renews Marx's vision of a capitalism expanding constantly on a world scale and subsuming other modes of production. For Luxemburg 'capital needs the means of production and the labour power of the whole globe for untrammelled accumulation, it cannot manage without the natural resources and the labour power of all territories' (Luxemburg 2003, 345–346). There is no such thing as 'capitalism – in-perpetuity' Luxemburg argued and, as it sought to expand to survive it found that 'primitive conditions allow for a greater drive and of far more ruthless measures than could be tolerated under purely capitalist social conditions' (Luxemburg 2003, 346). It is the study of those 'ruthless measures' that stand at the core of her enterprise and make Rosa Luxemburg so relevant in the era of globalisation and its contestation.

In his introduction to Marx's *Capital* Vol. 2, Ernest Mandel concludes that 'the final balance – sheet of Luxemburg's critique, then, must be a nuanced one. We cannot say baldly that she is right of that she is wrong' (Mandel 1978, 68). While her critique may have been technically flawed, the question of 'disproportionality' (between production and mass consumption) does need to be incorporated into any theory of capitalist crisis. Her stress on the contradictory nature of capitalist growth stands in stark contrast to the 'neo harmonicist' logic of the Austro-Marxists (such as Hilferding and Otto Bauer) who thought capitalism could overcome those contradiction (see Rosdolsky 1980, 569–580). In that sense Luxemburg did not cave into the charms of capitalist reformism which, of course, was the driver of all her political work. Above all, Luxemburg initiated a non-Eurocentric interpretation of Marxism that emphasised the way in which central capitalism extracted wealth and value from non-capitalist communities. 'Pure' capitalism has never existed, and never could as Luxemburg showed, and its subsequent extension on a global scale has only accentuated its contradictions as we shall see in the following chapters.

A further very contemporary note in Luxemburg's' work is the often-neglected chapter on international loans in *The Accumulation of Capital*. In the imperialist era, the foreign loan 'played an outstanding part as a means for young capitalist states to acquire independence' (Luxemburg 2003, 401). But, argues Luxemburg, 'though foreign loans are indispensable for the emancipation of the rising capitalist states, they are yet the surest ties by which the old capitalist states maintain their influence, exercise financial control and exert pressure on the customs, foreign and commercial policy of the young capitalist states' (Luxemburg 2003, 401). Luxemburg refers to the way in which between the 1830s and 1860s 'railway building and the loans necessary for it, mainly served to oust natural economy and to spread commodity economy' (Luxemburg 2003, 402). Whereas this could serve the development of America and Russia, 'railway construction in Africa and Asia during the last twenty years [1890–1910], on the other hand, almost exclusively served the purpose of an imperialist policy, of economic monopolisation and economic subjugation of the backward countries' (Luxemburg 2003, 402). Not only do we get a glimmer of the 'Third Worldism' that would emerge mid-twentieth century, but we see also a precursor of contemporary theories of critical finance. International wars can generate the conditions for economic development and eventual political independence but financial dependence on the early industrialising countries would continue. As Toporowoski comments the view of finance and loans portrayed by Luxemburg 'of a financial system that visits repeated catastrophes on the traditional economy, in the course of incorporating it in the modern international capitalist economy, anticipates much of the experience of the developing countries since the 1970s' (Toporowski 2009, 90).

As with all Marxist's writings it is important to note what Luxemburg's political objective was in criticising Marx's schema of expanded reproduction. In Russia, while Lenin argued that capitalist development would produce a bourgeoisie and a potentially revolutionary proletariat, the so-called Legal Marxists argued that Marx's reproduction schema in *Capital* Volume 2 implied an equilibrium model of capitalist development and thus precluded a breakdown of capitalism. Rosa Luxemburg dedicated considerable space to refuting Tugan-Baranovsky the leading Legal Marxist for whom 'if *social production is proportionally organised, there is no limit to the expansion of the market other than* the productive forces available' (cited in Luxemburg 2003, 299). Luxemburg effectively demolished the arguments of the neo-harmonicists in Russia or at least any pretence that these views were based on Marx's *Capital*. Capitalist production for Luxemburg cannot 'create unlimited markets and [be] independent of consumption' (Luxemburg 2003, 303). This optimistic theory believed not only that capitalist development was possible but argued that 'capitalism can go on for ever' (Luxemburg 2003, 304) something no Marxist who understood Marx could possibly argue.

More broadly, Luxemburg's theory of imperialism needs to be situated in the context of the shift by most of German social democracy failure to deal with the rise of militarism in Germany and eventual support for the German war effort and the vote for the granting of war credits in 1914. As Lukacs put it in a 1922 essay on Rosa Luxemburg's Marxism 'Social Democracy was the ideological exponent of a workers' aristocracy turned petty bourgeois. It had a definite interest in the imperialist exploitation of the whole world in the last phase of capitalism but sought to evade its inevitable fate: the World War' (Lukács 1968, 32). The intensity of the critique of Luxemburg's book on imperialism can thus be explained by the intense hostility of the 'revisionists' towards her politics. This hostile tone was reciprocated in Luxemburg's '*Anti Critique*' (Luxemburg 1972) that was written in prison in 1915 though not published until 1921. While conceding that her numerical treatment of Marx's reproduction schema could be set aside, she repeated the main points of *Accumulation* in a clear and more coherent way. In brief 'accumulation is impossible in an exclusively capitalist environment. Therefore, we find that capital has been driven since its inception to expand into non-capitalist strata and nations, ruin artisan and peasantry, proletarianize the intermediate strata the politics of colonialism, the politics of "opening-up" and the export of capital' (Luxemburg 1972, 145). This understanding of how capitalism is driven to expand into the non-capitalist domains is central to our understanding of the accumulation of capital on a global scale.

We also need to understand why Luxemburg's theory of imperialism was so fiercely criticised by other Marxists such as Bukharin, especially after her death at the hands of proto-fascists in 1919. By way of background, we note that Luxemburg had been very close to the Russian Marxists led by Lenin until when he caused the Bolsheviks to split from the Mensheviks, a move she condemned. She then went on to articulate a fierce critique of the anti-democratic politics of the Bolsheviks. Bukharin, a close ally of Lenin, was widely regarded as a leader in theory and was tasked with a critique of Luxemburg's *Accumulation* (Bukharin 1972). Bukharin questioned whether the great military and economic apparatus of imperialism could be explained by the effort to realise surplus value. Bukharin then goes on to posit the emergence of a single world capitalist corporation that could maintain proportionality (between means of production and consumption) and thus abolish the anarchy of the market. At that time, most Marxists contrasted capitalism/anarchy with socialism/plan as the main counterposed routes for society. Bukharin questioned Luxemburg's somewhat voluntarist definition of imperialism as a political choice, that implied society could avoid these pre-determined paths. Lenin, for his part, in his notes on Luxemburg's *Accumulation* openly derided the moralism of her critique of colonialism in the non-European world e.g. 'The description of the torture of negroes in South America is noisy, colorful and meaningless. Above all it is "non-Marxist".' (cited in Nettl 2019, II 333).

If we stand back from the more technical controversies raised by Luxemburg's critique of Marx we can draw several conclusions. First of all, we must note Luxemburg's questioning of Marx's theory of primitive accumulation: ' "Sweating blood and filth with every pore from head to toe" [in Marx's words] characterises not only the birth of capital but also its progress in the world at every step' (Luxemburg 2003, 433). This epistemological breakthrough that we can call *Permanent Primitive Accumulation* is the subject of the next section. For now, we stress that Rosa Luxemburg moved beyond a nation state-centred analysis of the global economy to focus squarely on capital accumulation as the driver of development. What also gives Rosa Luxemburg a very contemporary ring is her scathing attack on the corruption of democracy even in the early days of the Russian Revolution and the clear limits on Lenin's party-based vanguardism against a more organic conception of socialist democracy in keeping with Marx's theorising of radical democracy around the 1848 revolution.

In the appraisal of Rosa Luxemburg's contribution to Marxism there has been a tendency to separate out *The Accumulation of Capital* (Luxemburg 2003) from her political writings and in particular her sharp comments on the Russian Revolution. Thus, her biographer J.P. Nettl argued that these aspects of her work were found in different compartments and that there was no obvious connection between the two: 'on the one hand we have a rigorous economic causality of the enemy's being, on the other a series of pamphlets of tactical combat' (Nettle 2019, II 532). The underlying idea is that whereas the economic writings were in a determinist mode (the breakdown theory for example), the political writings denied all forms of determinism and extolled the virtues of spontaneism. For other commentators, Luxemburg's work suffered simultaneously from an optimistic fatalism (the inevitability of socialism) and a passive fatalism (the inevitable breakdown of capitalism). To clarify this misunderstanding, we need to grasp the relationship between Luxemburg's critique of political economic and her vision of how socialism could be achieved.

Luxemburg's view of the Russian Revolution, largely from a German prison cell, explains, to some extent why her politics and economic analysis were so fiercely contested by the Bolsheviks and others. Firstly, Luxemburg very clearly supported the bold move to take power in Russia, albeit 'prematurely' according to the doctrinaire Marxists of the era. She argued that 'for every thinking observer, these developments [in Russia] are a decisive refutation of the doctrinaire theory... according to which Russia, as an economically backward and predominantly agrarian land, was supposed not to be ripe for social revolution and proletarian dictatorship. This theory, which regards only a *bourgeois* revolution as feasible in Russia… the Russian Revolution should have called a halt at the stage which German imperialism in its conduct of the war had set as its noble task… it should have stopped with the overthrow of Czarism. According to this view, if the revolution has gone beyond that point and has set as its task the dictatorship of the proletariat, this is simply a mistake of the radical wing of the Russian labor movement, the Bolsheviks' (Luxemburg 1970, 367). There was, for Luxemburg, a more general lesson to be learnt from Russia that continues to have relevance today, namely that 'the masses must learn how to use power by using power. There is no other way… The workers today will learn in the school of action' (Luxemburg 1970, 426). There is nothing particularly spontaneist about these positions: there was, certainly, a clear rejection of the stages theory of socialism and the notion that action is secondary to political calculation.

Rosa Luxemburg went on to launch a fierce attack on the way socialism was being built in Russia though fully cognisant of the constraints under which it was operating. For Luxemburg 'public control is indispensably necessary. Otherwise, the exchange of experiences remains only with the closed circle of the officials of the new regime… No one knows this better, describes it more penetratingly; repeats it more stubbornly than Lenin. But he is completely mistaken in the means he employs. Decree, dictatorial force of the factory overseer, draconian penalties, rule by terror – all these things are but palliatives. The only way to a rebirth is the school of public life itself, the most unlimited, the broadest democracy and public opinion' (Luxemburg 1970, 393). And, in words that still resonate today Luxemburg concludes, in an address to the founding conference of the German Communist Party in 1919, concludes that 'socialist democracy is not something which begins only in the promised land after the foundations of socialist economy are created; it does not come as some sort of Christmas present for the worthy people who, in the interim, have loyally supported a handful of socialist dictators. Socialist democracy begins simultaneously with the beginnings of the destruction of class rule and of the construction of socialism' (Luxemburg 1970, 394). Luxemburg was, of course aware of the constraints under which the Bolsheviks operated but that did not mean she muted her criticisms: 'Doubtless the Bolsheviks would have proceeded in this very way were it not that they suffered under the frightful compulsion of the world war, the German occupation and all the abnormal difficulties connected therewith, things which were inevitably bound to distort any socialist policy, however imbued it might be with the best intentions and the finest principles' (Luxemburg

1970, 394). The challenge posed by Luxemburg was how to be able to act within these constraints to build a democratic socialism and not a new type of dictatorship as happened in practice.

The reason why Luxemburg was so harshly criticised by the Bolsheviks—her economics were portrayed as over-deterministic, and her politics were supposedly spontaneist—was because they wished to erase the imaginary 'deviation' of Luxemburgism. The critique above of the way in which socialism was being built in Russia cut to the quick and showed how far 'Leninism' was straying from the conception of Marx himself on the nature of socialist democracy. Thus, prominent Bolshevik theorists such as Bukharin had to undermine both Luxemburg's economics and politics alike. What was at stake was the very nature of socialism. In that regard, we note the verdict of Luxemburg that is still relevant today, namely that 'Without general elections, without unrestricted freedom of press and assembly, without a free struggle of opinion, life dies out in every public institution, becomes a mere semblance of life, in which only the bureaucracy remains as the active element. Public life gradually falls asleep…' (Luxemburg 1970, 391).

Permanent Primitive Accumulation

For Marx, 'primitive accumulation' is about the accumulation of the necessary assets for capitalist development and the creation of 'free' labour. The standard account in political economy was that 'long, long ago there were two sorts of people; one, the diligent, intelligent and above all frugal elite; the others lazy rascals, spending their substance, and more, in riotous living' (Marx 1976, 873). This 'original sin' explains for them why, the majority had nothing to sell but themselves (Marx 1976, 873). Marx explains things differently in examining the creation of free workers, in the double sense that they are 'free from, unencumbered by any means of production of their own' (Marx 1976, 874) and that they are 'free' to sell their labour power. The process 'which creates the capital-relation can be nothing other than the process which divorces the worker from the ownership of the conditions of his own labour' (Marx 1976, 874). So-called primitive accumulation, therefore, for Marx 'is nothing else than the historical process of divorcing the producer from the means of production. It appears as "primitive" because it forms the pre-history of capital, and of the mode of production corresponding to capital' (Marx 1976, 874–875).

The theoretical breakthrough that Rosa Luxemburg achieves is in demonstrating that 'primitive accumulation' was not just part of the formative stage of the capitalist mode of production but was, rather, a permanent feature. Capital accumulation, for Luxemburg, has two facets 'one concerns the commodity market and the place where surplus value is produced' in which 'accumulation is a purely economic process' (Luxemburg 2003, 432). The other aspect of capital accumulation that Luxemburg focused on 'concerns the relationship between capitalism and the non-capitalist modes of production….Its predominant methods are colonial policy, an international loan system….and war. Force, fraud, oppression, looking are openly displayed without any attempts at concealment, and it requires an effort to discover within the tangle of political violence and conquests of power, the stern laws of the economic process' (Luxemburg 2003, 432). We could question this apparent separation of economics and politics, but the point is clear: capitalism always depends on 'primitive' (as in backward) accumulation that cannot just be cast back to its pre-history. The 'stern laws' of the economy that Luxemburg refers to do not, of course operate independently, outside the context set by historical processes and political struggles.

Rosa Luxemburg detects an 'organic connection' between the 'normal' capitalist process of exploitation and accumulation and the pathological (which is also normal) process of primitive accumulation. This dynamic relationship was an integral part of capital accumulation on a global scale and thus Marx was wrong, in Luxemburg's view, to restrict it to the origins of capitalism. Colonialism and imperialism, the dispossession of rural populations, the continuity of slavery (albeit in different forms) and debt peonage all point towards the permanence of 'primitive' accumulation. For Luxemburg this process of robbery and plunder occurred mainly in the periphery of global capitalism. Today we might ask if this process is more general and where Luxembourg, among other, underestimated the persistence on non-capitalist of non-market forms of production and distribution.

It is only relatively recently that we have local access to Luxemburg's 1906 writings on non-capitalist societies, that formed part of her course for the social democratic party school '*Introduction to Political Economy*' (Luxemburg 2014). In these lectures Luxemburg showed a keen awareness of communal social relations outside of Europe, particularly in Africa. Compared to other Marxists of the period, Luxemburg showed considerable sympathy for these societies. At a time in which many European commentators—including leading members of the Second International—praised the civilising mission of colonialism and the 'backwardness' of other cultures, Luxemburg was writing about the 'extraordinary tenacity and stability – elasticity and adaptability' (Luxemburg 2014, 226) of these societies. Traditional villages in India, the Lunda Empire of Central Africa, the Inca Empire in the Andes, were all societies, for Luxembourg, with complex structures and positive factors.

Luxemburg particularly engaged with the story of pre-conquest societies in South America. There we find a reference to 'the age-old agrarian communist constitution' and to belief that 'among the Amerindians, living traces were found of a communism so far-reaching as seemed quite unknown in Europe' (Luxemburg 2014, 155). The clan owned the land in each village, arable land was distributed by lot, the village head was elected and all public affairs were settled by the village community. This 'age-old agrarian communist constitution' was alive and local in the Inca Empire when the Spanish invasion took place. The bourgeoisie, for Luxemburg, 'clearly affected in their class interests, scented an obscure connection between the ancient communist survivals that put up stubborn resistance in the colonial countries to the forward march of the profit-hungry "Europeanization" of the indigenous peoples, and the new gospel of revolutionary impetuousness of the proletarian mass in the old capitalist countries' (Luxemburg 2014, 163). In brief, social development did not require capitalist development and the market was not an eternal element in all human societies.

Luxemburg was closer to Marx in her analysis of pre-capitalist commune forms. Engels in his *Anti-Dühring* (Engels 1955) tended to adopt a somewhat romanticised view of the commune and believed that hierarchical differences were imposed from the outside. There Luxemburg was more in line with Marx's nuanced reading of the Russian commune that acknowledged its social potential but also its serious limitations (see Chapter 3). In particular, Luxemburg stressed the internal generation of inequalities with positions becoming hereditary and private property reasserting itself. In relation to sub-Saharan Africa Luxemburg referred to how 'Primitive communist society, through its own internal development, leads to the formation of inequality and despotism….such societies….sooner or later succumb to foreign occupation and then undergo a more or less wide-ranging social reorganization' (Luxemburg 2014, 233). Engels, for his part, mainly stressed the *external* factors creating social differentiation, something we would see in a different context with the Latin American dependency lens on development (see Chapter 7).

It is worth pointing out that Luxemburg's main source for the study of the Russian commune was the same one Marx used, namely Maxim Kovalevsky (see Hudis 2010) though she was seemingly not aware of this connection. An interesting footnote of history is that Karl Kautsky had asked Luxemburg to help prepare Marx's unpublished manuscripts for publication, but she declined (Hudis 2014, xvii footnote +). The lessons we can draw from Luxemburg and Marx in terms of their analysis of non-capitalist societies do seem to be quite independent. What this means is that it is up to us to draw out the parallels, bearing in mind, for example, that Luxemburg does not seem to have been familiar with Marx's writings on India where he showed a keen awareness of the dialectic between capitalism's 'progressive' role in destruction of communal modes of production and failure to generate a 'normal' capitalist society (see Chapter 2). Luxemburg's route was a different one.

For Luxemburg, capitalism had, throughout its historical expansion, engaged in a fierce struggle against the non-capitalist milieu. And as van der Linden remarks it is worth always bearing in mind that 'this happened first in Europe, with the struggle against feudalism's serfdom economy and guild crafts, then moved outside of Europe against societies that varied in development, from small groups of hunter-gatherers to formations based on small-scale commodity production' (van der Linden 2016, 141). Where Luxemburg was very clear in laying out the various factors that drove capitalism's struggle against the natural economies, namely: '1. To gain immediate possession of important sources of productive forces such as land, game in primeval forests, minerals, precious stones and ores, products of exotic flora such as rubber, etc. 2. To "liberate" labour power and to coerce it into service. 3. To introduce a commodity economy. 4. To separate trade and agriculture'. (Luxemburg 2014, 349–350). We thus see how integrated the processes of commodification, dispossession and plunder were in the making of the modern world and in the development of capitalism.

It is in relation to permanent primitive accumulation that Rosa Luxemburg makes a signal contribution to our understanding of capitalist development today. Unlike her comrade Clara Zetkin (founder of the German socialist feminist movement) Luxemburg was not explicitly a feminist, and did not extend her analysis of primitive accumulation to gender relations. However, if we draw out the links between the oppression of women and the questions of colonialism, militarism and brutalism that concerned Luxemburg we can see clear links. Thus, Maria Mies refers to women as 'the last colony" and argues that "her analysis of capital-accumulation helped us…to gain a better understanding of the status of homework under capitalism' (Mies 2014, 217) for example. Like the exploited peasants of the majority world, the outworkers and other 'non-standard' workers, women's work (in the home particularly) is both a cheap and efficient way of reproducing capitalist relations of production. Capital accumulation on a world scale today depends on the so-called informal sector outside the control of the state and formal labour relations that represents between half and two thirds of employment outside of the advanced industrial societies. It is Luxemburg, among all the classical Marxists, who speaks most directly to this present anomaly of the onward march of industrial capitalism as inevitable destiny.

Gender-based violence both today and historically also confirms that force is not only the 'midwife' of capitalist society but a continuous feature of its existence and reproduction. Male based capitalism continues to rely on non-capitalist reactions of production to provide inputs for the reproduction of labour power. And it is violence, especially violence against women, argues Mies that 'is the secret of accumulation which cannot be fully understood if reference is made only to wage-labour that is orderly, legally protected, unionised and usually male' (Mies 2014, 217). Luxemburg was unique among classical Marxist in recognising that violence is an economic factor. There was also a keen awareness by her of the myriad forms of labour and she had little of the factory bias, to put it that way of other Marxists of her era. Nor was she infatuated by the trade union model of working-class organisation and was cognisant of other forms of mobilisation. By extending these insights to a socialist feminist analysis of the gender division of labour and the position of Third World women in particular, we are going very much with the grain of Luxemburg's problematic and the socialism she fought for.

Rosa Luxemburg, finally, was both right and wrong in relation to capitalism's interaction with the non-capitalist world. She wrote that 'historically, the accumulation of capital is a ***kind of metabolism*** between capitalist economy and those pre-capitalist methods of production without which it cannot go on' (Luxemburg 2003, 397, emphasis added). This 'kind of metabolism' could be interpreted in terms of capitalism's articulation, even synergy, with non-capitalist forms of production. While

Marx also showed how capitalism 'corrodes and assimilates' those modes, Luxemburg goes to argue that capitalism cannot 'tolerate their continued existence side by side with itself' (Luxemburg 2003, 397). In common with a whole strand in Marxist thought then Luxemburg could only see the onward march of capitalism as it trampled over earlier forms of production and not the very real synergies that would develop and their persistence both in the developing world and at the heart of the advanced capitalist countries as well. While conscious that 'capital cannot accumulate without the aid of non-capitalist organisations', Luxemburg still concluded that 'only the continuous and progressive disintegration of non-capitalist organisations makes accumulation of capital possible' (Luxemburg 2003, 397). It would take the theory of uneven and combined development of capitalism (see Chapter 5) to resolve this seeming contradiction between the non-capitalist both necessary and something that needed to be overcome for the development of capitalism to occur. We would also need to move beyond a capital-centric form of analysis and understand capitalism in all its complexity which includes the continued reproduction and expansion of non-capitalist forms of production.

Accumulation by Dispossession

Following Luxemburg's lead, David Harvey has argued for a modernised version of the thesis of 'permanent primitive accumulation' as 'accumulation by dispossession'. This involves, according to Harvey 'a general re-evaluation of the continuous role and persistence of the predatory practices of "primitive" or "original" accumulation within the long historical geography of capital accumulation' (Harvey 2003, 144). The basic argument is that the specific processes of primitive accumulation identified by Marx and followed through by Luxemburg—the enclosure of the commons, the dispossession of rural population and the use of state power to place assets in the hands of a capitalist class—not only continue to this day but have even become more prominent. Harvey goes further in arguing that while these processes were seen by Luxemburg as characteristic of the capitalist periphery, today we can see them as an integral element of global capitalism everywhere. Thus, we can no longer think in terms of 'primitive' or 'original' accumulation of capital as a historical phase of capitalist development only.

Accumulation by dispossession as a concept had considerable resonance in the alter-globalisation movement since the 1990s. It also struck a chord, with all those who prioritised 'the commons' in the era of privatisation and neoliberalism. The shift from a variety of property rights-state ownership, collective ownership and communal rights—to an absolute priority for private property rights (for example in intellectual property) symbolised this turn. Above all, as Harvey puts it, we are now in an era when 'capitalism internalizes cannibalistic as well as predatory and fraudulent practices' (Harvey 2003, 148). As to its operation we are far from the structural causality of classical Marxism—with its laws of capitalist development—when Harvey argues that 'accumulation by dispossession can occur in a variety of ways and there is much that is both contingent and haphazard about its *modus operandi*' (Harvey 2003, 149). Where that leaves us in terms of understanding the dynamics of contemporary capitalism is not entirely clear, but it is an interesting insight nonetheless.

Where Harvey's analysis is most directly relevant potentially is in his distinction between struggles against capitalist exploitation (the working class) and capitalist dispossession. The violent struggles of primitive accumulation—against the enclosures, machinery and bonded labour—are back among us. Harvey questions the primacy of the central contradiction between capital and labour in the realm of production and whether the proletariat is still now 'the key agent of historical change' (Harvey 2003, 169). While he is correct in noting that traditional Marxism downplayed reproduction struggles (for example in the city) and simply assumed proletarian primacy, it is not clear if the struggles over dispossession are now to the fore either quantitatively or qualitatively. We might thus question his conclusion that the alter-globalisation movement 'must acknowledge accumulation by dispossession as the primary contradiction to be confronted' (Harvey 2003, 177) although to be fair, Harvey goes on to say that 'it ought never to do so by ignoring the dialectical relation to struggles in the field of expanded reproduction' (Harvey 2003, 177).

The concept of 'accumulation by dispossession' has been criticised from a number of perspectives. There is an orthodox Marxist view, exemplified by Raju Das for whom Harvey has effectively extended Marx's original concept of primitive accumulation but for whom 'accumulation by dispossession' is not Marxist, it is a 'chaotic concept: it puts together processes under its scope which should not be put together as they do not have a mutual relation of necessity, and it separates processes which should not be separated because they are internally related' (Das 2017, 598). We have certainly seen above that Harvey produces a very wide-ranging list of processes he puts down to accumulation by dispossession. The second criticism is essentially about Harvey's apparent move beyond the accepted parameters of historical materialism. In fact, though, Harvey recognises the impressionistic nature of the concept and would probably accept that it is 'chaotic' and even, maybe pre-theoretical; the point remains as to whether it is useful to a critical development theory.

There has also been a criticism based on the notion that 'dispossession' does not displace 'exploitation' as the main mechanism of capitalist development. The vast expansion of the term 'accumulation by dispossession' with Harvey can lead to imprecision and the conflation of distinct processes. In essence it is seeking to capture the 'extra economic' aspect of the accumulation of capital, the element of force and violence. So, for example, in the massive industrialisation of China's south-east over recent decades we can discern both the 'dispossession' of the peasants who migrated to the area but, also, a very classically Marxist process of capitalist development and exploitation subsequently of an industrial working class. If we elide these two, we are in danger of not seeing the main dynamic at play in China's 'great leap forward' in recent decades through a quite classic Marxist process of market forces assisted or enabled by an interventionist state.

Perhaps the most persuasive critique of Harvey's schema is that it does not foreground the gender dimension of dispossession. In Rosa Luxemburg the question a gender division of labour did not loom large in her analysis of pre-capitalist societies and their divisions, it was not central to her focus. And yet her framework can readily be applied for example to women and housework as we saw above. Harvey has, for his part, been criticised from a feminist perspective. At one level his enterprise can be seen as economistic with its fierce and unremitting focus on the process of capital accumulation. Doreen Massey for example criticises Harvey for taking a position that is 'white, male, heterosexist, Western: and one in which the male is not recognised as gendered' (Massey 1991, 43). A more specific gendered critique is articulated by Nancy Hartsock who has articulated a feminist historical materialism (Hartsock 2006) but who is also a critic of postmodernist or standpoint theories.

Hartsock carries out more of an 'internal' critique of Harvey on 'accumulation by dispossession' sharing the overall objective of better understanding current patterns of capital accumulation. Hartsock's points on the gender dynamics of accumulation are, basically, unarguable: 'primitive accumulation is not gender neutral but involves differential treatment of women and men' (Hartsock 2006, 177). Furthermore, the fact is that most women working worldwide do so outside the realm of market relations. Thus, as Hartsock reminds us, we must constantly bear in mind that 'women are involved in social reproduction to a greater extent than men' (Hartsock 2006, 177). The creation and maintenance of communities under non-capitalist modes of production (and, of course later) had women at the core of reproduction both in a biological sense and socially through the feeding and caring of the young. An understanding of primitive accumulation that is not gendered will, at best, be partial.

We should also take a wider look at that accumulation by dispossession means for development theory today. In particular, we need to consider critically Harvey's statement that 'accumulation by dispossession can be interpreted as the necessary cost of making a successful breakthrough into capitalist development with the strong backing of state power' (Harvey 2003, 154). Other radical students of development processes have queried this view. Thus, Giovanni Arrighi and co-authors has applied the general paradigm to the case of South Africa but concludes that 'such dispossession has in fact become the source of major development handicaps for at least some and possibly in any countries of the global South' (Arrighi et al. 2010, 410). Under apartheid South Africa was perhaps one of the most clear-cut cases of 'accumulation by dispossession' and we have seen since 1994 how it has produced dramatic handicaps for South Africa's democratic development.

What South Africa shows most clearly is how accumulation by dispossession undermines the prospects for long-term development and is not a simple necessity as many development theories assumed. Without land redistribution and the creation of a mass internal market, development can only ever be fitful and partial. As Gillian Hart shows, comparing South Africa to the more successful development models in South East Asia, we can conclude 'the most spectacular instances of industrial production in the second half of the twentieth century have taken place without dispossession of peasant-workers…[and have] a powerful and direct bearing on South African debates, not as models that could be emulated but rather because they denationalize dispossession' (Hart 2002, 201). This leads us to reject any teleological notion of development as necessarily going through a phase of primitive accumulation or dispossession as some sort of natural growing pain.

Finally, we might reconsider what Rosa Luxemburg contributes to our understanding of development and its limitations. Above all, Luxemburg contributes to our understanding of classic imperialism from a non-Eurocentric perspective. Consistent with Luxemburg's unrelenting commitment to a radical socialist democratic politics we see a non-state perspective emerging. The voices of the colonised, the enslaved and the exploited are heard clearly through her writings. We should also be aware of the limitations of Luxemburg's perspective based, as it was, on the accepted paradigms of the Second International. The evolutionism and stages theory of development is part and parcel of that paradigm that Luxemburg does not explicitly break with, unlike the late Marx. There is also a failure to fully understand the right of self-determination of the non-European peoples and a persistent belief that the inexorable march of capitalism would inevitably obliterate non-capitalist relations of production.

While Marx and her Marxist contemporaries tended to assess the destructive and violent aspects of capitalist expansion in an ambivalent fashion, Luxemburg placed more emphasis on the purely negative aspects of this development: the misery of many men, women and children who were uprooted and had become its victims. For her, primitive accumulation was not a stage that preceded actual capitalist development (as Marx said in the wake of Adam Smith's thoughts on previous accumulation), but a process that endured throughout the entire history of capitalism. 'At the time of primitive accumulation, i.e. at the end of the Middle Ages, when the history of capitalism in Europe began, and right into the nineteenth century, dispossessing the peasants in England and on the Continent was the most striking weapon in the large-scale transformation of means of production and labour power into capital. Yet capital in power performs the same task even today, and on an even more important scale – by modern colonial policy. It is an illusion to hope that capitalism will ever be content with the means of production which it can acquire by way of commodity exchange'. (Luxemburg 2003, 350).

Finally, Luxemburg always stressed that the working class needed to stand in solidarity with the anti-colonial struggles. This was important at a time when the leaders of social democracy articulated an openly pro-colonialism approach, bordering on the racist. Yet as van der Linden remarks 'she understands this solidarity to be a one-sided activity. It never occurred to her to directly establish contact with those who took part in the Herero uprising' (van der Linden 2016, 155). Luxemburg pushed

European Marxism to its outer limits but, ultimately remained imprisoned by its view of the world that had Europe at the centre of civilisation and viewed the 'natural economic societies' as on a lower plane. It would take the postcolonial turn (see Chapter 8) for Marxism to fully lay that world-view to rest.

References

Arrighi, Giovanni, Nicole Aschoff, and Ben Scully. 2010. Accumulation by Dispossession and Its Limits: The Southern African Paradigm Revisited. *Studies in Comparative International Development* 45: 410–438.

Bukharin, Nikolai. 1972. Imperialism and the Accumulation of Capital. In *Rosa Luxemburg and Nikolai Bukharin, Imperialism and the Accumulation of Capital*. London: Allen Lane The Penguin Press.

Das, Raju. 2017. David Harvey's Theory of Accumulation by Dispossession. *World Review of Political Economy* 8 (4) (Winter), 590–616.

Engels, Frederick. 1955. *Anti-Dühring*. Moscow: Progress Publishers.

Hart, Gillian. 2002. *Disabling Globalization. Places of Power in Post-Apartheid South Africa*. Berkeley, CA: University of California Press.

Hartsock, Nancy. 2006. Globalization and Primitive Accumulation: The Contribution of David Harvey's Dialectical Marxism. In *David Harvey: A Critical Reader*, ed. Noel Castree and Derek Gregory. Oxford: Blackwell.

Harvey, David. 2003. *The New Imperialism*. Oxford: Clarendon Press.

Hudis, Peter. 2010. Accumulation, Imperialism and Pre-capitalist Formation. Luxemburg and Marx on the non-Western World. *Socialist Studies / Études Socialistes* 6 (2): 75–91.

Hudis, Peter. 2014. Introduction. In *The Complete Works of Rosa Luxemburg*, vol. 7, Economic Writings 1. London: Verso.

Lukács, George. 1968. *History and Class Consciousness. Studies on Marxist Dialects*. London: Merlin Press.

Luxemburg, Rosa. 1970. The Russian Revolution. In *Rosa Luxemburg Speaks*, ed. Waters Mary-Alice. New York: Pathfinder Press.

Luxemburg, Rosa. 1972. The Accumulation of Capital—An Anti-Critique. In *Rosa Luxemburg and Nikolai Bukharin, Imperialism and the Accumulation of Capital*. London: Allen Lane The Penguin Press.

Luxemburg, Rosa. 2003. *The Accumulation of Capital*. London and New York: Routledge.

Luxemburg, Rosa. 2014. The Industrial Development of Poland. In *The Complete Works of Rosa Luxemburg*, vol. 1, Economic Writings 1. London: Verso.

Mandel, Ernest. 1978. Introduction. In *Capital*, vol. 2, Karl Marx. London: Penguin.
Marx, Karl. 1976. *Capital*, vol. 1. London: Penguin.
Massey, Doreen. 1991. Flexible Sexism. *Environment and Planning: Society and Space* 9 (1): 35–57.
Mies, Maria. 2014. Housewifisation-Globalisation-Subsistence-Perspective. In *Beyond Marx. Theorising the Global Labour Relations of the Twenty First Century*, ed. Marcel Van der Linden and Karl Heinz Ruth. Chicago IL: Haymarket Books.
Nettle, John. 2019. *Rosa Luxemburg. The Biography*. London: Verso.
Rosdolsky, Roman. 1980. *The Making of Marx's 'Capital.'* London: Pluto Press.
Toporowski, J. 2009. Rosa Luxemburg and Finance. In *Rosa Luxemburg and the Critique of Political Economy*, ed. Riccardo Bellofiore.
Van der Linden, Marcel. 2016. Rosa Luxemburg's Global Class Analysis. *Historical Materialism* 24 (1): 135–159.

PART II

Contemporary

CHAPTER 7

Dependent Development

The so-called 'dependency theory' that emerged in Latin America during the 1960s and received worldwide attention as the main alternative to the dominant paradigm, is undoubtedly the main Southern contribution to development theory. This chapter recounts how the activist intellectuals driving it saw themselves *Completing Lenin* by adding the view of how imperialism was perceived in the county being dominated, something hitherto missing in the Marxist classics, with the partial exception of Rosa Luxemburg. We explore in this section the various Marxist and neo-Marxist attempts to create a new paradigm of dependent development and establish its own 'laws of motion' distinct from those of metropolitan or central capitalism. The following section on the *External/Internal Dialectic* explores the varying emphasis placed on internal and external causation by various dependency theorists, after an early almost total focus on the external element. This debate continues to rumble on in international political economy and the critique of globalisation, as different schools grapple with the dilemmas of a predominantly external lens on capitalist development and the need to incorporate the internal dynamics and class struggle of the dependent condition. Finally, I turn to the *Achievements and Limits* of the dependent development approach that has in recent years been making something of a comeback. Its undoubted economism and methodological nationalism in many cases needs to be balanced by its creative use as a comparative historical methodology in its

R. Munck, *Rethinking Development*, Marx, Engels, and Marxisms,
https://doi.org/10.1007/978-3-030-73811-2_7

best hands. I argue for the continued relevance of dependency today as a methodology and as a lens to apprehend the contradictions of capitalist development on the periphery of the world system.

Completing Lenin

Lenin, in his famous pamphlet *Imperialism* made reference to 'dependent countries' and named Argentina as an example. This is a minor point but maybe worth using as a starting point for our analysis of the dependency approach. Lenin noted that 'not only are the two main groups of countries, those owning colonies, and the colonies themselves, but also the diverse forms of dependent countries which, politically are formally independent, but in fact are enmeshed in the net of financial and diplomatic dependence, typical of this epoch…An example is provided by Argentina' (Lenin 1970, 734). Argentina was, indeed, when Lenin was writing, widely perceived to be part of Britain's informal empire, independent since the start of the nineteenth century but enmeshed in British finances, loans, banks and railways to promote and capitalise on its dynamic agro-export economy. But that was it, one paragraph and it was clear that Lenin was mainly focused on imperialism in terms of its impact in Europe and the looming inter-imperialist war. Since the 1950s, however, a number of Marxists in Latin America had already begun to articulate a view from the South to put it that way (see Bagú 1949; Frondizi 1955) that clearly offered a distinct Marxist perspective on development.

Within Latin America economic planning circles there had also been an analysis following the Second World War that was not dissimilar to what later emerge as the dependency approach. The analysis of the Economic Commission for Latin America (ECLA) and its chief economist Raúl Prebisch exemplified this break with economic orthodoxy (see Kay 1993). It advocated an early version of the centre-periphery paradigm based on the unequal nature of the world economy and its social and spatial impact. The originally industrialising countries had increased productivity with the diffusion of technological progress globally which was very uneven. The peripheral economy only integrated technology in a fitful manner and then mainly in the agro-export sector. Whereas development was supposedly homogenous and integrated at the centre it was inevitably both disarticulated (due to the importing of technology) and dualist (in the gap between advanced and traditional sectors) at the periphery. This unequal situation is both deepened and perpetuated by the international terms of trade that shaped the world economy. This perspective was not a Marxist one, but it did represent an epistemological break in relation to the hitherto orthodox international trade theory.

It was politics, though, that would prompt the emergence of a new radical development paradigm in Latin America. The Cuban Revolution of 1959 had formally declared itself socialist in 1961. There was an example now in Latin America that capitalism was not necessarily the only path to development. When the early dependency theorists started meeting in Chile in 1964 after the military coup in Brazil drove many of them out, Cuba was uppermost in their minds. In the midst of military repression across the continent, a radical development alternative presented itself. The alternative to dependency became, quite simply, Cuba and that meant, in the context of the US boycott, a policy of autarchy or delinking (Amin 1985). If 'socialism in one county' as Stalin had preached for Russia was not possible, it was certainly not possible to build 'socialism on one island'. Cuba thus in many ways provided a solution for the dependency theorists as to what 'non-dependency' would look like, but it also posed an ultimatist politics of development, encapsulated in the slogan 'dependency or socialism', that was reminiscent of Luxemburg's 'socialism or barbarism'.

The simplest definition of dependency was coined by Theotônio dos Santos for whom: 'Dependence is a *conditioning situation* in which the economies of one group of countries are conditioned by the development and expansion of others....the basic situation of dependence causes these countries to be both backward and exploited' (Dos Santos 1978, 76). In other words, underdevelopment is the form development takes in these countries. In a comment reminiscent of Marx when he said it was not classes that he had discovered but the class struggle, Cardoso and Faletto argued that 'the originality of the hypothesis [of dependence] is not in its recognition of the existence of external domination—an obvious process. It is in its description of the forms and the effects of this type of dependence on classes and state with reference to past situations' (Cardoso and Faletto 1979, 174). In other words, it was a methodology for the study of the dialectal relationship between development and dependency through class formation and class struggle.

An explicitly revolutionary Marxist analysis of dependency is articulated by Ruy Mauro Marini (Marini 1974) which was based on an acceptance that the Marxist classics had not uncovered the laws of motion of the countries dominated by colonialism and imperialism. However, they accepted much of the current analysis of the capitalist world economy and its domination by monopoly capital for example. Building on Dos Santos's succinct definition of dependence as a 'conditioning situation', Marini went on to show how the relations of production of the dependent nation are continuously recreated to secure the extended reproduction of dependence. Key to this process is, for Marini, the overexploitation or super-exploitation of labour in the subordinate countries as local capitalists seek to recover the losses they make on the international market due to unequal exchange. This over-exploitation of labour means that dependent capitalism cannot move from exploitation based on absolute surplus value to one based on relative surplus value as characteristic of developed capitalism.

This rather absolutist schema was followed through politically by Dos Santos for whom the requirements of dependent capitalism left only the stark option of 'socialism or fascism' (Dos Santos 1972). Radicalisation and deepening class conflict are inevitable and intermediate options are deemed to be utopian. It was not hard for Cardoso (this time writing with José Serra) to effectively critique this vision in the late 1970s (Cardoso and Serra 1978) as Brazil was moving into a dynamic phase of associated dependent development. Marini was criticised for conflating unequal exchange with international terms of trade. As against Marini's argument that relative surplus value is not an option on the periphery, they show that the phase then opening-up of internationalisation of the internal market was based precisely on the extraction of surplus value and an increase in the organic composition of capital. While not doubting that unequal exchange and over-exploitation of labour benefitted central capitalism it was not seen as essential for its reproduction.

A less orthodox Marxist version of the dependency approach was that articulated by F.H Cardoso and E. Faletto in their 1969 landmark *Dependency and Development in Latin America* (Cardoso and Faletto 1979) against the economistic tendency of some dependency writers. They were keenly aware of the social dimension: 'our approach is both structural and historical: it emphasizes not just the structural conditioning of social life, but also the historical transformation of structures by conflict, social movement and class struggles' (Cardoso and Faletto 1979, x). Their understanding of social class is more Weberian than Marxist, but it is richly sociological rather than economistic. *Dependency and Development* is above all, a 'concrete analysis of a concrete situation' as called for by

Lenin and was not just a logical unfolding of abstract economic categories. Politically it signalled an engagement with the electoral arena when most other dependency writers continued to advocate the armed struggle and the clung to the shining example of Cuba.

Cardoso (with others) effectively critiqued the strong underconsumptionist tendency among the dependency writes and the general stagnationist take on further prospects. Social class was brought back into the equation albeit in a sociological manner as Marini pointed out in a fierce rebuttal (Marini 1978). He is also criticised for lacking a firm underpinning in Marxist political economy. The main differences are, however, political and early on he separated himself from those who argued that 'the local bourgeoisie becomes *lumpen* incapable of national accumulation, dilapidated in their consumerism, blind to their real interests' (Cardoso 1977, 58). For him the national bourgeoisie was quite conscious of its social interests except that it preferred to forge an alliance with the international class rather than lead a struggle for 'national liberation'. Cardoso most certainly took a reformist path in practice and not a revolutionary one but that does not invalidate his analysis of dependency.

From the perspective of the English-speaking world, dependency is most often associated with the writings of Andre Gunder Frank (1969). In reality, Frank was only loosely associated with the dependency school and had more in common with the world systems approach (Wallerstein 1979) then emerging. While he coined some of the most memorable phrases of this period—such as 'the development of underdevelopment'—he was more influential in his critique of modernisation theory than in developing an alternative dependency paradigm. Frank's understanding of development was heavily dependent on the neo-Marxist frame of Paul Baran (1957) not based on the concept of 'surplus value' but, rather, the 'potential surplus' a rational society could generate. While capitalism was once a relatively efficient engine of growth it was no longer so, and socialism could, in theory be more efficient and maximise the 'potential surplus'.

Gunder Frank was probably most influential in Latin America through his earlier critique of Communist Party dualism (Frank 1966). This was quite similar to the dualism posed by the modernisation theorists between the traditional and modern sectors. For the official Marxists, the socialist task in the countryside was the eradication of 'feudalism' and the building of 'democratic capitalism' through the 'national bourgeoisie'. For Frank, the Latin American haciendas and plantations had always been capitalist through their role in the mercantile global economy. In a reprise of the earlier transition to capitalism debate in relation to England, Ernesto Laclau argued against Frank, from an equally dualist perspective, that the colonial mode of production was not capitalist and that non-capitalist relations of production persist to the present day (Laclau 1971). Frank's focus on commercial relations led him to neglect the importance of production relations in creating the patterns of uneven and combined development of capitalism.

The Latin American debate on modes of production tried to contribute to our understanding of dependent capitalism. The Stalinist communist parties had for long referred to the rural relations prevailing since the colonial era as 'feudal', largely to bolster a political position that argued for a national democratic revolution led by the 'national bourgeoisie' against the 'feudal' landowners. Gunder Frank and others came into the debate in the 1960s arguing that Latin America had been 'capitalist' since the colonial era and thus the tasks of the upcoming revolution would have to be socialist and not capitalist. But, of course, participating in an international capitalist market did not make all social and economic relations in all countries capitalist. To say this was a 'circulationist' error was perhaps obvious (see Laclau 1971) but it did at least open up a dense historiographical debate around the precise nature of the modes of production that had characterised Latin America since the colonial era.

Moving on from Pierre Vilar's throwaway phrase cited above (Chapter 4) that Spanish colonialism represented the 'highest stage of feudalism' and not capitalism we saw a more nuanced analysis emerge (see Assadourian 1973) Spain at the time of the American conquest was undergoing a process of combined and uneven development marked by feudal institutions and an emerging commercial bourgeoisie focused on the external market. This incipient, still commercial, form of capitalism was the driver of the conquest even if feudalism was still the dominant mode of production in the Spanish socio-economic formation. This process did not, however, mean that either feudalism or capitalism was somehow transplanted to the Americas. There, especially in the plantations and mines extra-economic coercion would prevail as the main means of exploiting labour. The prevalent form of relations of production was thus decisively non-capitalist, with 'free labour' only very slowly and in limited areas making a breakthrough.

Ultimately the modes of production debate in Latin America was carried out at a level of abstraction where it could not provide clear answers. That is because the 'combination' of modes of production could not provide the answers that only an analysis at the more concrete level of socio-economic formation could provide. Thus, there was a long debate on whether we could discern a 'colonial' or 'dependent' mode of production in Latin America (Cardoso 1973) given that supposedly Marx had left the colonial world out of his analysis. But there no way to show a distinct 'colonial' mode of production let alone a dependent one without a much more concrete analysis of the whole social and political framework of the situation that could not be reduced to the economic relations of production. It was an advance on simply copying the European 'transition to capitalism' debate (see Hilton 1976) but it still got caught up in a type of formalism that Balibar later recognised in an autocritique (Balibar 1973) of his own earlier influential approach to modes of production (Balibar 1970).

Balibar's autocritique of the earlier Althusserian formulation of modes of productions recognised that this theory of modes of production in general with just some variations was 'in short, a theory of typologistic or structuralist inspiration, however consistent' (Balibar 1973, 58). The Latin American debates and the later ones in South Africa (see Wolpe 1980) did, indeed suffer from this formalistic structuralism and the development of typologies that did not necessarily add to our understanding of the colonial difference. While the analysis of the 'conjuncture' was meant to be at the heart of Althusserian Marxism (in the spirit of Lenin as it were) when Balibar sought to generalise the Althusserian mission to create a comparative theory of modes of production this displacement was to have serious negative consequences as he later realized, insofar as these 'topographical' concepts introduced an ambiguity and then 'instead of social formations, it is now (and anew) a question only of modes of production, i.e. of a still 'abstract' generality, of which, in practice, the social formations will appear only as particular and concrete 'realizations'' (Balibar 1973, 60). The result was a theory of modes of production that was seen as engendering history and reproducing the social formation rather than understanding that it is 'the history of the social formation that reproduces the mode of production on which it rests and explains its development and its trans formations. The history of the social formation, i.e. the history of the different class struggles of which it is composed, and of their "resultant" in successive historical conjunctures, to use a metaphor frequently employed by Lenin' (Balibar 1973, 70).

Achievements and Limitations

The dependency approach in Latin America came in for a lot of criticism in the 1980s, often because it became so broad as to be practically an 'empty signifier' that anyone could pour any argument into. In the English language literature this was partly to do with its very partial or tendentious incorporation into the secondary literature, often mediated by particular English language 'translators' or interpreters. We can note in this respect that F.H. Cardoso wrote a neglected piece on 'the consumption of dependency' (Cardoso 1984) in the North, which was quite revealing. The dialectical analysis of internal/of external determinants (see section below) was lost as the 'new theory' was portrayed as giving absolute priority to the external dimension. Furthermore, argued Cardoso, 'the paradigm of dependency is consumed in the US as though the contribution to the historical debate had been centred on a critique of Latin American feudalism' (Cardoso 1984, 77). In the United States in the late 1960s the dependency frame was taken to be expressing a domination by foreign capital, the machinations of the CIA and the dark underhand manoeuvres of the multinational corporations and/or a generic imperialism.

Mainstream academia tended to interpret dependency as a model, with variables, to be tested and, inevitably, then it has been found wanting. That missed the point-deliberately as part of the metropolitan academy perhaps—that this was explicitly a methodology not a formal model, and included a 'radically critical viewpoint' (Cardoso 1984, 80). We also, however, saw a significant international spread of the dependency approach with the early work by activist-intellectual Walter Rodney who wrote *How Europe Underdeveloped Africa* (Rodney 1972). It might also be said that the prolific output of Samir Amin from Egypt came to be seen internationally as the main dependency spokesperson (Amin 1985). It is interesting that Amin came to the dependency frame from a quite orthodox analysis of accumulation on a world scale and the various aspects of unequal exchange that also helped 'mainstream' the dependency approach within Marxism. These developments were welcome, but they also changed the strongly methodological emphasis of the Latin American originators of the approach. Clearly the discursive polysemy of dependency meant that it took various forms and these cannot be reduced to one clear unified development theory.

Dependency as a framework, or theory or paradigm, continues to be productive in Latin America despite this variegated context. For example, in Brazil a new generation of analysts are returning to the work of Ray Mauro Marini to seek their bearings in a country that is the 8th largest economic power in the world by (purchasing power parity) but which still suffers from the symptoms of underdevelopment. With the onset of globalisation in the 1990s and the emergence of new concepts such as 'risk society' (Beck 1999), 'network society' (Castells 1996) and 'Empire' (Hardt and Negri 2000), the dependency perspective went through a bit of a renaissance. In Latin America, the transnationalisation of economic power reached new heights but the level of social contestation also increased dramatically with a wave of left-of-centre governments being elected after 2000. Analysts asked whether this was a return to the national-popular regime of accumulation of the 1960s or whether it was something new. A renewed dependency approach acted as a compass to guide debates during this period.

We should never underestimate the importance of the emergence of a radical development theory from the global South. It paved the way, certainly in Latin America, for the various post-development and post-colonial approaches of the 1990s. It shifted the epistemological terrain from the day in which it queried Lenin's theory of imperialism for its neglect of the perspective of the colonised. Also, in recovering the history of dependent development in Latin America this wave of activist research helped empower the indigenous movement's recovery and articulation of a new indigenous development perspective. Any criticisms we might have need to be set aside such undoubted gains in epistemological, political and knowledge terms. Above all, dependency needs to be placed in his proper historical context of Latin America in the 1960s and not viewed as an abstract intellectual production only.

Despite its undoubted originality and path breaking role, the dependency paradigm came in for a lot of criticism, some of it justified. In his review of Latin American theories of development Cristóbal Kay lists just some of these accusations: 'tautological, economistic, historical, utopian, devoid of class analysis populist or Narodnik, nationalist, myopic, one-dimensional, ideological, eclectic, mechanical, sophist, a negative teleology, idealist, anticapitalistic, a marxified structuralism, non-Marxist or non-materialist, careless on the use of Marxist theory, unable to break with bourgeois development theory, without empirical grounding, theoretically imprecise, unclear, contradictory, too global or holistic, deterministic, methodologically and conceptually eclectic, lacking in clear policy recommendations for overcoming dependence, stagnationist, circulationist, and so on' (Kay 1993, 175). This extensive and varied charge sheet alone would tell us that the dependency theory had considerable impact. For my part, I will just discuss some salient problems while cognisant of the overall positive contribution it made.

The first issue that struck me when engaging with dependency theory when it began was how much it mirrored the modernisation theory (Development I) it critiqued. It seemed to be simply turning it on its head: integration with the world economy good (no, it's bad), diffusion of technology creates development (no, it created underdevelopment). It did not seem as of the end objective was any different from that of modernisation: some version of the good society. Much later I was able to interpret this problem in terms of Derrida's (1994) notion of logocentrism, referring to a Western tendency to impose a hierarchy when dealing with oppositions such as tradition/modernity. In terms of development theory, it helps us grasp, as Kate Manzo puts it that 'even the most radically critical discourse easily slips into the form, the logic and implicit postulations of precisely what it seeks to contest' (Manzo 1991, 70). Thus, dependency remained trapped within a modernist discourse and its horizon of possibilities was thus limited.

The second, quite obvious, flaw in the dependency frame was its methodological nationalism. It was national development strategy-dependent or not—that was being debated. This was in fact pointed out at the time by Francisco Weffort in an early debate with F.H. Cardoso (Weffort 1971). By posing the relations of exploitation as one between nations—the rich countries exploit the dependent countries/colonies—the theory was inevitably placing itself on the nationalist terrain. While dependency theory oscillated between a national approach and a class approach the first tended to be given priority. There was also a lack of clarity as to where dependency fitted in the Marxist theory of imperialism. Was it just an addendum to Lenin who once mentioned the word dependence? More likely, it was a decisive break with orthodox Marxism in Latin America that picked up an indigenous tradition of revolutionary nationalism encapsulated in the Castroist slogan '*Patria o Muerte*' (nation or death) then part of general left culture in Latin America.

The third, I think clear, flaw of dependency theory is its economism, at least taken as a whole. Economism or economic reductionism is a tendency in Marxism to reduce complex issues to their economic 'roots' and think always in terms of determination by the economic base, albeit 'in the last instance'. Jorge Castañeda and Enrique Hett wrote a sharp analysis of '*dependentista economism*' (Castañeda and Hett 1978) from an Althusserian Marxist perspective, drawing attention to the way in which it does not permit us to develop theory of the political (Castañeda and Hett 1978, 131). It simply short-circuited the political domain in arguing that 'development' was not the answer to economic underdevelopment, only 'revolution' was. If the political domain was drastically curtailed and simplified the cultural domain had no place in this economistic discourse and was thus going to find its way back in through the post-development theories and the practices of the new social movements.

The fourth issue I would take up would be dependency theory's political voluntarism. Of course, all currents within this paradigm did not share equally this feature, but the 'left' current certainly did. Dependency was seen in a necessitarian way, only socialism could overcome this condition. There was no need to plot a path through the complex politics of the region, socialism simply needed to be realized. Economism and voluntarism are seen as quite opposed ideologies—one is reductionist the other is idealist—but they often go hand in hand. During the 1970s, democracy was missing from the left lexicon and there were few mediations between the condition of dependency and the salvation of socialism. And with politics not being a central feature of most dependency workers (except for F.H. Cardoso who look a decidedly social democratic turn) there was no need to critically examine whether socialism in Cuba could even be a suitable model for the big semi-industrialised countries like Brazil, Mexico and Argentina.

In terms of a balance sheet of the dependent development approach, it needs to first be situated in its historical context to be understood: 1960s Latin America. It swept away the old Marxist orthodoxy as represented by the Communist Parties and their stages view of development. It based itself on the best of mainstream development knowledge, namely the Economic Commission for Latin America (ECLA) intellectual production of the 1950s. Above all, it operated in the shadow of the Cuban Revolution that cast its glow over all intellectual and political currents on the left. Its weaknesses, as outlined above, are very much a product of the period, above all its voluntarism. That it was severely criticised, even ridiculed by the international development mainstream is not surprising. It was also, however, not treated too seriously by the 'metropolitan left' who were focused on the problems of neo-capitalism in the North Atlantic. Today, dependency theory is going through a revival and we have yet to see what the result will be.

One possible way forward would be to work in 'spirit' of dependency much as Derrida bid us work in the spirit of a certain Marx. This approach can be seen, for example, in the approach by Peter Evans who had originally worked in the tradition of 'dependent development' (Evans 1979) that saw a state, national capital and foreign capital triple alliance promoting industrialisation in the 1970s as a way to go beyond classic dependence in which the south was simply condemned to agrarian production for the global economy. More recently, Evans has come round to the view that industrialisation is a development path with diminishing returns and maybe not even necessary to achieve development. Evans now argues that industrialisation is not sufficient for development for two major reasons. First, the evolution of technology has meant that industrialisation cannot absorb a large portion of the population in gainful employment. It simply does not provide sufficient market-based support for jobs...The second major reason for why industrialisation is not sufficient for development any more, according to Evans, is that the character of capitalism has changed. It was difficult to find a strong link between industrialisation and human well-being in the 1960s, but it is even more difficult today. As the power of capital is increasingly global, the options and space for local capital are few and far between (Evans 2007). For Evans the main issue now is to seek new opportunities for the creation of decent jobs, a direction also taken by Manuel Castells who was once close to dependency theory but now advocates participation in the new global economy on its terms as the only option for the global South (see Castells and Himanen 2014). The new global order (see Chapter 10) has undermined any idea that industrial transformation would secure human capabilities and generate a new 'great transformation in the global South'. We can go in the direction of Evans and Castells in promoting a much greater role for the state in the development process and the need to create more jobs in the service sector and the 'new' economy. We can also, of course, follow the spirit of the dependency approach into the post-development approach (Chapter 8) or the indigenous development thinking around alternatives to development (Chapter 9).

External/Internal Dialectic

One way to recover the 'spirit of dependency' would be through an effort to develop a dialectical understanding of dependent development so that we can move beyond internal versus external determination as binary opposites. Clearly external factors can become 'internalised' through the class structure for example. We can argue that the essence of dependency is the transfer of surplus value through internal social relations conditioned by external relations. What we have learnt is that it was not just a question of 'extending' Marx's model of capitalist development to the periphery. This work had to be completed insofar as Marx had simply not dealt with it in any detail. On the other hand, against Third World Marxism and nationalist temptations, we have learnt that there is not a dependent capitalist mode of production with different 'laws of motion'.

Against the popular simplistic 'externalist' dependency frame, some analysts in the 1980s and 1990s moved to what we might call an 'internalist' reading of development in the periphery, although this move was barely registered in the English language literature. Particularly important was the decisive move by Cardoso de Mello in his *Capitalismo Tardio* (*Late Capitalism*) (Cardoso de Mello 1982) dedicated to a critical review of the formation and development of the Brazilian economy. For him the dominant ECLA interpretation is cast in terms of its dynamic being set by the imperatives of the international diversion of labour and external demand. While outward-oriented growth prevailed, dependency and poverty would be the dual result of this peripheral social formation. However, a different picture would emerge if one simply accepted that Latin American history was the result of the development of a certain type of capitalism.

For Cardoso and Faletto the development of the capitalist mode of production in Latin America 'is determined in the first instance by internal factors and, in the last instance by external factors, from the moment that the national state is established' (Cardoso and Faletto 1979, 6). In the colonial period, Brazil (like the rest of Latin America) produced precious metals and clonal agricultural products for the metropolitan mercantile bourgeoisie under conditions of commercial monopoly. The new international division of labour created by the Industrial Revolution and the formation of the nation states in Latin America led to the emergence of a primary-export economy. This was not imposed but was 'the result of the emergence of organized export economies based on wage labour and the development of capitalism in Latin America' (Cardoso de Mello 1982, 31). The reproduction of these capitalist relations of production is not ensured endogenously and required participation in the world economy.

In the course of the twentieth century, capitalism developed in Brazil with the generalisation of capitalist relations of production and the creation of an internal market from the 1930s onwards. The formal subsumption of labour, previously dominant, was replaced by the real subsumption of labour from the 1950s onwards. What were external obstacles to the development of capitalism now became internal obstacles as late industrial capitalism developed. The development of a capital goods sector from the 1950s onwards meant it was not appropriate to think in terms of a 'different' capitalism, albeit late and peripheral in its origins. For Cardoso de Mello, in brief, 'Brazilian and Latin American history is the history of Capitalism' (Cardoso de Mello 1982, 176). This way we can rethink the development of a particular type of capitalism in Latin America that cannot be reduced to singular characteristics such as 'outward looking' or 'backward' for that matter.

From within the dependency theory orbit we saw emerging in the 1980s a more nuanced reading and one that had a better grounding in the Marxist classics. Thus, in Colombia, Salomón Kalmanovitz moved from an orthodox dependency frame to one more shaped by classical Marxism (Kalmanovitz 1986). He broke decisively with the false dichotomy between internal and external contradictions. Kalmanovitz was not optimistic about the possibility of reconstructing Marx's understanding of the laws of notion of capitalism as a global system. What he did add to the study of dependency was the need to continuously bear in mind the conditions of its reproduction. Indeed, most exponents of dependent development saw it in fairly static terms and did not place it in its complex overall dynamics.

Kalmanovitz sought to go beyond the static and merely comparative theory of underdevelopment by postulating a 'late' development in historical terms. The specific nature of capitalist development in Latin America was due to the fact that it emerged later than that of the imperialist countries reflecting the uneven development of capitalism (Kalmanovitz 1986, 11). His dialectical logic led him to focus on the totality that became an over determinant presence over the logic of its parts. From that perspective he could undermine the logic, that gave priory to either these 'internal' or 'external' factors causing development and underdevelopment. The peripheral social formation is not a malleable entity on which external factors operate. The internal and external do not exist within a unidirectional world where one is passive and the other passive. Rather, they are in a complex dialectical relationship where 'the external confronts a given material structure with its own dynamic logic' (Kalmanovitz 1986: 32).

To the dialectic of the endogenous and exogenous causation of 'dependent development' we can add with Kalmanovitz the need to distinguish between the structural and conjunctural factors. So, for example the relative economic stagnation in many countries of Latin America in the early 1960s was interpreted by the likes of Gunder Frank as a structural feature denoting the expansion of the dominant capitalist model. Conjunctural shifts in the terms of trade were also read as structural signs of stagnation and decline. It was thus inevitable that some dependency theorists would simply miss the massive industrialisation of the 1960s and a shift in the nature of the development model and the emergence of powerful urban working class. The 'totality' we needed to consider was not reducible to the 'world system' and had to include the shifting political economy of the periphery and the changing class composition that would determine its subsequent dynamic.

While Ruy Mauro Marini's attempt to ground dependency theory in Marx's theory of capital accumulation may not have succeeded, he opened the way for a productive engagement by others. Enrique Dussel is one of those who have engaged closely with Karl Marx's *Economic Manuscripts 1861–63* (Dussel 2001). Dussel's innovative development of dependency theory centres around Marx's theory of completion and the distribution of surplus value. While we cannot derive a theory of unequal exchange at the international level from Marx's abstract of capital accumulation in *Capital*, we can, he argues, if we move into a more concrete terrain extending Marx's concepts. Dussel thus extends Marx's theory of intra-industry competition and market value to the question of 'dependency' which sees a transfer of value from the low-productivity producers of the peripheral countries to the high-productivity producers in the centre countries (Dussel 2001).

Marx's theory of capitalist development did not explicitly consider the international distribution element, but we can discern how he might have approached that issue. Rosa Luxemburg also helped to fill that gap with her analysis of international loans and how central Capital expanded to the periphery to realise surplus value and how surplus value is extracted from the periphery. To be clear, Marx in *Capital* was studying 'capital in general' and so could not be expected to be so concrete. It is only through an analysis of the world market that we can understand there is not an exchange of equivalents on international trade. So 'dependency' could never be established by an application of Marx's categories as most writers in that tradition believed. Marx did refer to in his *Economic Manuscripts* to how 'From the fact that the profit may be less than the surplus value, and hence that capital [may] exchange at a profit without being valorised in the strict sense, it follows that not only individuals but nations too may continuously exchange with one another and continuously repeat the exchange on an ever-growing scale, without gaining equally thereby. *One nation may continuously appropriate part of the surplus labour of the other and give nothing in exchange for it*, except that here the measure is not as in the exchange between capitalist and worker' (Marx and Engels 1989, 244, emphasis added).

The competition between capitalist nations is thus not one of exploitation but, rather, the extraction of surplus value by the stronger one from the weaker or dependent one. Competition says Marx 'executes the inner laws of capital; it forms them into coercive laws in relation to the industrial capital but it does not invent them' (Marx and Engels 1989, 136). And, for Marx, Adam Smith 'is correct to the extent that it is only in competiton – the action of capital on capital – that the immanent laws of capital, its TENDENCIES are realised' (Marx 1987, 136). Dependent development can thus be seen, from Marx's perspective, as a moment in the competition of capital. This capital on capital competition works at the horizontal level while the 'vertical' plane of capital/wage-labour exploitation determines the 'laws of motion' of the capitalist mode of production. The problem of dependency is thus not caused by monopoly capitalism and will not cease if monopoly is reined in either.

Arguably, Antonio Gramsci, who provides a link or bridge between classical Marxism and the modern underdevelopment theories through his incipient model of internal colonialism. His last article before he was arrested and imprisoned was precisely on *Some Aspects of the Southern Question* (Gramsci 1978) that deepened his analysis of uneven development in Italy that lay at the core of the programmatic 'Lyons Theses' of the new Communist Party (Gramsci 1978). The 'Southern Question' was the context within which state formation and nation-building occurred in Italy through what Gramsci called a 'passive revolution' defined as 'molecular changes which in fact progressively modify the pre-existing composition of forces and hence become the matrix of new changes'

(Gramsci 1971, 109). As with all development contexts as we understand them today, Italy was riven by acute regional disparities and weak economic, political and social integration. Addressing these tasks was crucial for the working class movement if it was to achieve cultural and political hegemony.

Gramsci's analysis of the Southern Question is of great contemporary relevance in terms of constructing a critical development theory that is historically grounded and dialectical in terms of the relation between external and internal factors. The relations between agriculture and industry can be posed as class relations but also now need to be seen as spatial or territorial ones. Gramsci posed a close analogy between the way coloniser countries dealt with the colonised and the way uneven development emerged and was reproduced in a peripheral country such as Italy during the Risorgimento. Gramsci posited a semi-colonial relationship between the Italian North and South that can be transposed or scaled up to the global North and South. It was also the inspiration for the 'internal colonialism' school that emerged in the 1960s (see Gonzales Casanova 1965) which posited race/ethnicity as the main marker of social inequality on a regional basis. Internal colonialism, in a Gramscian idiom, highlights the specific nature of capitalist development in the capitalist periphery and the way in which combined and uneven development depends on the reproduction and integration of 'archaic' social relations within its logic.

Gramsci's research agenda around the Southern question in Italy has also had a major impact on the postcolonial paradigm (see Chapter 8), not least through the concept of internal colonialism. We see evidence of this in the work of leading postcolonial figure Edward Said, particularly in his book *Culture and Imperialism* (Said 1979) where he foregrounds Gramsci's materialist approach to uneven development in *Some Aspects of the Southern Question.* Said adapts much of Gramsci's language and understanding of culture, arguing that 'ideas, cultures and histories cannot seriously be understood or studied, without their force, or more precisely their configurations of power, also being studied' (Said 1979, 5). Antonio Gramsci in his person and in his politics can, in fact, be seen as postcolonial activist-intellectual as Robert Young argues (Young 2012, 17).

As with Lenin's *Development of Capitalism in Russia* (Lenin 1967) subsequent historiography has questioned much of Gramsci's analysis of the Southern Question. The development of capitalism in Italy and the significance of the Risorgimento has been the subject of much research and debate. Rosario Romeo (1974) had early on cogently criticised the Gramscian notion that there had been a missed opportunity for an agrarian revolution in 1860 and that this could have accelerated the development of capitalism in Italy. We could also question Gramsci's traditional Marxist view of the 'bourgeois revolution' and the way in which the French revolution is elevated to iconic status and benchmark against which other experiences are judged and found wanting. In Latin America it was the Communist parties, following Gramsci's death, who took this model of the bourgeois revolution to its ultimate dogmatic consequences and hinged their whole strategy around the emergence of a 'national bourgeoisie' that simply could not exist.

The actual course of capitalist development and the 'bourgeois revolution' in Italy was not a deviation from the French model as Gramsci saw it but has its own dynamic. Likewise, those processes in Latin America had their own hybrid dynamic and would never follow a pre-determined path. Nothing could be further from an open Marxism attuned to the multiple paths history could take as Marx fully realised in his late engagement with development in Russia (Chapter 3) External involvement was key to the various phase of the bourgeois revolution in Italy with its weakness also shown in its inability to resolve the 'agrarian question' according to the models of democratic development led by an emerging industrial class. The revolution of 1796–1799 did lead to agrarian reforms but, as Paul Ginsborg notes, 'the reforms of this period tended more to unite the bourgeois and aristocratic landowners than to confront the peasant problem' (Ginsborg 1979, 45). Thus Gramsci's 'historic bloc' between Northern industrialists and Southern landowners was consolidated rather than a 'classic' bourgeois revolution that confronted feudal/or aristocratic economic and political power. Much the same pattern can be discerned in Brazil between the emerging São Paulo industrial class and the coffee barons. In this situation it was futile for the Communist parties to persist in calling for a democratic bourgeois revolution to overthrow feudal remnants in the belief that workers should first support the 'national bourgeoise' before even thinking about socialism.

References

*Cardoso, Fernando Henrique, 1977.
Amin, Samir. 1985. *Delinking: Towards a Polycentric World*. London: Zed Books.

Assadourian, Carlos Sempat, ed. 1973. *Modos de producción en América Latina. Cuadernos de Pasado y Presente 140*. Córdoba: Siglo XXI.
Bagú, Sergio. 1949. *Economía de la Sociedad Colonial*.
Balibar, Étienne. 1970. The Basic Concepts of Historical Materialism. In *Reading Capital*, ed. Louis Althusser and Étienne Balibar. London: New Left Books.
Balibar, Étienne. 1973. Self-Criticism: An Answer to Questions from 'Theoretical Practice.' *Theoretical Practice* 7–8: 56–72.
Baran, Paul. 1957. *The Political Economy of Growth*. New York: Monthly Review Press.
Beck, Ulrich. 1999. *World Risk Society*. Cambridge: Polity Press.
Cardoso, Ciro. 1973. Sobre los modos de producción coloniales de América Latina. In *Modos de producción en América Latina. Cuadernos de Pasado y Presente 140*, ed. Carlos Sempat Assadourian. Córdoba: Siglo XXI.
Cardoso de Mello, João. 1982. *O Capitalismo Tardio : Contribuicao a Revisao Critica da Formacao e do Desenvolvimento da Economia Brasileira*. Sao Paulo: Brasiliense.
Cardoso, Fernando Henrique. 1984. The Consumption of Dependency Theory in the United States. *Latin American Research Review* 12 (3): 7–24.
Cardoso, Fernando Henrique, and Ernesto Faletto. 1979. *Dependency and Development in Latin America*. California: University of California Press.
Cardoso, Fernando Henrique, and José Serra. 1978. Las desventuras de la dialéctica de la dependencia. *Revista Mexicana De Sociología* 40: 9–55.
Castañeda, Jorge, and Enrique Hett. 1978. *El Economismo Dependentista*. Mexico: Siglo XXI.
Castells, Manuel, and Pekka Himanen, eds. 2014. *Reconceptualising Development in the Global Information Age*. Oxford: Oxford University Press.
Castells, Manuel. 1996. *The Rise of the Network Society*. Oxford: Blackwell Press.
Derrida, Jacques. 1994. *Spectres of Marx*. New York and London: Routledge.
Dos Santos, Theotônio. 1972. *Socialismo fascismo. El Nuevo carácter de la dependencia y el dilema latinoamericano*. Buenos Aires: Perifería.
Dos Santos, Theotônio. 1978. The Structure of Dependence. *The American Economic Review* 60 (2): 231–236.
Dussel, Enrique. 2001. *Towards an Unknown Marx. A Commentary on the Manuscripts of 1861–63*. London and New York: Routledge.
Evans, Peter. 1979. *Dependent Development. The Alliance of Multinational, State and Local. Capital in Brazil*. Princeton, NJ: Princeton University Press.
Evans, Peter. 2007. The Relevance of Dependent Development Then and Now. In *Dialogues on Development* (ISSN 2472-6966). Institute for New Economic Thinking.
Frondizi, Silvio. 1955. *La Realidad Argentina. Ensago de interpretación sociológica*.

Ginsborg, Paul. 1979. Gramsci and the Era of Bourgeois Revolution in Italy. In *Gramsci and Italy's Passive Revolution*, ed. John Davis. London: Groom Helm.
Gonzales Casanova, Pablo. 1965. Internal Colonialism and National Development. *Studies on Comparative International Development* 1 (4): 27–37.
Gramsci, Antonio. 1971. *Selections from the Prison Notebooks*. London: Lawrence and Wishart.
Gramsci, Antonio, 1978. Some Aspects of the Southern Question. In *Selections from Political Writings (1921–1926)*. London: Lawrence and Wishart.
Gramsci, Antonio. 1986. *"The Lyons Theses" in Selections from Political Writings (1921–1926)*. London: Lawrence and Wishart.
Gunder Frank, Andre. 1966. *The Development of Underdevelopment*. New York: Monthly Review Press.
Gunder Frank, Andre. 1969. *Latin America: Underdevelopment or Revolution*. New York: Monthly Review Press.
Hardt, Michael, and Antonio Negri. 2000. *Empire*. Harvard: Harvard University Press.
Hilton, Rodney, ed. 1976. *The Transition from Feudalism to Capitalism*. London: New Left Books.
Kalmanovitz, Salomón. 1986. *El Desarrollo Tardio del Capitalismo*. Bogotá: Siglo XXI.
Kay, Cristobel. 1993. *Latin America Theories of Development and Underdevelopment*. London: Routledge.
Laclau, Ernesto. 1971. *Feudalism and Capitalism in Latin America*. New Left Review I (67) (May–June).
Lenin, Vladimir Illich. 1967. *The Development of Capitalism in Russia*. Moscow: Progress Publishers.
Lenin, Vladimir Illich. 1970. Imperialism: The Highest Stage of Capitalism. In *Selected Works*, vol. 1. Moscow: Progress Publishers.
Manzo, Kate. 1991. Modest Discourse and the Crisis of Development Theory. *Studies in Comparative International Development* 26 (2).
Marini, Ruy Mauro. 1974. *Subdesarollo y Revolución*. Mexico: Siglo XXI.
Marini, Ruy Mauro. 1978. Las razones del neodesarrollismo (respuesta a F.H. Cardoso y J. Serra). *Revista Mexicana de Sociología*, 41, 57–106.
Marx, Karl, and Frederick Engels. 1989. *Collected Works*, vol. 29 (1857–1861). London: Lawrence and Wishart.
Rodney, Walter. 1972. *How Europe Underdeveloped Africa*. London: Bogle-L'Ouverture Publications.
Romeo, Rosario. 1974. *Risorgimento e Capitalismo*. Bari: Laterza.
Said, Edward. 1979. *Culture and Imperialism*. New York: Vintage.
Wallerstein, Immanuel. 1979. *The Capitalist World Economy*. Cambridge: Cambridge University Press.

Weffort, Francisco. 1971. Nota Sobre a 'Teoría da Dependencia': Teoria de Classe ou Ideologia Nacional? *Estudos CEBRAP* No. 1. Sao Paulo: CEBRAP.

Wolpe, Harold, ed. 1980. *The Articulation of Modes of Production*. London: Routledge.

Young, Robert. 2012. Postcolonialism "Il Gramsci Meridionale". In *The Postcolonial Gramsci*, eds Neelam Srivastava and Baidik Bhattacharya. London and New York: Routledge.

CHAPTER 8

Post-Development

In the 1980s there was a perceived general impasse in terms of Marxism's influence on the development problematic (see Booth 1985). The dependency approach was also seen to have diminishing purchase with the rise of the East Asian 'tiger' countries that seemed to disprove the simplistic version of the theory as articulated by Andre Gunder Frank among others. From out of this situation, we saw the gradual emergence of a broad 'post-development' problematic that was to seek not just a more democratic form of development but to go beyond it in some way. This also reflected the crumbling of the post-war modernisation theory that simply had not delivered the progress it promised. Likewise, the 'crisis of Marxism' was also coming to a head and post Marxist variants came to the fore.

We begin our survey of this radical questioning of both development and Marxism by considering the *After modernity* problematic. How would Marxism respond to the postmodernist theories then gaining currency? Why was Marxism considered to be Eurocentric? We also add into the equation, the more 'political' postcolonialism approach then gaining currency. We find new themes emerging such as the importance of culture, the neglected role of 'race' in the making of the modern world and the role of agency and voice in the making of development. We turn next to presentation of the *Decolonial option* that foregrounds the continuing role of colonialism, not least in epistemic terms. What does

R. Munck, *Rethinking Development*, Marx, Engels, and Marxisms,
https://doi.org/10.1007/978-3-030-73811-2_8

it mean to decolonise development? How do issues of identity, otherness and language relate to the world of inequality, exploitation and poverty? If development has been discerned to have failed as a socio-economic endeavour what do the post-development and postcolonial theories offer as an alternative?

We finally turn to the *Politics* of post-development/colonialism. We consider whether it has undermined the Marxist understanding of capitalism as a universalising mode of production. Does the colonial difference mean that Marxism has been superseded as a framework for understanding the global system? We posit two version of the postcolonial paradigm, one eminently co-optable by the World Bank that has adopted the themes of identity empowerment and the importance of the local, and one not so co-optable namely the revolutionary anti-imperialism of Franz Fanon that may serve to bridge the gap between Marxism and anti-colonialism.

After Modernity

The post-development discourse emerged as a reaction against the notion that Development II could, in reality, take the majority of the world's population into the affluent lifestyle enjoyed in the West. It was also clearly an anti-colonial discourse insofar as it rejected the assumption that the West could or should administer development and democracy in the rest of the world. The post-development paradigm is critical of the 'truth regime' (Foucault 2000) of Northern development theory, how it defines poverty and seeks to impose a universal blueprint for development worldwide. This mission is clearly a continuation of the colonial discourse and the notion of the 'white man's burden' (Kipling 2012) to create civilisation by force if necessary. Thus, post-development builds on the insights of postcolonialism, albeit more focused on the social and economic aspects of development rather than the cultural domain where postcolonialism made its name, at least in the academy.

The post-development perspective takes an absolutist stance towards 'actually existing development' to call it that. 'Development stinks' says Gustavo Esteva (Esteva 1987, 135) or 'there is something rotten at the core of the very concept of development' as Zia Sardar puts it (Sardar 1996, 37). These blunt statements served notice that post-development was not just seeking to reform or improve development. As with postcolonialism, these theorists focus on the Eurocentrism of the development drive from Development I onwards. As with dependency theory (Chapter 7) they reject the Northern focused definition of development needs worldwide and the platitudes of modernisation theory (Development II). But they simply do not see, or leave out of the debate, the non-Western development models such as those prevailing in China and South East Asia which somewhat blunts the universal aspiration of the critique. They tend to see development as a malevolent monolith and do not seek out its ambiguities, variations and contradictions. Above all, the local, bottom-up and social movement-based alternative development model, implicit in this approach is rarely spelt out or translated into the political or policy domain. We are thus left with a critique but not really with an alternative theory of capitalist development.

Given the double theme of this book—Marxism and development in their inter-relationships—it is important to trace the origins of post-modernism from within Marxism, insofar as it permeates all the 'posts' be in post-development or other versions. It began with the study of so-called 'post-industrial' societies in the 1970s, which saw knowledge becoming the main driver of economic development. This flow of knowledge would bypass national boundaries and also question traditional disciplinary boundaries between the natural sciences, social sciences and art and literature. The very foundations of knowledge in the European Enlightenment would be questioned. From knowledge as the path to truth (and salvation) there was a shift to the notion of knowledge as unstable, and fragile. The promise that modernity and ever-increasing knowledge would liberate humanity from ignorance and irrationality was beginning to look quite threadbare, with global capitalism in long-term crisis and the anti-colonial revolution in full flow as in the 'blowback' of the colonial possessions in Portugal in 1975.

There are many ways into the debate around postmodernism (and ways to get lost in a veritable maze) but the work of Jean-François Lyotard is as good as any way in and has been foundational. Lyotard was an influential member of the far-left group *Socialisme ou Barbarie* from the mid-1950s to the mid-1960s and a perceptive commentator on the anti-colonial struggle in Algeria. In the early 1970's he engaged with the work of Freud and began to go beyond even his own unorthodox Marxism. For Lyotard 'reason is already in power in kapital. We do not want to destroy kapital because it is not rational, but because it is reason and power are all one' (cited in Anderson 1998, 27). Recall that around this time neo-Marxism had shifted to a critique of capitalism based on it its irrationality and not its inherent contradictions (Chapter 1). There was to be no dialectic, for Lyotard, leading to the supersession of capitalism, only the libidinal power of the 1968 generation could change the world, power came from the imagination.

Lyotard's landmark text *The Postmodern Condition* (Lyotard 1984) began life as a technical report on knowledge for the government of Quebec. Much of the report was about the studies of science, technology and the arts and the ways in which the flow of knowledge is controlled in the West. In terms of how we legitimated the criteria for distinguishing between true and false statements Lyotard argued that the modern era narratives were exhausted as its metanarratives collapsed. Simplifying in the extreme, wrote Lyotard 'I define *postmodern* as incredulity towards metanarratives...[due to] the crisis of metaphysical philosophy and of the university institution which in the past relied on it' (Lyotard 1984, xxiv). Among the key metanarratives of the twentieth century, we would have to mention both establishment Marxism and development theory would both be characterised by a teleology, that is heading towards pre-defined ends. How would they respond to this fundamental critique of their legitimation procedures?

Another current we need to mention is the 'cultural' take of Frederic Jameson also from within Marxism, albeit it a Hegelianized version. His late 1990s *Postmodernism, or the cultural logic of late capitalism* (Jameson 1991) offered a sweeping survey of how Western Marxism was essentially exhausted as a critical theory. For Jameson, postmodernism was the new cultural dominant for the stage of late capitalism. Modernism had responded to incomplete modernisation and the ongoing conflicts between the city and the countryside. The culture of postmodernism was to be less elitist and tended to dissolve the frontiers between 'high' and 'low' culture. Postmodernism was part of the market dominance of neoliberalism but it was also 'populist' and potentially liberatory. For Jameson there was little point in lamenting the effects of postmodernist or wallowing in nostalgia for the certainties of modernism.

Postmodernism was thus consolidated with globalisation and the complete triumph of capitalist relations of production in the 1990s. The prospect of an alternative social order—always a constant in modernism—now faded even as possibility. This was the 'truth' behind Lyotard's incredibility towards metanarratives and the deconstruction of all dominant discourses. Collective endeavours of large social group—be they workers, peasants or nations—fade in an era of individualism. In an era celebrating hybridity and crossover 'the Manifesto becomes outdated' as Perry Anderson puts it, 'a relic of an assertive purism at variance with the spirit of the age' (Anderson 1998, 93). The crisis of modernism was real and its impact decisive, but it also unleashed new liberatory impulses and ways of rethinking utopia outside of the constraints of modernity which was also, of course, the era of coloniality.

Given that there is no clearer metanarrative than development, it was not surprising to see a 'post-development' approach emerging out of the ferment of postmodernism and its engagement with development. It emerged essentially as a critique of Development 2 as we have called the particular constellation of thinking/policy making that emerged in the United States in the immediate post-war period to manage the post-colonial order. Arturo Escobar's mid-1990s *Encountering Development: The Making and Unmaking if the Third World* (Escobar 1995) was a landmark exposition of this thesis. Post development, as he wrote, 'was meant to convey the sense of an era in which development would no longer be a central organiser of social life' (Escobar 1995, xiii). Heavily influenced by Foucault's method of discourse analysis, Escobar effectively dismantled the ethnocentric and managerial assumptions of the United States aided state-led development model. Attaining a middle-class 'developed' lifestyle was simply not possible (or even arguably, desirable) for the majority of the world's population. We needed to think beyond development given the way it was not perceived as a totally negative enterprise.

Post-development theorists were fiercely critical of the positivist and empiricist methods of the 'development industry' that embraced the World Bank, the IMF, the international NGO's and the academic specialism known as development studies in an integrated power/knowledge system. As against the assumed universality and scientificity of this paradigm, the post-development theorists posited the importance of place, subjectivities and identity formation. Post-development breaks decisively with the Eurocentrism of the dominant development paradigms and articulates the need for a subaltern Southern knowledge to emerge. It is a far more fundamental break with development compared to all the various critiques of the 1980s from a feminist, environmentalist and 'bottom-up' perspective. To be clear this dismissal of the very term 'development' would apply to Development 2 and not, necessarily, Development 1 as the unfolding of human progress along the lines of industrialisation and the development of capitalism more generally. The post-development theory emphasis on the US post-war moment is, arguably, exaggerated and creates an epistemological break in development theory that is not really there from a more long-term perspective.

A quite distinct, but related, current of thought crystallised around the concept of 'post colonialism'. While sharing some of the post-structuralist and culturalist origins of post-development it was also much more directly political in its intent. In terms of the development of capitalism (Development I) this approach would stress the formative and enduring impact of colonialism in the colonial countries but also in the colonising countries (renewing Luxemburg's quest without being explicit about it, see Chapter 5). The postcolonial condition thus refers to the complex economic, political and cultural legacies of colonialism that do not evaporate the day a new national flag is hoisted. There is a link here to the sharp analysis carried out by Franz Fanon on the deep-rooted nature of colonialism and the obstacles that an independent Algeria would inevitably face (Fanon 1970). In terms of their politics, the postcolonial theorists are also, unambiguously, anti-colonial and they are committed to deconstructing the ending legacies of colonialism in social and cultural life and discourses.

A central contribution to develop a broad postcolonial theory of development would be Dipesh Chakrabarty's drive to 'provincialize Europe' (2007) and Edward Said's expose of orientalism, both of which had a huge impact on development studies and the postcolonial school in particular. As against the dominant view of 'Europe' as the sovereign, theoretical centre of all historical discourse against which others are measured, we need to relativise its role. The mythical figure of Europe was seen as the benchmark against which all other routes to development were judged against and inevitably found lacking. The Industrial Revolution and the Enlightenment, or versions of the real history of same, became unattainable ideals and condemned all others to a secondary position. To 'provincialise' Europe meant recognising the limitations of Western social science in terms of explaining the historical experiences of political modernity in the tricontinental worlds of Asia, Africa and Latin America. Chakhrabarty offers a critique of the Enlightenment concepts of a universal human experience and of secular modernity. However, his project is not about rejecting European thought as a whole but, rather, represents an effort to renew European thought 'from and for the margins' (Chakrabarty 2007, 16). While this project has sometimes been accused of being a simple cover for nationalism (as the dependency approach was, see Chapter 7) it is much more a move to pluralise the history of global political modernity of which 'development' is a key element giving all subaltern actors a role and a voice.

As to Orientalism, this was a colonial power/knowledge device to further 'other' the non-European world. The merit of Said's work—despite all the criticisms it has attracted—is that it showed *colonialism* and colonial modernity was not only about military and political strategy, but also operated a historical discourse of knowledge. As Robert Young sums it up: 'Colonization, in short, involved epistemic as well as physical violence' (Young 2001, 383). Said was instrumental in mainstreaming the idea that colonialism was not only a form of economic exploitation and military oppression as the classic Marxists had shown, but also at the same time created a discourse of domination, a historically specific discourse of knowledge and power. It is worth noting given the polarisation between a certain Marxism and the postcolonial theorists that Said uses many of Gramsci's key concepts, and *Orientalism*'s main argument is that 'ideas, cultures, and histories cannot seriously be understood or studied without their force, or more precisely their configurations of power, also being studied' (Said 1978, 5); thus, in Rosengarten's view, 'Gramsci helped open the way for the most far-reaching and dynamic aspects of postcolonial thought' (Rosengarten 2015, 65–66).

If both Marxism and development are seen as inextricably bound up with modernity where do, they stand 'after modernity'? Marxism has, by and large, settled its accounts with postmodernism after an initial period of intense hostility from a 'proprietorial' position towards anyone seemingly questioning its revolutionary credentials. Marxism is now more conscious of its modernist roots and its limitations. Marxism has also shared in the critique of Eurocentrism as articulated by the post-development current of thought. Much of the ferment of the 1980s and 1990s has settled and now questions are asked as to where post-development is going. This is an issue we must now address as we study in more detail what a 'decolonial' political option might mean for both development studies and for Marxism. What is now to the fore, compared to a previous era is the importance of culture—no longer relegated to a 'superstructure' determined 'in the last instance' by the economic base—the critical role of race in shaping colonialism and the modern world system and the irrepressible role of voice and agency against all forms of structuralism.

Decolonial Option

As a way of taking forward these themes around post-development and postcolonialism we usefully might consider what 'decolonizing' development means. The postcolonial problematic has shown us how development is constructed as a discourse it is not natural or a given. The post-development optic for its part, also places the dominant development discourse both historically and geographically; it is not universal. They both respond to the limited success the Marxist political economy of development/underdevelopment had in the 1970s in terms of influencing the mainstream development perspective. By introducing the discursive formation of 'development' it could be seen as furthering the original Marxist objective. But it did so without taking up explicitly (and often opposing) the nationalism of the colonised, something and had characterised Marxism since the 1920s. What we need to trace now is the main ways in which the decolonial option unsettled the dominant Marxist development theories and to what extent they opened up the debate for a renewed radical problematic.

There is an interesting continuity between the dependency optic of the 1960s and the decolonial approach of the 1990s in the work of Aníbal Quijano who was an active participant in the Latin American debate in the 1970s and thus poses an interesting bridge with his 'coloniality of power' writings of the 1980s. Modernity is seen as an order which is not European but when Europe meets America in conquest. Thus is born the 'coloniality of power' (as against colonialism) in which 'the social category of "race" is the key element of the social classification of colonized and colonizers' (Quijano 2007, 171). Capitalism provided the new structure for the control of labour in this new global order spanning slavery, serfdom, the petty commodity mode of production, reciprocity and community, to wage labour. The critique of the coloniality of world power is now urgent for Quijano, it entails epistemological decolonisation and the exchange of experiences to construct another rationality to surpass the European paradigm of rationality/modernity. Implicit is the sense that a 'decolonised' Marxism would play a role in this process of reconstruction.

From this perspective, the original conquest of the Americas and the long rule of coloniality have marked all its subsequent development trajectory. There have been continuities and transformative ruptures through to the present day. Where dependency focused primarily on the economic domain and the relation with the external world, the decolonial perspective directed our attention to the element of direct and epistemic violence and its cultural impact. It was and is through violence that the labour force was subjected to the will of capital and it was violence that terminated many democratic experiences before they could threaten the stability of the established order. It was 'coloniality at large' (see Moraña et al. 2008) that represented the underside of modernity and exposed the nature of 'development' on the capitalist periphery; a Marxism that is not itself decolonial has difficulty in grasping this situation, let alone effectively intervening in it.

We can thus argue with Quijano and others that modernity was not born in Europe but in its violent encounter with America. The universalising discourse that legitimised capitalist expansion was, also a racialised one at its very core. The classification of the global population was a racial as much as class hierarchy. That is a very different starting point for modernity than an idealised version of the European enlightenment so cherished by Development I. The very formation of the state and of the nation in the Americas was marked by the colonial difference that Marx failed to recognise or understand as we saw in Chapter 3 when dealing with Latin America. Thus, argues, Quijano, 'the process of independence for Latin American states without decolonizing society could not have been, and it was not, a process towards the development of modern nation-states but was instead a rearticulation of coloniality of power over new institutional bases' (Quijano 2008, 215). Without achieving that process of decolonisation, it will not be possible to achieve either development or democracy.

The epistemic decolonial turn was bound to take its, often Marxist, proponents beyond a political economy paradigm. The seemingly universal European paradigms of development were subverted by both feminist and race critical perspectives. In the global North, Marxism had accommodated, to some extent, this critique with the promotion of the class/race/gender trinity. In the global South, these critiques would prove more corrosive of Marxist political economy and its dependency variant in particular. As Ramón Grosfoguel notes 'many leftist projects in Latin America following the *dependentista* under-estimation or racial/ethnic hierarchies have reproduced, within their organizations and when controlling state power, white creole domination over non-European peoples' (Grosfoguel 2008, 327). Essentially, no radical project of transformation can be successful without dismantling the colonial/racial hierarchies, something that can occur only outside of a nationalist/dependency frame that pits the 'nation' versus the world.

More broadly, and in a positive vein, we can pose the decolonial opt on that can emerge once we recognise the centrality of the 'colonial difference'. As Arturo Escobar articulates this question, we may envision alternatives to the totality we call modernity, not necessarily another totality leading to a new global design but, rather, 'a network of local/global histories constructed from the perspective of a politically enriched alterity' (Escobar 1995, 37). This means examining modernity through the lens of a coloniality that is always/already a constant element. We thus begin to rethink both the spatial and temporal origins of modernity in a way that can, potentially, unlock the radical potential of difference. This entails, of course, rethinking radical political economy that has been constrained by its Eurocentric origins and its inability, until recently, to foreground gender differences.

There is much that a renewed Marxist perspective on development could take from the 'decolonial' critique. Inevitably Marxism shares philosophical and epistemological terrain with Eurocentrism. The national question detour to the East and then the South (see Chapter 5) inevitably turned it into something else, best exemplified in the dependency approach (Chapter 7). In the next section I will try to draw out some of the main insights of the decolonial approach that can be incorporated into a renewed Marxism. For now, I just wish to note that this perspective is much stronger on critique than it is on offering an alternative. Thus, we have a 440-page long *Post-Development Reader* (Rahnema 1997) that covers a wide range of topics from a diverse group of scholars but when it comes to producing a way forward in the final chapter, the editor can offer only two pages *Towards new paradigms and a new language* (Rahnema 1997, 400–402) that can only urge us to embrace 'the passion of witnessing one's Truth'.

What we can take from the decolonial turn is the need for a much greater appreciation of the role of culture in the development process. Certainly, in modernisation theory there was an instrumental emphasis on 'culture' as in the 'Western values' deemed necessary for successful development such as self-motivation, entrepreneurialism belief in science, thrifty habits, etc. These are essentialist and ethnocentric views of culture exemplified best perhaps by Huntingdon's *Clash of Civilisation* (Huntingdon 2002) who defines culture as 'ancestry, religion, language, history, values, customs and institutions' (Huntingdon 2002, 21). As to the radical dependency theory, it took a neo-Marxist political economy approach that downplayed cultural and ideological determinations. As Grosfoguel puts it 'culture was perceived as instrumental to capitalist accumulation processes' (Grosfoguel 2008, 326). The economic reductionism of dependency was quite marked, but also typical of much neo-Marxist work on development.

The post-development and postcolonial schools of thought brought a 'cultural Marxism' influenced understanding to bear on development studies. Culture was seen as the set of practices whereby meanings, values and subjectivities are constituted in a given social order. As Raymond Williams had put it, much earlier, culture is 'the signifying system through which necessarily (through among other means) a social order is communicated, reproduced experienced and explored' (Williams 1981, 13). The shift towards this understanding of culture in the 1980s helped to overcome the earlier dependency approach neglect of Latin America's racial/colonial hierarchies. The 'economy' was no longer the privileged site for social analysis and political focus. To overcome dependency, the left would also have to embrace the need to overcome the 'coloniality of power' through a second decolonisation.

The other element that can be gained for a renewed Marxist perspective is a better understanding of the importance of territoriality. As Arturo Escobar puts it 'the struggle for territory is…a cultural struggle for autonomy and self-determination' (Escobar 1995, 68). Territory is the site for place-based social relations and cultural constructions. This is, of course, crucial in understanding how social movements form around development issues. It also moves our attention beyond the simple or single 'nation' as the privileged place where opposition to the 'global' is built. We are now much more aware of the politics of scale, from the household to the community, the local and the regional and the various dimensions of the transitional. Understanding development in this complex way is essential if we are to escape unilinear and teleological conceptions of development.

Postcolonial theory has allowed us to radically rethink the importance of territoriality, joining the effort begun by Marxist geographies like Henry Lefebvre (Lefebvre 1991). The production of space and the division of territory through colonialism and imperialism are now an integral part of radical political economy. We now have a more complex understanding of state, nation and territory in relation to the development process. Edward Said in his, writings on Orientalism and on imperialism and culture (Said 1978, 1994) showed how territory was created through colonial discourse and how the spatial fix of territory involves the production of socio-spatial difference. This approach also allows us to grasp the particular importance of nationalism in the postcolonial world insofar as the process of territorialisation was also a process of national identity formation.

Finally, in terms of epistemology we should now be better placed to refuse debilitating binary oppositions. The simplistic dualism of development-underdevelopment, centre-periphery, dependence-autonomy have now been decisively subverted. We are less drawn to the totalising perspective and understand the value of more regional or piecemeal knowledge. The idea of a social totality should not blind us to an understanding of social heterogeneity. The co-presence of different historic logics points us away from all reductionism. In terms of how we might understand the postcolonial lens I would argue against its unity as a 'school', a label that did so much harm to the dependency lens. As Fernando Coronil puts it 'post colonialism is a fluid and polysemic category, whose power derives in part from its ability to condense multiple meanings and refer to different locations' (Coronel 2008, 416). It is more effective if we do not fix its meaning through formal definitions.

Robert Young's wide-ranging historical introduction to postcolonialism (Young 2001) allows to look at ways to bridge the gap between cultural and political analysis that often bedevils debate on this topic. Postcolonialism, from Young's perspective, is not post as in 'after the end of colonialism' but, rather in the sense of 'after the onset of colonialism'. This is a global discourse that subsumes Marxism in its revolutionary, but not in its Eurocentric modalities. It reflects new forms of knowledge that emerge from anti-colonial political and cultural practice. It goes further, argues Young, insofar as 'postcolonial cultural critique integrates its Marxism with the politics of international rights, in doing do focusing on the central problematic for Marxism as a political philosophy, namely how socialism can be developed in a popular rather than coercive form' (Young 2001, 7). From this perspective it does not make sense to counterpose Marxism and the postcolonial paradigm we might argue.

Our conclusion to this section would be that postcolonialism and Marxism are not, or should not be, opposed to one another. Third world nationalists and revolutionaries like Nehru, Cabral and Marti for the first and Ho Chi-Minh, Fanon and Castro for the second, drew their inspiration from Marxism and other sources. What unifies them is that the hybrid postcolonial politics they articulated was directed at the decolonisation of the Third World peoples. Thus, for Young, 'postcolonialism designates the perspective of tricontinental [Africa, Asia and Latin America] theories which analyse the material and epistemological conditions of postcoloniality and seek to combat the continuing, often covert, operation of an imperialist system of economic, political and cultural domination' (Young 2001, 58). Marxism would be poorly served if it continued to stress its doctrinal purity against the postcolonial approach, defending a Second World (actually existing socialism) against the messy encroachment of the Third World.

Politics

The political significance and reception of postcolonial theory needs to be considered critically. We cannot simply leave it as it presents itself. We will therefore consider postcolonialism from a Marxist and then from a development perspective.

Despite its origins in Marxism as much as in poststructuralist theory the postcolonial approach has come in for fierce Marxist attack. One issue we are particularly interested in here, given the subject matter of this book is the defence of the universalising mission of capitalism by some Marxists against the postcolonial attack. Thus, we find Vivek Chibber stating unambiguously that Western categories can and, indeed, must be applied to postcolonial societies like India: 'There has been no prominent body of thought associated with the left in the last 150 years or so that has insisted on denying the scientific ethos and the applicability of categories coming out of the liberal Enlightenment – categories like capital, democracy, liberalism, rationality and objectivity…. postcolonial theorists are the first to do so' (Chibber 2013b).

The critique by Chibber of the postcolonial approach is more accurately described as directed against the Indian subaltern history school. It can also be seen—over and above the fireworks—as a debate within Marxist pivoting around the science culture divide (see Brennan 2014). Since Sorel took on the mechanistic Marxism of his day and Gramsci called 1917 the 'revolution against *Capital*', Marxism has had a clear scientific side and a 'warm' side more attuned to culture and human agency. The Indian subaltern studies were, for example, engaged in bottom-up and culturalist reading of labour history against the Stalinist orthodoxy of party, unions and state. While Chibber may have effectively undermined the 'postcolonial studies' pretensions in the US academy he does not obliterate a very valuable strand of Marxist cultural labour history.

In terms of the postcolonial take on global development, Chibber makes many valuable points. Just like dependency theory's assumption that there was a non-dependent autonomous and auto-centric development model to compare to, so the subaltern school sometimes assumed a 'West' that was more coherent and a bourgeoisie that was more dynamic than its counterpart in the 'East'. In setting up a mythical and coherent original path to capitalist development the dependency and subaltern approaches will, of course, find their Latin American and Indian paths to catalyst development not 'normal'. This flaw does not mean, however, that we need to accept Chibber's claimed left heritage of universalism, totality, reason, truth, progress and science. Nor can we deny that the Marxist view of development has, indeed, been teleological, stageist and deterministic in many authoritative statements. In short, we need to be very wary of dismissing the 'colonial difference' globally through a polemic.

Marxism's engagement with the postcolonial problematic has been a fraught one. While there have been collaboration, confluences and crossovers, some damaging polemics have also been a feature of this relationship. Vivek Chibber's *Postcolonial Theory and the Spectre of Capital* (Chibber 2013a) was widely seen by Northern Marxists as a definitive burial of the postcolonial enterprise. For Chibber postcolonial theory was complicit in the neoliberal capture of diversity and difference in the academy, becoming a new 'radical' orthodoxy that stifled dissent. The postcolonial theorists were seen to be articulating a Southern version of Orientalism in their denial of universality and stress on the colonial difference. In a similar vein Žižek had launched a polemic against 'Multiculturalism, or, The Cultural Logic of Multinational Capital' (Žižek 1997) which complained about 'this multiculturalist ideological poetry embedded in today's global capitalism', that he saw as part of 'Western cultural imperialism' and reflecting a 'self-referential form of racism'. The enemy of both multiculturalism and postcolonialism is seen as a universalism that Marxism should reclaim for socialism.

What this polemic shows is how Marxism and postcolonial theory are taken to be unified and stable discourses. There is a failure to deconstruct, to put it that way. The 'Marxism' that goes into battle here against postcolonialism to defend its 'radical' position in the academy from competitors, is an openly universalist ideology with a firm belief in causality and a faith in the inevitability of socialist revolution. The vision of 'postcolonial theory' targeted by these Marxist critics is focused, rather, on contingency and hybridity and its critique of Eurocentrism. Western capitalism and imperialism were targeted by both discourses but in different ways. Marxists argued that the postcolonial theorists made a category error in seeing capitalism as a civilisational category rather than an economic mode of production. For Marxists such as Lazarus and Varna 'the intersection of postcolonial and multicultural politics provided a domain in which radicalism could be espoused within the constraints of a seemingly undefeatable global order' (Lazarus and Varna 2008, 311).

Behind the Marxist critique of the postcolonial frame was the need to remove its radical credentials in the academy and this led to an ill-tempered exchange from which neither side emerged with much credit, the only exception being those Marxists who worked within the postcolonial paradigm. One way of approaching the issue was to seek the subsumption of postcolonialism within Marxism. Thus, Vasant Kirwan argued that 'to the extent that postcolonial studies has the ability or ambition to enrich Marxism, it must perforce become an aspect of Marxism' (Kaiwar 2014, xviii). This was reminiscent of an earlier Marxist engagement with feminism that saw a similar refusal to engage on equal terms, instead assuming a quasi- hegemonic (to not say imperialistic) position. At least this position understood that Marxism and postcolonialism 'fished in the same (radical) pond' and could learn from one another. For that to be possible Marxism would need to come to terms with its Enlightenment heritage and its relationship to the concept of universalism. We find that within Marxism this interrogation has been ongoing, not least among the Marxist currents within the postcolonial movement in its broadest sense so that both the concepts of 'Europe' and the 'universal' are now in question.

Ettiene Balibar (co-author with Louis Althusser of *Reading Capital* in the mid-1960s, Althusser and Balibar 1970) provides a good example of a Marxism that engages, in the spirit of postcolonialism, with both the problem of Europe and the complex nature of universalism (Balibar 1991). Balibar clearly uncouples the concept of Europe from that of universalism and also shows how the latter (as against the simplistic Marxist critics of postcolonialism) is an unstable category that cannot be simply counterposed to the difference and particularity of the postcolonial approach. Europe, furthermore, was not just constituted by the 'Europeans' from the era of slavery to the current era of mass migration. It is in these more concrete terrains for example in the new subaltern labour studies (see Chaturvedi 2000) that we see an intense and productive engagement between Marxist and postcolonial approaches to the extent that we can no longer see them as separate let alone counterposed.

Returning now to the Marxist critique of the postcolonial lens I think one of its main weaknesses is to counterpose the 'culturalist' reading of the postcolonial theorists to the political economy approach, seen as the proper domain of Marxism. Thus, in the debate around Chibber's critique (see Warren 2016) we see the need to question the apparent standoff between universalism and cultural particularism. While people are undoubtedly all shaped by culture, we need to ask how far does cultural particularity go. In other words, there is always somewhere more local than the localism we deploy to understand the impact of culture on a collective identity. What we call 'Europe' is not just a 'provincialising' entity but itself contains many provinces (and peoples). To deal with this complexity of the real we need a cultural political economy (see Sum and Jessop 2015) and not a return to a crude political economy against culture.

The argument for Marxism to engage in a more open, less aggressive manner with postcolonialism seems persuasive to me if we are to avoid what Derrida referred to as Marxism's 'propietorialism'. Kolja Linder (2010) has put forward a number of positive arguments for this dialogue: it would reinforce the growing realisation that capitalism is not as totalising as some think, also certain social spaces are outside of its reach. Marxism would also be able to achieve a definitive break with evolutionism and the notion of inevitable human progress. As with post-structural variants of Marxism, it allows us to create the theoretical space for contingency, specifically historical contingency, for example in relation to the role of Europe and the emergence of the capitalist mode of production. Certainly, many of the critiques of Marx as a Eurocentric thinker betray an ignorance of his later work (see Chapter 3) but, equally, many Marxists have chosen to fight the postcolonial approach from an openly universalist and economically reductionist perspective that should, by now, have been overcome.

The other engagement we need to track is the development theory response to postcolonialism. From a dependency perspective we could say, following Ilan Kapoor that 'postcolonial theory does not adequately appreciate the role of capitalism, resulting in significant political problems' (Kapoor 2008, 14). Certainly, in the work of Edward Said one finds few references to capitalism, with his main focus being the politics of representation. The issue of social-economic inequalities—so central to the mission of the dependency lens—is marginalised by a semiotic approach to politics. While anti-colonial cultural practices could, indeed, be transgressive they were ultimately successful through a very modernist political-and sometimes armed struggle-movement for independence and the construction of nationhood. Dependency's tendency to become subsumed under nationalism cannot be overcome by ignoring it.

Aijaz Ahmad has directed our attention to postcolonialism's tendency to approach capitalism epistemologically and its 'literary-critical habit of seeing all history as a contest between different kinds of narrative, so that imperialism itself gets described not in terms of the universalisation of the catalyst mode as such but in terms of the *narrative* of this mode' (Ahmad 1997, 376). Economic reductionism cannot be replaced by a discursive reductionism. The theoretical deconstruction of 'development' as discourse does not displace it politically or the material issues it addresses: inequality, exploitation and poverty. While a cultural political economy can bring both elements together, a purely culturalist reading of development leaves much of its underpinnings intact. A more root and branch critique is still called for, which we address in Chapter 9 on indigenous development.

A further weakness of the post-development approach is its lack of reflexivity on its own theoretical assumptions. There is, for example, an unintended parallel between the neoliberal attack on 'developmentalism' for its reliance on the nation state, and the post-development critique. Its emphasis on grassroots politics and empowerment carries with it a profoundly anti-state message. Yet it was the national development state that was the main enemy for the neoliberal offensive of the 1980s and 1990s. Likewise, the post-development emphasis on civil society was perfectly congruent with the World Bank turn in the 1990s towards civil society engagement and empowerment. The international NGO's—the international civil society counterpart to the global financial institutions—were enthusiastic propagandists for a domesticated, official civil society. Post colonialism, in brief, was less inclined to deconstruct this particular variant of its own politics in practice.

In terms of the politics of postcolonialism, there are two main variants we can explore: a reformist co-option by the development mainstream and a revolutionary option around Franz Fanon's work and practice. Already in the 1980s the dominant neoliberal development paradigm had been questioned from within as it were. What some have called a neopopulist development paradigm (see Blaikie 2000) began to emerge that promoted a 'new agenda'. Bottom-up development was promoted, small-scale production prioritised and popular participation was promoted. Indigenous technical knowledge was to be more appreciated, community-based research was to be a priority and grassroots empowerment was to be the main objective. It is easy to see how the post-development agenda dovetailed with this new mainstream agenda into which it fed, albeit shorn of its literary origins.

Postcolonialism has drawn attention to the unreflexive nature of development theory. In its post-development variant, it associated this theory almost exclusively with US President Truman's post-war international development strategy to replace European colonialism, in both cases the theoretical discourse has found a niche in the academy but have not had a big influence on development policy. In fact, they do not present an alternative to mainstream development strategy as Marxism at least seeks to do. Their emphasis on 'race', gender, territoriality, the local and culture are all themes the mainstream—which is much more porous that they assume—can absorb. What seems to emerge from these critical approaches to development, as Michael Watts argues 'is an often uncritical celebration of difference, an emphasis on local knowledge, and on writing and self-reflexivity' (Watts 1995, 54).

Franz Fanon appears as a major figure in the postcolonial canon as an articulator of 'difference'. Fanon was also, of course, a Marxist revolutionary in the anti-imperialist struggle who was sharply critical of the postcolonial regimes. Looking from Algeria to nominally independent Latin America, he wrote of 'the incapability of the national middle class to fulfil its historic role of bourgeoisie' (Fanon 1970, 122). He wrote eloquently about 'the pitfalls of national consciousness" and how "from nationalism we have passed to ultra-nationalism, to chauvinism, and finally to racism' (Fanon 1970, 125). Fanon was a critic of Eurocentric and 'race-blind' approaches to revolution on the periphery. But he was equally critical of the nationalist leaders who 'believe it lies in their power to give the initial impulse to the nation, whereas in reality the chains forged by the colonial system still weight it down heavily' (Fanon 1970, 89). This also, like traditional Marxism, meant following an 'a-priori schedule' as Fanon put it.

It is Fanon's chapter 'Countering violence' in *The Wretched of the Earth* (Fanon 1970) first delivered to the historic 1958 'All Africa People's Conference' in Accra that sets him apart from all culturalist readings of postcolonialism. Fanon was opposed equally to the 'African socialism' of Leopold Senghor and the 'Marxist Leninist' socialism of Nkrumah the host. As against the uncompromising violence deployed in Algeria against the colonial regime, leaders such as Senghor 'had managed quietly to negotiate independence from France in the context of French fright at the situation in Algeria' as Young recounts (Young 2001, 280). Fanon captured a new mood of anti-colonial revolutionary militancy that would grow in the decades after his death in 1962. The remaining white settler colonies in Rhodesia, South Africa and Portuguese Africa would only fall through protracted deployment of mass resistance and revolutionary violence.

For Homi Bhabha in his influential Foreword to Fanon's *Black Skin White Masks* (Bhabha 1986) notes how 'Memories of Fanon tend to the mythical. He is either revered as the prophetic spirit of Third World Liberation or reviled as an exterminating angel, the inspiration to violence' (Bhabha 1986, viii). This binary opposition risks misinterpreting Fanon, and Bhabha rightly urges us to think of how 'it is not for the finitude of philosophical thinking nor for the finality of a political direction that we turn to Fanon', rather we need to see 'Fanon [as] the purveyor of the transgressive and transitional truth' (Bhabha 1986, ix). Fanon is replete with unresolved contradictions, for example between culture and class, and areas of deep ambivalence as in his discussions around race and sexuality. In terms of the theme of this chapter on post-development, Fanon reminds us how colonialism dislocated the psyche of the colonised. Fanon also reminds us that Marxism needs 'stretching' to comprehend the colonial difference and that for him Marxism was a tool for liberation and the furthest thing from a closed philosophical system.

References

Ahmad, Aijaz. 1997. Postcolonial Theory and the 'Post'—Condition. *Socialist Register*, 353–371.

Anderson, Perry. 1998. *The Origins of Postmodernity*. London: Verso.

Balibar, Étienne. 1970. (with Louis Althusser) *Reading Capital*. London: New Left Books.

Balibar, Étienne. 1991. *Race, Nation and Class*. London: Verso.

Bhabha, Homi. 1986. *'Foreword': Remembering Fanon in Fanon, Franz, Black Skin, White Masks*. London: Pluto Press.
Blaikie, Peter. 2000. Development; Post Anti and Populist; A Critical Review 2. *Environment and Planning A* 32 (6): 1033–1050.
Booth, David. 1985. Marxism and Development Sociology: Interpreting the Impasse. *World Development 13* (7).
Brennan, Timothy. 2014. Subaltern Stakes. *New Left Review* 89 (September–October): 17–87.
Chakrabarty, Dipesh. 2007. *Provincializing Europe: Postcolonial Thought and Historical Difference*. Princeton: Princeton University Press.
Chaturvedi, Vinayak, ed. 2000. *Mapping Subaltern Studies and the Postcolonial*. London: Verso.
Chibber, Vivek. 2013a. *Postcolonial Theory and the Spectre of Capital*. London: Verso.
Chibber, Vivek, 2013b. Interview with Vivek Chibber: How Does the Subaltern Speak? *Jacobin* (10) (April).
Coronel, Fernando. 2008. Elephasity in the Americas? Latin American Post-colonial Studies and Global Decolonization. In *Coloniality at Large. Latin America and the Postcolonial Debate*, ed. Mabel Moraña, Enrique Dussel, and Carlos Jauregui. Durham: Duke University Press.
Escobar, Arturo. 1995. *Encountering Development: The Making and Unmaking of the Third World*. Princeton: Princeton University Press.
Esteva, Gustavo. 1987. Regenerating People's Spaces. *Alternatives* 12 (2): 125–152.
Fanon, Franz. 1970. *The Wretched of the Earth*. Harmondsworth: Penguin.
Foucault, Michel. 2000. Truth and Power. In *Essential Works of Foucault 1954–1984*, ed. Paul Rabinow. New York: The New Press.
Grosfoguel, Ramon. 2008. Dependency Theory in Latin America. In Moraña et al., *Coloniality at Large*.
Huntingdon, Samuel. 2002. *The Clash of Civilizations and the Remaking of World Order*. London: Simon and Schuster.
Jameson, Frederic. 1991. *Postmodernism, or the Cultural Logic of Late Capitalism*. Durham: Duke University Press.
Kaiwar, Vasant. 2014. *The Postcolonial Orient: The Politics of Difference and the Project of Provincializing Europe*. Leiden: Brill.
Kapoor, Ilan. 2008. *The Postcolonial Politics of Development*. London: Routledge.
Kipling, Rudyard. 2012. *The White Man's Burden and Other Poems*. New York: Barnes and Noble.
Lazarus, Neil, and Rashmi Varma. 2008. Marxism and Postcolonial Studies. In *Critical Companion to Contemporary Marxism*, ed. Jacques Bidet and Stathis Kouvelakis. Chicago: Haymarket.
Lefebvre, Henri. 1991. *The Production of Space*. Oxford: Basil Blackwell.

Linder, Kolja. 2010. Marx's Eurocentrism. Postcolonial Studies and Marx Scholarship. *Radical Philosophy*, 27–41.

Lyotard, Jean-François. 1984. *The Postmodern Condition: A Report on Knowledge*. Manchester: Manchester University Press.

Moraña Mabel, Dussel Enrique, and Jáuregui, Carlos A. (eds). (2008). *Coloniality at large: Latin America and the postcolonial debate*. Durham: Duke University Press.

Quijano, Aníbal. 2007. Coloniality and Modernity/Rationality. *Cultural Studies* 21 (2–3) (March–May): 168–178.

Quijano, Aníbal. 2008. Coloniality of Power, Eurocentrism and Social Classification. In Moraña et al., *Coloniality at Large*.

Rahnema, Majid. 1997. Towards Post Development: Searching for Signposts, a New Language and New Paradigms. In *The Post-Development Reader*, ed. M. Rahnema. London: Zed Books.

Rosengarten, Frank. 2015. *The Revolutionary Marxism of Antoni Gramsci*. New York: Haymarket.

Said, Edward. 1978. *Orientalism*. Harmondsworth: Penguin.

Said, Edward. 1994. *Culture and Imperialism*. New York: Vintage.

Sardar, Zia. 1996. Beyond Development: An Islamic Perspective. *European Journal of Development Research* 2: 36–55.

Sum, Ngai-Ling, and Bob Jessop. 2015. *Towards a Cultural Political Economy. Putting culture in its Place in Political Economy*. Cheltenham: Edward Elgar.

Warren, Rosie, ed. 2016. *The Debate on Postcolonial Theory and the Spectre of Capital*. London: Verso.

Watts, Michael. 1995. A New Deal in Emotions: Theory and Practice and the Crisis in Development. In *Power of Development*, ed. Jonathan Crush. London: Routledge.

Williams, Raymond. 1981. *Culture*. Glasgow: Collins.

Young, Robert. 2001. *Postcolonialism. An Historical Introduction*. Oxford: Blackwell.

Žižek, Slavoj. 1997. Multiculturalism, or, the Cultural logic of Multinational Capitalism. *New Left Review* I (225) (September–October).

CHAPTER 9

Indigenous Development

At the start of the twentieth century a new, alternative, development theory emerged in Latin America some thirty years after the dependency approach. It was focused on an indigenous development model known variously as *Buen Vivir* (loosely translated as living well), *Sumak Kawsay* (in Kichwa) or *Suma Qumaña* (in Aymara). There is a wide range of post-development discourses articulated under the general title that we will explore critically in the section below *Buen Vivir*. They offer something as radical as post-development but more grounded in the history of the global South pre-colonialism. While this theory was created outside (even in opposition to) the Marxist paradigm there is also a *Marxist Indigenism* we need to explore in terms of its relevance for current Marxism and development debates. We present here the political writings and practice of José Carlos Mariátegui (1889–1930) who was in many ways a Latin American Gramsci, in the sense that he promoted an original development of Marxism for a situation that was different from the capitalism of Marx's day. While Gramsci grappled with a renewed Marxism and socialist politics in the context of a developed economy parliamentary democracy, Mariátegui was seeking to make Marxism relevant to a society characterised by underdevelopment, the need to forge a nation and to build on the pre-capitalist communism of the Inca society.

Finally, we examine the potential impact of *Buen Vivir* and Mariátegui's legacy for a renewed Marxist development theory. The

R. Munck, *Rethinking Development*, Marx, Engels, and Marxisms,
https://doi.org/10.1007/978-3-030-73811-2_9

section below, *Back to the Future* posits the possibility that pre-capitalist societies can offer lessons for the transition to socialism today, much as Karl Marx considered in this late re-evaluation of the socialist potential of the Russian commune. We consider whether this approach is simply utopian or whether another development is actually possible, based on the persistence of non-capitalist relations of production today. Is the solidary economy, for example, a form of prefigurative socialism or, simply, a place of refuge in a world dominated in all aspects by the market?

Buen Vivir

Coinciding with the rise of left-of-centre governments in Latin America after 2000, a new development discourse emerged from within the indigenous and environmental social movements. There are at least three ways we can approach Buen Vivir: as an indigenous political philosophy opposed to the Western development paradigm, as a Latin American contribution to the broader alter-globalisation of the commons or as an environmentalist project articulating a new relationship between nature and humanity. It broke decisively with the economism and methodological nationalism of the dependency approach and foregrounded culture. Essentially, it spoke to the extended reproduction of life rather than that of capital. It advocates a different constitutional model than that of individualistic capitalism in which community values and respect for nature take priority. As a development paradigm, it was enshrined in the new constitutions of Ecuador and Bolivia under the new progressive governments of the early twenty-first century, and it acted, for a period, as a powerful signifying discourse.

After 2010 and the end of the commodity boon the apparent synergy between social movements and progressive governments in the Andean region around the concept of *Buen Vivir* began to turn into conflict. The government argued that large-scale extractive economic activities—mega mining in particular—would provide more employment and boost social spending. The environmental rights groups protested that this breached the constitution and did not benefit the poor and marginalised. Alberto Acosta resigned as the Minster for Mines and committed fully to *Buen Vivir* as against the government's vision of a 'Twenty-First Century Socialism'. In Bolivia also, Evo Morales continued to preach the virtues of *Buen Vivir* at an international level but at home joined the critics who were beginning to dub *Buen Vivir* an 'Andean cosmovision for the salon' that incorporated a 'pose of ancestral authenticity' (Stefanoni 2012, 10). *Buen Vivir* as window dressing met *Buen Vivir* as roadmap to a sustainable development.

We can thus pose Buen Vivir as an empty signifier that can be given different meanings depending on which social force is articulating it. There are points in common in terms of development or alter-development discourse. Buen Vivir represents a radical rethinking of Western ontology and epistemology replacing a binary view of the world with a relational one (Altman 2020, 89). Essentially, it refers to humans and nature living in harmony based on a reading of Andean pre-conquest society and not, necessarily, current indigenous community practices. It sees the relatively recent 100 years old transition to socialism being set in the context of a longer term transition from colonialism going back to the fifteenth century. Buen Vivir seeks to articulate an alternative to current development discourses (including Marxism) and promotes ethics of development that subordinates economic objectives to ecological criteria including food sovereignty, control of natural resources and water as a human right.

One of the early proponents of Buen Vivir who was affiliated to the indigenous movement in Ecuador was Alberto Acosta who, went on to become Chair of the Constitutional Assembly in 2008 albeit briefly. An orthodox economist by training, Acosta joined Pachakuti the political party formed by the indigenous movement. For Acosta 'it is clear that *Buen Vivir* does not offer a fully elaborated or definitive concept, nor does it emerge from academic thinking, nor partisan ideas' (Acosta 2018, 101). In fact, the genealogy of the current concept of Buen Vivir shows that while it did emerge from within the indigenous movement it was a process 'facilitated' by a Danish and an Italian NGO. While Buen Vivir does reflect, indirectly, elements of traditional Inca cosmovision it is hardly 'pure' and we need to be sceptical of statements such as 'Buen Vivir arises from an Andean-Amazonian millennial womb' (Acosta 2018, 102). Like all discourses, it is, in fact, a hybrid and does not spring unmediated from Pacha Mama (Mother Earth).

Alberto Acosta was also, of course, a political actor in Ecuador's left-of-centre process. Buen Vivir served as his political banner. It is a political position just like that of the Marxist Álvaro García Linera in Bolivia who articulated a Buen Vivir philosophy but as part of what he saw as long-term development of Amazonian capitalism before socialism could be on the agenda. As an economist, Acosta is well aware that *Buen Vivir* can only be a utopian horizon. It is not immediately operationalisable. We see here a different, less philosophical, interpretation of Buen Vivir emerging when Acosta calls in 'the foundation for another economy' (Acosta 2018, 108). Indigenous communities in the Andes have indeed been able to maintain a degree of economic organisation through practices of reciprocity and solidarity, community-level action and self-management. They have thus prefigured, to some extent, an alternative development model not based on capitalist relations of production and distribution.

Another key figure in the creation and international dissemination of Buen Vivir was Uruguayan 'deep ecologist' Eduardo Gudynas who is a biologist by training. His work on Buen Vivir, or the Bueno Vivires as he puts it, is set directly in the context of the 'extractivism' practised by the Andean progressive government in the 2000s. He is explicitly not Marxist and is a fierce critic of what he sees as the productivist biases of the socialist movements. Gudynas believes that those movements have created a '"compensatory state" that accepts capitalist development strategies, balancing concessions and limits on capital, tolerating social and environmental impacts, but offering compensation in exchange' (Gudynas 2018, 73). A post extractivist transition requires a radical challenge to the current development model with Buen Vivir as its horizon along with, according to Gudynas 'very pragmatic proposals of changes to move in that direction, for example in taxation, environmental assessment, a territorial ordering and citizen participation' (Gudynas 2018, 75).

What we see emerging is quite a pragmatic Green politics alongside the rather utopian vision of Buen Vivir. Marxism had long since made its adjustment to environmentalism and it would be wrong to counterpoise the two discourses. Where Marxism would have difficulty would be in the reformist implicit when utopian visions come down to earth. There is also an issue with the way in which Buen Vivir advocates orient towards power and their understanding of its mechanisms. It is not simply a matter of offering a vison of the Good Life that brings together all our favourite causes to effect change. Social movements for change always orient towards the state to effect this change and, of course, engage with political parties. Gudynas, along with Acosta, is affiliated to the Rosa Luxemburg Stiftung (https://www.rosalux.de/) a Rosa Luxemburg-oriented foundation and, in practice, they seek change through the interventions of the international development NGOs.

There were many criticisms articulated around the use of Buen Vivir as a counter to Marxist-influenced development politics. Some Marxists in the region referred disparagingly to *Pachamamismo* (Borón 2010) seen as purely mystical talk that ignored the very real development needs of the population. Alvaro García Linera, the Marxist activist, then Vice President of Bolivia under Evo Morales, referred to the 'creative tensions' in the revolution in regards to the 'communitarian socialism' of Buen Vivir and argued that it needed to 'use science, technology and industry to generate wealth, otherwise how could we build roads, set up clinics and schools, produce the food to satisfy the basic and growing needs of society' (García Linera 2012, 24). Here we see encapsulated the divide between a productivist Marxism and alternative environmental and communitarian politics. It became polarised, of course, around the issue of extractivism (the economic boom of the early 2000s was based on oil, gas and mineral extraction) around which both sides dug into their trenches.

There is an alternative, perhaps, in the *Sumak Kawsay* version of Buen Vivir that retains its roots within the indigenous social movements. It is more place-based, less transnational, it confronts both the market economy and the state. There is a will to build a real axis of self-determination around Sumak Kawsay and it has a real social base. As Philip Altman writes 'This turns Sumak Kawsay into an element of political struggle. As the state does not fulfil its responsibilities to the indigenous peoples, Sumak Kawsay establishes rules for an autonomous life without the state' (Altman 2020, 91). This is a far more radical programme of action than the Buen Vivir articulated by the international think tanks seeking new covers for their sustainable development policies. Within the indigenous movement there are of course debates between the more indigenist and the more socialist currents, for example, on the extent to which they should forge an alliance with the organised labour movement.

Buen Vivir is, undoubtedly, a powerful non-Marxist critique of mainstream development theory, particularly in its extractivist mode. There is also, however, a form of epistemic extractivism at play in the way it was taken beyond its indigenous roots and translated into a broad container concept that embraced ecology, feminism, degrowth and the commons. In its new incarnation within the German left of-centre think tanks (see Lang and Dunia 2013) it takes on a life of its own. Its origins in Andean indigenous life and struggles are lost as it becomes part of a generic counter—discourse in academic and NGO circles. Another way to look at Buen Vivir is as a living discourse under permanent construction. It can be seen as an ideal to be achieved, even as a utopia like that of the early socialists until they were displaced by Marx's more 'scientific' approach to the building of socialism. To follow through on this thread, we need to consider the 'indigenous Marxism' of José Carlos Mariátegui (see next section) that is making a revival today in Latin America.

We need to ask, finally, whether the Buen Vivir(es) can overcome the crisis of development theory and whether they can replace the Marxist paradigms. On both questions my conclusion will be in the negative but that does not mean, in my view, that the Buenos Vivires (plural) cannot play a useful and radical role in Marxism's ongoing engagement with the development problematic. As we have seen, Buen Vivir (and its associated paradigms) is very much a discourse in permanent construction and one that is continuously being resignified: it is an 'empty signifier' that takes on meaning depending within which development discourse it is integrated with or articulated with. This open meaning of Buen Vivir is both a strength and a weakness and its outcome depends on how the discursive struggle proceeds. My own sense, at least in relation to Latin America, is that Buen Vivir is a vital terrain for both Marxism and development theory.

Behind the Buen Vivir paradigm(s) lurks the shadow of post-development (see Chapter 7) that exposed the colonial roots of the development enterprise. Buen Vivir has articulated most clearly the values of reciprocity, solidarity and relationality (we are all related to each other, the natural environment and the spiritual world, and these relationships bring about interdependencies). It can lead both to an alternative development strategy and/or an alternative to development that would be a quite different thing. In practice, like feminism beforehand, it is a discourse that can be absorbed by national governments and international development agencies like the World Bank. The mainstream has considerable ability to absorb critique. Unai Villalba (2013) has aptly referred to the 'adaptation and hybridisation' of the Buen Vivir paradigm, not least in the case of the Andean countries where it became a part of the national constitutions in name only. From this perspective we can see how Buen Vivir can become an integral element of the standard development discourse much as human development, gender and development, sustainable development and 'bottom up' development have in the past.

Buen Vivir needs to be itself deconstructed before we can move towards a more nuanced ('dialectical') understanding of its significance. Overall, it does articulate an Andean indigenous ontology that is opposed to the European ontology of modernity. It stresses the reproduction of life as against the reproduction of capital accumulation. Yet there are major differences between the various strands of Buen Vivir: the indigenous one, that affiliated with an ecological Marxism and, finally that which falls into the post-development camp. Certainly, there is no 'pure' indigenous Buen Vivir, it is very much a constructed tradition. When it springs from a Marxist milieu it tends to morph into a different discourse and political tradition. When Buen Vivir relates to other 'post development' themes, such as the critique of the extractivist development model and joins the drive for food sovereignty, for example, then it can become part of a new chain of meanings and thus become particularly effective.

Marxist Indigenism

Latin America's first Marxist theorist, José Carlos Mariátegui (1894–1930) was the originator of what became known as dependency theory, and of the turn towards the Amerindian people as the basis on which to build both the nation and socialism. Formed in the Marxism of Gramsci (and others) in Italy he then grounded his Marxism in the Peru of the 1920s, still dominated by semi-feudal land structures and oligarchic politics. Mariátegui represents an original engagement with both Marxism and development theory.

Mariátegui's thought was against all forms of dogmatism. He was fervently opposed to the mechanical and evolutionist Marxism of the Second (social democratic) International. His Marxism was an 'open' Marxism in that it rejected historical inevitabilism (and its denial of agency) and in that he was also open to other critical philosophical or theoretical systems of thought. His was not a bookish Marxism, he was no Marxologist. Its basic outline was learnt in Italy, but it only became a praxis when it entered an aleatory relation with Peruvian reality. His Marxism was opposed to all forms of determinism, economism and the typical blind faith in progress characteristic of dogmatic Marxists. Mariátegui preached instead the virtues of voluntarism and understood the 'advantages of backwardness' in the Latin American context where pre-colonial themes could act as harbingers of a socialist future.

He was forced to leave Peru in 1919 for a period of exile in Europe though his exit was an arranged one as it were. He was to spend time in Germany where he began to learn German and became familiar with the work of Oswald Spengler, *The Decline of the West* (Spengler 1990) that had just been published. This was to have considerable influence in

Latin American cultural circles throughout the 1920s; in its own way it 'provincialised' Europe, placing it in the context of the rise and decline of other civilisations. The First World War was to mark the end of a certain vision of Europe in Latin America. He also engaged with the contemporary psychoanalytical movement in Vienna and was most enthusiastic about the council movement in Hungary. His was a vanguardist form of thinking, the new, the iconoclastic and the modern appealed greatly to him.

It was in Italy where Mariátegui ended up and where he would be shaped both philosophically and politically during his sojourn from 1919 to 1922. This was a revolutionary period in all regards. Here Mariátegui imbibed the idealist, anti-positivist and anti-evolutionist concepts of Benedetto Croce and Antonio Labriola who marked his distinctly idealist reception of Marxism. He also engaged passionately with the praxis of George Sorel, the driver of revolutionary syndicalism, creator of the notion of 'myth' and supposed champion of violence. Above all, Mariátegui engaged with the Antonio Gramsci of the *Ordine Nuovo* and the Turin factory occupations period. From *Ordine Nuovo* he took the model of a worker's periodical as an organiser. He participated in the XVII Congress of the Italian Socialist Party in 1921 when the breakaway Italian Communist Party was formed and may have met Gramsci there. Their thinking was to show some striking parallels though, of course, Gramsci's *Prison Notebooks* would appear long after Mariátegui died. His basic ideological coordinates were now formed.

When Mariátegui returned to Peru in 1923 it was a case of 'a theory in search of a subject' as Oscar Terán put it (Terán 1985, 79). His recently acquired Marxist theoretical frame was still quite orthodox and Eurocentric as he had not yet engaged closely with Peruvian reality to any great extent. He was basically operating within a workerist, syndicalist and classist paradigm. In the period 1923–1924, Mariátegui began to teach at the Universidad Popular Gonzalez Prada, an adult education worker's college. This resulted in a course on current affairs published as *History of the World Crisis* (Mariátegui 1980) as he renewed his journalistic calling at the request of Raúl Haya de la Torre who asked him to edit the journal *Claridad* (Clarity). He went on to become a member of Haya de la Torre's nationalist movement APRA (*American Popular Revolutionary Alliance*) when it was formed in 1924. This nationalist and anti-imperialist political movement was seen by the Third (Communist) International or Comintern, formed in 1919, as the Latin American equivalent of the Chinese Kuomintang. Meanwhile, there was a renewal of indigenous people's activation through a number of rebellions and Mariátegui was to make contact with some of their leaders.

A period of intense political activity followed from 1925 to 1928 during which Mariátegui crystallises his 'practical socialism' and embeds it in Peruvian reality. This period culminates with the publication of his main work the *7 Ensayos de Interpretación de la Realidad Peruana* (Mariátegui 1979) which appeared in 1928. The Peruvian reality and the indigenous problem now dominates Mariátegui's thought and practice even though he kept up his cultural analysis. His European period learnings are there in the background but central now is their engagement with the recalcitrant reality of Peru at that time. In 1926 Mariátegui launches *Amauta* (wise teacher) a journal dedicated to the confluence between political and cultural critique and, soon after *Labor* dedicated specifically to workers. He continues to be an active member of APRA until he splits with Haya de la Torre in 1928 when the latter turns a broad anti-imperialist front into a clearly petty bourgeois party. Both political and trade union contacts with the Comintern intensified, mainly through the latter's South American Secretariat based in Buenos Aires. In 1928 the Partido Socialista del Peru (Peruvian Socialist Party) was launched with Mariátegui as its first Secretary General.

When Mariátegui returned to Peru from Italy in 1923 a wave of indigenous uprisings had just subsided. In 1921 the population of Tocroyoc had called for the expulsion of the *hacendados* and the *mistis* (mestizos) but also for the restoration of Tawantinsuyu (the Inca Empire). These rebellions were part of a long cycle of indigenous resistance to colonialism that broke out sporadically. They often had a messianic or millenarian character. Mariátegui attended one of the *Congresos de La Raza* (Race Congresses) organised by indigenous leaders on his return. There he met with one of their leaders, Ezequiel Urviola, according to Flores Galindo 'a true new Indian (*nuevo indio*), a rebel, defender of his culture but capable of assimilating the best elements of the West' (Flores Galindo 1980, 45). Mariátegui now began a serious research programme based on official documents but also through the collection of oral testimony. A new phase in his thinking and action opened.

Mariátegui expressed his early thoughts on the 'indigenous question' in the collection of articles in *Peruanicemos al Perú* (Mariátegui 1981) the title of which expresses well his intention when returning to the country. Referring to the indigenous people's congress he had attended,

Mariátegui declares that 'the indigenous congresses do not yet represent a programme, but they do already represent a movement. They indicate that the Indians are beginning to acquire a collective consciousness of their situation... A people of four million, conscious of its numbers, never despairs on its fate: these same four million, while they are but an inorganic mass, a dispersed multitude, are incapable of decoding their historic path' (Mariátegui 1981, 46). From then on Mariátegui would work tirelessly with the indigenous movements to construct a new worker–indigenous peasant alliance that could forge a counter-hegemony while also constructing the Peruvian nation. The role of Inca culture and religion would play a key role in that process according to Mariátegui.

It is in the *7 Ensayos* that Mariátegui outlines his mature thinking on the indigenous question and sets it in the context of Marxist theory. Mariátegui discusses the specific nature of the Peruvian social formation through an approach that prefigures, to some extent, the dependency approach of the 1960s, especially its critique of dualism. For him 'all the theses around the indigenous question that ignore or seek to circumvent this socio-economic frame..are condemned to absolute discredit' (Mariátegui 1979, 56). The indigenous question is also a land question for Mariátegui and he castigates all the liberal, moral and humanistic readings in the *indigenista* discourse. What is most original perhaps in Mariátegui is his recovery of pre-conquest modes of reciprocity and mutuality in the indigenous communities which could prefigure the socialist future. Reclaiming these revolutionary traditions and translating them into the present conjuncture were key tasks for Mariátegui.

The final phase of Mariátegui's brilliant but fleeting political career runs from 1929 to his death in April 1930. On the one hand, Mariátegui helps consolidate the Peruvian labour movement with the formation of the *Confederación General de Trabajadores Peruanos* (General Confederation of Peruvian Workers) which, will also, against prevailing orthodoxy seek to organise the peasant leagues and the federations of indigenous communities. But, on the other hand, this period saw him move fully into a position of active (no longer just passive) opposition to the politics of the Comintern. Thus, while it mandated that the indigenous question was simply a class question this was at odds with Mariátegui's more complex and nuanced understanding. They also objected strongly to his refusal to create an orthodox communist (as against broader socialist) party subject to the centralised discipline of the Comintern and the vagaries of its political strategies and tactics. Even before his death, Mariátegui was moved aside and replaced by a functionary under direct orders of the Buenos Aires Secretariat. When he died he was accused of numerous political sins from populism to Europeanism, utopianism and Sorelianism, but the masses of Lima turned out in their thousands to follow his coffin through the streets. What are we to make today of this political ideology dubbed 'Mariáteguismo' (or Amautismo) that was castigated by the Comintern and APRA alike?

In 1929 Mariátegui, by then leader of the Peruvian Socialist Party, sent to a regional Comintern Congress held in Buenos Aires a document (co-written with Hugo Pesce) entitled '*The Problem of the Races in Latin America*'. The analysis contained in these theses was a codification of the *7 Ensayos* approach set in a more Marxist idiom, and with a broader continental sweep. It notes that "an indigenous revolutionary consciousness may take time to form; but once the Indians have made the socialist ideas theirs, they will serve it with a discipline, a tenacity and a strength, that few proletarians elsewhere could match' (Mariátegui 1978, 46). Furthermore, 'it is imperative to give the indigenous or black proletariat, be it agrarian or industrial a clear-cut class struggle character' (Mariátegui 1978, 46). These formulations fell foul of the plans of the Third International (represented by Italian-Argentine Vittorio Codovilla) for which the very term 'Peruvian reality' was anathema, focused as they were on the somewhat reductionist 'semi-colonial' category for the whole of Latin America, and whose current policy for indigenous peoples was to call for self-determination.

Mariátegui was part of an intellectual generation for whom indigenism was crucial but in very different ways. Inca communism was in many ways an empty signifier into which different classes or political currents could inscribe different meanings. There was a paternalist indigenism that preached the integration of the indigenous peoples through education, an official, rhetorical indigenism, a sentimental culturalist reading, and finally, a radical indigenism focused on the contesting of exploitation and oppression through self-emancipation (Mazzeo 2013, 245). Mariátegui came to his indigenism through Marxism and, as he put it, the Inca past was 'revindicated not by the traditionalists but by the revolutionaries' (Mariátegui 1978, 121). Today we see paternalist, official, sentimental and radical indigenisms taking up political positions that can be related to Mariátegui's thought.

Mariátegui obviously understood that the 1920s indigenous revolts could not return Peru to the days of the Inca empire. Likewise, Sumak

Kawsay and Suma Quamaña in the 2020s realise that there will be no simple return to the agrarian communism of the Inca era. But in both cases politics and not a utopia is at the core of the debates. When Mariátegui returned to Peru in 1923 he engaged closely with leaders of the revolts and with the *indigenista* intellectuals. He was conscious of the ongoing resistance of the indigenous communities, the *long durée* of social struggles going back to the era of the Conquest. In 1923 an indigenous congress was held in Lima that brought some of the concrete demands ensuing from these struggles into the open. These included: defence of the community, adequate schooling, abolition of free labour and freedom of assembly and religion, all within a strong anti-feudal frame (Flores Galindo 2010, 181). Today we can look at the programmes of the various Buenos Vivires and see how the various programmes for action and demands for indigenous autonomy are the concrete manifestations of the ongoing indigenous resistance to colonisation and exploitation.

Today of course, the indigenous question is central to the theory and practice of Andean socialism and to development theory. A link between Mariátegui and the current conjuncture is perhaps the work of Flores Galindo, notably *In Search of an Inca: Identity and Utopia in the Andes* (2010), strongly influenced by Mariátegui. The legendary Túpac Amaru and Mariátegui were, for Flores Galindo, indispensable guides for a radical transformation in the Andes and for the creation of alternative visions that looked to the future through the lens of the pre-colonial past. Against all forms of messianic leadership Flores Galindo channels Mariátegui to declare that 'To avoid dictatorship, revolutions cast workers as the true protagonists. It had to spring from the interior of the country and Marxism had to find expression in Quechua' (Flores Galindo 2010, 193). It is not the providential leader who will create a utopian future but only the creative energy and innovation of mass politics.

Mariátegui's 'Peruvian' Marxism centred the indigenous question and that is probably his main relevance to contemporary politics. In his engagement with the organic intellectuals of the indigenous movements he avoided all nativist readings of the revolts of the 1920s. But against the prevailing wisdom of the Comintern he understood that there was a cultural dimension to the 'indigenous question' that could not just be reduced to a 'class question'. The Indian was a peasant but also, undeniably, indigenous. Socialism in Peru (and in Latin America) would be indigenous or it would not be socialism. As Miguel Mazzeo puts it 'socialism, Andean utopia and myth intervene to denounce the existing order and announce a new order, emerging as dream and desire at the heart of historical conflictedness' (Mazzeo 2013, 206). In this way, Mariátegui is at one with contemporary moves towards prefigurative socialism based on communities and practices of reciprocity in the past.

The main focus of Mariátegui's critique of Marxism was the evolutionist, mechanical and scientistic version of the Second (Social Democratic) International. Sorel and his theory of the revolutionary 'myth' served to translate Marxism into a locally relevant paradigm. What Peru needed, for Mariátegui, was not a theory, but a 'myth' that would energise and channel the discontent of the masses. Marxism was not a doctrine for him but a set of ideas or tools that would be reinterpreted in the light of Peruvian reality. Against the fatalism of mechanical Marxism (the unfolding of the contradictions of capitalism as an objective process) Mariátegui emphasized the importance of will, agency and even messianic politics. In this, he was closest to Walter Benjamin who, according to Michael Löwy (also, not coincidentally a Mariátegui scholar) promoted a 'historical materialism sensitive to the magical dimension of the cultures of the past, to the "dark" moment of revolt, to the lightning flash that rends the heavens of revolutionary action' (Löwy 2008, 11).

Finally, Mariátegui was further away as could possibly be from traditional Marxist economism, he was a '*marxismo arielista*' (Kohan 2000), providing a cultural matrix for transformation. This Marxism opposed to Shakespeare's Caliban (capitalist imperialism) was based on Ariel's spirit of the air. In the pages of *Amauta* and his practice, Mariátegui sought to bring together artistic and political praxis. His engagement with the European cultural vanguards of the 1920s continued in Peru. Amauta was a project to accumulate cultural and political energies and, as Flores Galindo puts it 'it represented a magical movement of synthesis, which has maybe not been repeated since, at that level, in the whole of Latin America' (Flores Galindo 1980, 147). When cultural and political vanguards are at odds it is not possible to develop a Mariátegui inspired socialism or build a counter-hegemonic force to the dominant order of capitalism imperialism.

In conclusion, Mariátegui's 'open' Marxism was the opposite of the dogmatic and mechanical schema of historical evolution that prevailed in official circles. He was conscious of Marxism's Eurocentrism and understood the need to ground in the local reality of the periphery, as with Fanon, it had to be 'stretched'. His being grounded in national reality did not preclude him being a staunch internationalist, his drive to recover the Inca past did not deter him from a commitment to all things modern and futurist. He would have agreed with Gramsci's scathing critique of Bolshevik theoretician Nikolai Bukharin's manual of Marxist sociology that would reduce a living and critical way of thinking to the 'evolutionist positivism' of sociology (Gramsci 1970, 419). As with Georg Lukács, he viewed Marxism not as a fully formed system of thought but, rather as a *method* (Lukács 1971, 1) for critical analysis, something Mariátegui always focused on, even if it took him to thinkers like Sorel and others outside the Marxist orbit. That allowed him to carry out an original analysis of the indigenous question in Latin America and the foregrounding of the pre-existing communist forms that could inspire a struggle for communism in his era. That is the theme we will now seek to go deeper into in the next section.

Back to the Future

When we consider the way in which Marx dealt with the pre-capitalist Russian commune and Luxemburg engaged with non-capitalist societies beyond Europe, we are driven to the question of whether Buen Vivir represents a viable strategy, taking us 'back to the future'. We have seen how Mariátegui began to articulate such a perspective in the 1920s but this was a theme also taken up by Alberto Flores Galindo in the 1980s in his '*In search of the Inca Identity and utopia in the Andes*' (Flores Galindo 2010). He found in Mariátegui and in legendary Inca leader Tupac Amaru, precursors for a project of radical social transformation and alternative visions for the nation. Flores Galindo outlined, on the basis of extensive anthropological and literary research, what an Andean utopia might look like, based on a pre-Hispanic past characterised as an era of social justice, harmony and prosperity.

Flores Galindo did not set out to 'find an Inca' in the dim and distant past but, rather, sought a creative appropriation and recreation of the past to build socialism in the present. It was a very real utopia: 'Andean people [could] imagine a kingdom without hunger, without exploitation and where they ruled once again. It represented the end of disorder and darkness. Inca became an organising idea or principle' (Flores Galindo 2010, 27). Peasant revolts had continued from the postcolonial era, through the 1920s (when Mariátegui wrote) to the 1980s (when Flores Galindo was active). In a country with an indigenous peasant majority there could be no nation without them or, for that matter, no socialism. As Flores

Galindo writes (taking up a theme of Mariátegui's) 'To avoid dictatorship, revolution cast workers as the true protagonists. It had to spring from the interior of the country, and Marxism had to find expression in Quechua. Utopia expanded its horizons toward the future' (Flores Galindo 2010, 193).

Our recovery of potential indigenous development models does not mean that we can take indigenous identity as a given. The rise of new *indigenismo* in the 1990s coincided with the hegemony of neoliberalism in Latin America. Neoliberalism openly promoted the development of indigenous identity and a new modality of neoliberal citizenship. Whereas the old nationalist developmentalist statepromoted assimilation of the indigenous, neoliberalism promoted a more decentralised view where individual identity was supposedly valued. There was thus a kind of elective affinity between neoliberalism and the neo-*indigenismo* it promoted through multiculturalism and the rejection of assimilation. In practice neoliberal multiculturalism accepted, even valorised, the folkloric other while denouncing the bad other (the indigenous social movements) as fundamentalists. This confused ideological scenario is part of the explanation as to why there was not a greater confluence between *indigenismo* and Marxist socialism.

Nor was the emergence of *Buen Vivir* carried out in opposition to neoliberalism and the international financial institutions. Indeed, the World Bank came to embrace Buen Vivir much as it had a version of feminism in the 1980s. The dominant development discourse—Development III as we have called it—was well able to co-opt alternative discourses and incorporate them into the mainstream. As Hidalgo-Capitan and Cubillo-Guevara recount 'without a doubt the focus on good living (as a translation of Sumak Kawsay) was adopted by the Interamerican Development Bank beginning in 2004 when the Kochira anthropologist from the Amazon, Carlos Viteri was an officer of this international body' (Hidalgo-Capitan and Cubillo-Guevara 2017, 23). Its international systematisation was furthered by local and foreign anthropologists working in the Ecuadorian Amazon in the 1990s. As Hidalgo-Capitan and Cubillo-Guevara put it 'the genuine discourse of *Sumak Kawsay* from the Amazon was quickly assimilated by intellectuals in the Andean worlds' (Hidalgo-Capitan and Cubillo-Guevara 2017, 24) through their connections with the international NGOs. Thus, very modern networks helped (re) create this supposedly ancestral discourse.

The Marxist left also engaged with indigenous society and identity in different ways from the 1920s to the present in the Andean countries. The communist parties of the region engaged in particular with education issues, being joined by Catholic Church-affiliated groups in the 1960s. Neither the state nor the big landowners had any interest in literacy for the indigenous labourers. By the 1980s in some countries, it was the indigenous movement itself that was tasked with bilingual intercultural education. The period of neoliberal reforms that opened up in the 1980s accentuated the disadvantages of the indigenous communities and many entered into opposition. Decentralisation and the encouragement of civil society (as a counter to the state) actually facilitated this mobilisation. Many of the indigenous groups were motivated more by access to social and economic mobility more than cultural identity. It was in this context that Buen Vivir emerged as an alternative development strategy.

The demands of the indigenous organisations in the Andean countries were centred in the 1990s around issues of cultural recognition and in particular the demand for a plurinational constitution that was, indeed, achieved in Bolivia. However, the formal recognition of cultural identities was part of a broader set of issues around the distribution of resources (land, access to jobs, health and education) and full political participation. The left was divided on those issues and did not really pose a clear way forward unifying both dimensions. The new indigenous movements have, in practice, placed the state under interrogation. A key question was whether the nation state as currently constructed, and with its colonial origins, could properly represent all citizens. Multiculturalism from above has not provided the answers and there has been an increasing shift towards socio-economic and development projects.

In terms of alternatives to mainstream development theories how do the various indigenous development approaches fit in? My own view of Buen Vivir is that it is the most significant Latin American contribution to global development theory since the dependency theory of the 1960s. Dependency pointed towards a gap in Marxist theories of imperialism: they were almost totally viewed from the North and not from the global South. For all its various inconsistencies—a downplaying of class struggle for example—dependency was an epistemological breakthrough at the time. Buen Vivir is also a quite diverse-even contradictory—set of discourses. It is also, arguably, utopian insofar as it is hard to envisage it as a programme for government in the context of underdevelopment. Nevertheless, it breaks the northern grip on development theory and the dominant approach to ecology in the shape of a vague sustainable development strategy.

Where the Marxist version of indigenous development as developed originally by Mariátegui has serious prospects is in relation to the social movements that contest the dominant development paradigm in practice. An indigenous ecology that has already made serious inroads into the peasant movements could yet relate to the concerns of urban workers if suitably 'translated' this becoming a unifying and inspiring social force. Indigenous social movements have been strong enough to bring down governments but have often struggled to form durable hegemonic alliances let alone govern on their own. The indigenous political project has struggled to go beyond a condemnation of neoliberal politics. In recent years we have seen greater attempts to link with the urban labour movement in an alternative development project that goes beyond ethnicity with a concrete call for transitional social and economic demands.

Returning now to a broader perspective on the indigenous development model we thus need to consider how it might relate to the debate on 'another production'. Given the prevalence of the informal economy across the global South it was not surprising that alternative models of production would emerge such as the 'popular economy' and the 'solidarity economy'. Aníbal Quijano—who made the transition from dependency to a postcolonial frame—has been among those promoting these alternative production systems as a means to create a non-exploitative society (Quijano 2006). For Quijano the key issue here in terms of forging an alternative development strategy is that in these popular/solidarity economies 'working relationship and product and resource distribution are mainly organized around reciprocity and social life, around everyday social practices – in short, around the community' (Quijano 2006, 426).

Indigenous development theory is this part of a broader set of debates around the popular economy as an alternative or complement to the catalyst mode of production. We are back to the debate in classic Marxism as to whether capitalism needed to engage with the non-capitalism or would eventually supersede it everywhere and at every level. The evidence from the popular/solidarity/cooperative movements across the global South is that we need to be wary of both enthusiastic endorsements of their revolutionary, anti-capitalist potential and hasty negative dismissals of their potential alike. Forced labour based on extra-economic coercion and alternative relations of production based on reciprocity is increasing in importance, albeit still under the general sway of capital as a world system.

In recent years there has been a significant shift, particularly within post-structuralist Marxist feminist writings to consider the potential of non-capitalism in the transformation project. As Gibson-Graham put it 'In the hierarchical relation of capitalism to noncapitalism lies (entrapped) the possibility of theorizing economic difference, of supplanting the discourse of catalyst hegemony with a personality and heterogeneity of economic forms' (Gibson-Graham 1996, 11). The indigenous development theories we have examined in this chapter may help us further deconstruct the capitalism–non-capitalism dialectic. We can thus move beyond an essentialist reading of capitalism with a stable and coherent identity to explore the possibilities of alterity and the creation of a non-post capitalist order.

The indigenous development model deliberately places itself on the margins of the world economy picking where to engage, for example in migration practices that build the community economy. The management of the local ecosystem is based on principles of self-sufficiency, self-management and political autonomy. Gibson-Graham have broadened out this problematic to a general consideration of an alternative set of dynamic principles of development to include:

> choosing to meet local *needs* by delivering increased well-being directly… using *surplus* as a force for constituting and strengthening communities…. recognising *consumption* as a potentially viable route to development….creating, enlarging, reclaiming, representing, and sharing a *commons*. (Gibson-Graham 1996, 197)

When we consider the massive extension of market mechanism under globalisation in the next chapter we must constantly bear in mind the ways society protects itself from its untrammelled rule. The mechanisms of self-protection, so well articulated by Karl Polanyi from a semi-Marxist perspective, have a great role currently in the various ways in which accumulation by dispossession takes place. It is not a question of substituting the local for the national terrain or self-protection for the class struggle but of recognising that submerged socialist tradition of co-operativism reflected in current attempts to create a solidary economy within but opposed to capitalism. Only a dogmatic Marxism would simply reject these old/new modalities of creating working class strength, not least in a development context.

References

Acosta, Eduardo. 2018. Living Well from an Ecuadorian Perspective: Philosophies Without Philosophers Actions Without Theories. In *Reframing Latin American Development*, ed. Ronaldo Munck and Raúl Delgado Wise. London and New York: Routledge.

Altman, Philipp. 2020. The Commons as Colonisation-the Well-Intentioned Appropriation of Buen Vivir. *Bulletin of Latin American Research* 39 (1): 83–89.

Borón, Atilio. 2010. *Pachamamismo versus Extractivismo.* Quito: Luna de bolsillo.

Flores, Galindo. 1980. *La agonía de Mariátegui. La Polémica an la Komintern.* Lima: DESCO.

Flores, Galindo. 2010. *Search of an Inca. Identity and Utopia in the Andes.* Cambridge: Cambridge University Press.

García Linera, Alvaro. 2012. *Geoplolítica de la Amazonía: Poder hacendal – patrimonial of acumulación Capitalista.* La Paz: Vicepresidencia del Estado.

Gibson-Graham, J.K. 1996. *The End of Capitalism (As Wc Knew It): A Feminist Critique of Political Economy.* Oxford: Blackwell.

Gramsci, Antonio. 1970. Critical Notes on an Attempt as Popular Sociology. In *Selection from the Prison Notebooks.* London: Lawrence and Wishart.

Gudynas, Eduardo. 2018. Extractivism: Tendencies and Consequences. In *Reforming Latin American Development*, ed. Ronaldo Munck and Raúl Delgado Wise. London: Routledge.

Hidalgo-Capitán, Antonio Luis, and Ana Patricia Cubillo-Guevara. 2017. Deconstruction and Genealogy of Latin American Good Living (Buen Vivir). *International Development Policy* 9 [Journals, openedition.org/poldev/235].

Kohan, Nestor. 2000. Los caníbales de Mariátegui. In *De Ingenieros al Che: Ensayos Sobre el Marxismo.* Buenos Aires: Biblos.

Lang, Miriam, and Dunia Mokrani, eds. 2013. *Beyond Development. Alternative Visions from Latin America.* Quito: Fundación Rosa Luxemburgo.

Lowy, Michel. 2008. Communism and Religion: José Carlos Mariátegui's revolutionary Mysticism. *Latin American Perspectives* 35 (2): 71–79.

Lukács, Georg (1971). *History and class consciousness: Studies in marxist dialectics.* Cambridge: MIT Press

Mariátegui, José Carlos. 1978. *El problema de las Razas en América Latina.*

Mariátegui, José Carlos. 1979. *Suete Ensayos de la Realidad Pernana.* Lima: Amanta.

Mariátegui, José Carlos. 1980. *Historia de la Crises Mundial.* Lima: Amanta.

Mariátegui, José Carlos. 1981. *Peruanicemos el Peru*. Lima: Amanta.

Mazzeo, Miguel. 2013. *El socialism enraizado: José Carlos Mariátegui: vigencia de su concepto de 'socialismo práctico*. Mexico: Fondo de Cultura Económica.

Quijano, Aníbal. 2006. Alternative Production Systems. In *Another Production Is Possible: Beyond the Capitalist Canon*, ed. Bonaventura Sousa Santos. London: Verso.

Spengler, Oswald. 1990. *The Decline of the West*. Oxford: Oxford University Press.

Stefanoni, Pablo. 2012. ¿Y quién no querría "vivir bien"?: encrucijadas del proceso de cambio boliviano. *Crítica & Utopía* IV (7): 9–26.

Terán, Oscar. 1985. *Disculir Mariátegui Puebla: Editorial Universidad Autónoma de Puebla.*

Villalba, Unai. 2013. Buen Vivir vs Development: A paradigm shift in the Andes? *Third World Quarterly* 34 (8): 1427–1442.

CHAPTER 10

Globalisation and Development

With the collapse of the Soviet Union's development model and that of the national developmental states, the 1990s saw the emergence of neoliberal globalisation as a dominant development paradigm. Its advocates promised *A Flat World* where all economic differences would disappear as the magic of the market created a convergence of living standards. One Marxist reaction was to deny that globalisation was any different from imperialism, but others embraced this brave new world on the basis that it would hasten the ultimate demise of capitalism. We examine here both the promise of globalisation and its outcome from a critical cultural political economy perspective. Some radical critics of globalisation posited that those countries and regions that were left out of the vortex of globalisation would become *Black Holes*. We examine in this section the way in which globalisation has impacted the development in Sub-Saharan Africa and in Latin America. While the outcome was not the smooth world that was promised, it is different I would argue and more complex than classical imperialism in many ways.

Finally, we turn to *Development Futures* based on what we have learnt from the two sections above and from the 'rise of China'. Is Chinese development since the 1990s a simple illustration of Marx's theory of primitive capital accumulation? Can China (and India and Brazil) now finally 'develop' and 'catch up' with the originally industrialising countries? We stress the uneven and combined pattern of development as

R. Munck, *Rethinking Development*, Marx, Engels, and Marxisms, https://doi.org/10.1007/978-3-030-73811-2_10

outlined in the Marxist classics. We return to the contradictions of capitalist development. Finally, in an era where 'sustainable development' is becoming an ever more urgent concern, we reconsider the relevance of post-development and indigenous approaches to development.

A Flat World

The World Is Flat (Friedman 2007) won the inaugural Financial Times and Goldman Sacks Business Book of the Year Award in 2005. Friedman envisaged a Globalization 1.0 (1492–1800) based on imperial conquest and the search for resources, Globalization 2.0 (1800–2000) which shrank the world as companies globalised for markets and labour, are finally leading to Globalization 3.0 (2000 onwards) which shrinks the world further and levels the playing field as it were. The great 'flatteners', from this perspective, were the collapse of the Berlin Wall and the rise of the personal computer and workflow software. Open-source software was seen as the most disruptive force of all. More traditional capitalist methods such as outsourcing, offshoring and supply chinning were also enablers of this brave new world. Information technology and cheaper transport would shrink the world and the free spread of new technologies would level the world. Friedman, he tells us, owed this revelation to a visit to the 'Silicone Valley' of Bangalore in India.

Another, more academic, version of this thesis came from Financial Times lead economist Martin Wolf in his *Why Globalization Works* (Wolf 2004). Wolf acknowledged that IMF policies in the 1990s were to subservient to the United States and that the institutions of the global liberal market economy were far from perfect. Overall, however, the benefits of globalisation were too precious to be squandered: the poor globally could be lifted out of poverty and market reformers in China and India could change the world. But will in the aftermath of the Great Financial Crisis of 2007–2009 Wolf became far less optimistic. Globalisation could equally end up in collapse as the pre-World War I globalisation wave did between 1914 and 1945. Now Wolf was arguing that 'Globalisation has reached a plateau and, in some areas, is in reverse' (Wolf 2014, 5) not least with the United States turn towards protectionism. Global financial markets must also be regulated or stability of the global order would be jeopardised Wolf was now somewhat belatedly arguing.

What these authors from the neoliberal camp were responding to was the globalisation of capitalism we have called Development III insofar as it decisively supplanted Development II the modernisation theory advocated by the United States as it became the hegemonic power after European colonialism. In the post-development era the nation state was no longer the automatic envelope for development. With the rise of globalisation, the nation state was becoming too small to deal with global issues (e.g. migration and climate change) but at the same time too big to deal with the problems citizens faced on a daily basis. The 'globalisation project' as Mc Michael called it (McMichael 1996) represented a utopian vision of global liberalism that subordinated the old Second (socialist) World and Third (nationalist) World under the aegis of the transnational corporations and international corporations and international financial institutions. International integration would ensue albeit at the cost of national social disintegration.

Globalisation has, indeed, led to spatial barriers falling away, for example in the arenas of trade and communications. Time has also changed from being a reflection of natural processes to become instantaneous. Hence the term 'time–space compression' that David Harvey explains in terms of 'processes that so revolutionized the objective qualities of space and time that we are forced to later, sometimes in quite radical ways, how we represent the world to ourselves' (Harvey 1989, 240). Above all else, globalisation signifies a much greater interconnectedness of social fates across the globe. Held and Mc Grew who hewed a 'transformationalist' path between the globalisation true believers and the sceptics, argued that 'Globalization weaves together, in highly complex and abstract systems, the fates of households, communities and peoples in distant regions of the globe' (Held and McGrew 2003, 129). The transformative impact of globalisation on the existing capitalist mode of production reached all domains and unleashed a series of inter-linked transformative processes.

The rise of supra-territorial processes—e.g. global financial markets and the Internet-spell the end of methodological nationalism. Economic internationalisation is not new, but compared to the 1860–1914 period the post-1990 wave of globalisation has created a qualitatively more integrated economic order. Globalisation has driven a shift in the centre of gravity of capitalism around commercial and industrial capital to a new centre based on 'intangibles' such as finance, information and communication capital. The multinational corporations of the post-war era that drove Development 2 have been superseded by truly transnational corporations. The 'new' economy is nos, however, universal as the starry-eyed globalisers argued: the uneven and combined nature of capitalist development persists and, arguably, even deepens in this new phase of capitalism.

Marxist reactions towards globalisation varied. There was the obvious argument that Marx and Engels had 'predicted' this development in the Communist Manifesto: 'All fixed, fast-frozen relations....swept away... all that is solid melts away, the need for a constantly expanding market for its products chases the bourgeoisie over the whole surface of the globe' (Marx and Engels 1970, 70). Other Marxists were still in shock from the collapse of 'actually existing socialism' and the prospects for revolution in the West and became critical supporters of the globalisation revolution. Thus Charles Leadbeater, ex-member of the British Communist Party, in *Up the Down Escalator* berated what he called 'reactionary pessimists [who] bemoan technology and globalisation because they threaten to wreck tradition, dissolve ancient institutions and rob us of our identities' (Leadbeater 2002, 65). For the communist turned new ideas entrepreneur, society has improved in all aspects over the last 1000 years and we can expect that improvement to continue. Another reaction from traditional Marxists came from those who were determined to 'hold the line' as it were for traditional Marxist categories and thus argued that globalisation was simply 'globaloney' (Wood 2005). Capitalism had always tended towards internationalisation, technological advance was also an integral part of capitalism so that introducing the term globalisation had the effect of disgóuising these tendencies and pretending it was something totally new.

There was a strong Marxist argument that globalisation was simply, in fact, imperialism. Thus, Atilio Born launched a fierce critique of Hardt and Negri's iconoclastic *Empire* (Hardt and Negri 2000) as a libertarian pessimist product of the defeat of the socialist left in the 1980s and 1990s. For Borón, while the 'phenomenology' of imperialism may have changed in recent decades, 'the fundamental parameters of imperialism' as delineated by other classic Marxist writers (see Chapter 5) remain correct (Borón 2012). We have already seen to what extent Lenin's theory of imperialism was politically overdetermined by the First World War and how it was limited analytically. Going further than that we need to consider Jan Nederveen Pieterse's verdict that while the empire is 'primarily of a political nature, state-centred and territorial', globalisation in the late twentieth century 'is intrinsically multidimensional, involves multiple actors and is, in significant respects decentred and de-territorial, involving multiple and diverse jurisdictions' (Nederveen Pieterse 2001, 39). From the clear coloniser/colonised division we move into a more complex and decentred set of relations between social inclusion and exclusion mechanisms.

The main issue we need to address, here, though, is whether globalisation did indeed create a 'level playing field' as Friedman and many others or, whether, it simply increased poverty and inequality as its critics assumed. The promise of reducing or even eradicating poverty worldwide was an abiding promise of Development II and now it would be realised by the dynamic alongside globalisation according to Development III. For the World bank and others, it was a simple axiom that greater integration into the world economy would reduce poverty. Parts of China, parts of India and even Vietnam were cited as evidence for Dollar and Kray writing in 2002 '*the best evidence available* shows.....the current wave of globalization... has actually promoted economic inequality and reduced poverty' (Dollar and Kraay 2002, 123). The number of people living on the nominal figure used at the time of 1US$ per day as a measure of poverty had, indeed, declined but that did not mean too much.

The measurement protocols of the World Bank regarding poverty have changed over time and depending on how it is measured greatly affects the outcome. According to the Bank's 2015 data, 10% of the world's population lived on less than $2 per day (the new measure) compared to 36% in 1990 (World Bank 2020). Despite doubts on the data or measurement protocols, we can conclude that the economic growth associated with the accelerated spread of capitalist relations of production has reduced absolute poverty levels worldwide. However, the results are volatile and if we take the more realistic measure of 39 per day an increase in poverty is predicted. Furthermore, after the COVID-19 crisis, the Bank predicts a recrudescence of global poverty insofar as 'by 2030 up to two thirds of the global extreme poor may be living in fragile and conflict afflicted countries making it evident that without intensified action, the global poverty targets will not be met' (World Bank 2020).

The question of global inequality is hugely complex and there is still considerable debate, particularly around the data on China which depending on how it is interpreted can swing the conclusion either way. It is, of course, quite possible for poverty levels to reduce while inequality levels climb. According to the United Nations in 2020 report on inequality in a rapidly changing world two-thirds of the world population lives in countries where inequality is increasing. Only Latin America has bucked the trend and that is down to decisive international by left-of-centre governments since 2000. Overall, the share of income going to the richest 1% of the population increased dramatically between 1990 and 2015, while the bottom 40% of the population earned less than 25% of all income in all countries surveyed (United Nations 2020). While international inequality has declined in relative terms, the absolute gap between the average incomes of people living in high and low-income countries has doubled between 2000 and 2020 so, for example, the average income in North America, is now 16 times higher than that of people in Sub-Saharan Africa.

An interesting angle on the social/spatial implications of inequality is provided by Branko Milanovic. He compares inequality in the mid-nineteenth century when Marx and Engels were active to inequality today. In 1850 the Gini coefficient was around 53 Gini points composed almost equally of between country and within county inequities. As Milanovic explains this means that half of an individual's inequality level was explained by international uneven development (between countries), and half by income differences between workers and capitalists (Milanovic 2012, 127). Today, by contrast, on a global Gini coefficient of 65 points, 85% is due to differences in mean country incomes and only 15% by social class differences. This tells us that the 'colonial difference' is very real and also explains some of the difficulties which stand in the way of international working class solidarity.

There is no simple answer to the question of whether global capitalism has produced greater poverty and inequality of not. We often find that global trends between different countries and within countries show divergent paths. Overall, we cannot accept that there has been a great convergence in the level of development between countries or that the great divide between rich and poor countries has somehow become irrelevant. There has been a reduction in the levels of global absolute poverty, an indicator that the World Bank has focused on. But, there is also now a recognition by the World Bank and others that the current high levels of inequality both within and between countries is to the detriment of economic development but also political stability. There is also a general acceptance that the increase in within-country inequality is due mainly to the impact of economic deregulation, corporate tax cuts and the decline of trade union power and welfare provision.

Mainstream economics has always searched for the cause of economic growth with a view to develop universally valid and objective strategies for capitalist development. This Holy Grail has never been found despite the countless confident strategies articulated, the last one being the neoliberal revolution in economic thinking. Recently however there has been a recognition by economists associated with the World Bank that this quest has been a failure and that there is no agreed causation for development to be found in the mainstream policy circles. As Kenny and Williams put it 'the current search for the cause or causes of economic growth appears to be frequently informed by a commitment to producing objective, scientific, and universal knowledge of economic growth, and this is underpinned by the view that all economies are substantially similar in their components and processes that there is but one basic production function driving all economies at all times and in every time-frame' (Kenny and Williams 2001, 20). That is the theory and the public presentation of development data by the World Bank and most mainstream economists.

However, it is now becoming clear after 50 years of 'development' that the World Bank itself now recognises that this quest has been a failure, and that there is no agreed causation for development to be found in the mainstream policy circles. So now, as Kenny and Williams acknowledge 'while there are problems and inadequacies in the statistical techniques frequently used to assess these theories, the universal failure to produce robust, causally secure relations predicted by models might suggest a broader problem than statistical methodological weaknesses'...[In reality] the evidence appears to suggest that country growth experiences have been extremely heterogeneous, and heterogeneous in a way that is difficult to explain using any one model of economic growth' (Kenny and Williams 2001, 21). We cannot therefore assume that the process of economic growth is the same everywhere and at all times as the neoclassical but also critical economists portray things. The ahistoricism of the mainstream theories is seen as a major cause of the failure. In a damning indictment of the whole *raison d'etre* of the whole basis for the economics of development, the World Bank affiliated authors acknowledge that 'a review of the available evidence suggests that the current state of understanding about the causes of economic growth is fairly poor. Clearly there have been development "successes" just as there have been development "failures". What we are arguing is that we are in a weak position to explain why some countries have experienced economic growth and others not. This should, we think, induce us all to be a little more cautious in the certainty with which we hold to present models and modes of thinking' (Kenny and Williams 2001, 22). Nicely understated this study in fact undermines the whole edifice of development economics and leaves the door open for more historically grounded political economics including Marxism.

At a regional level we see a similar recognition that the hitherto accepted wisdom about development is simply wrong as can be seen in the testimony of Alicia Barcena, general secretary of ECLA (Economic Commission for Latin America) that undermines the long-term development strategy of that organisation, widely seen as progressive compared to the neoliberal strategy, and states bluntly that it has failed. Barcena now admits that Latin America 'has lost two trains, that of industrial policy and that of innovation, allowing decisions to be taken by the market. It is clear that this development model has run out of steam' (Bárcena 2020). The ECLA general secretary recognises that Latin America not only continues to show low growth rates but also is still the most unequal region in the world. The dominant extractivsit economic model concentrates wealth in a few hands and is the opposite of the much-vaunted need to be innovative. The market is not going to lead Latin America out of this morass and greater state intervention is clearly called for. Barcena admits that 'the levels of disenchantment and anger are mounting as people see a rent earning policy prevailing, widespread tax evasion and a culture of privilege that normalizes inequality and discrimination' and then the head of Latin America's strategic economic think tank concludes that 'the model is broken…people are fed up' (Bárcena 2020). This admission does not mean automatically that radical critics, for example of the extractivist development model, are correct, but it does open the door for more creative and open thinking around the future of democratic development.

Black Holes

Globalisation has clearly accentuated inter-country inequalities as the great vortex of growth since 1990 sucked many into its orbit but also cast others aside. For Manuel Castells it is not only poverty and inequality that is at stake with globalisation: 'There is also an exclusion of people and territory, which from the perspective of dominant interests in global, informational capitalism, shift to a position of structural irrelevance' that he calls "the *black holes* of informational capitalism' (Castells 1998, 162).

These are areas and social groups that are cut off both socially and culturally from the new global order. They may, of course, still be linked into the international circuits of capital through various branches of the criminal economy. There is a debate around whether we can, in fact, talk about surplus populations in this way, but it does lead Castells and others, to refer to a Fourth World to replace the Third World of the 1960s. This would be the underside of the much-vaunted new informational economy.

There is little doubt that much of Sub-Saharan Africa is asymmetrically integrated into the new global order. Most African countries are unable to compete on the global markets through manufacturing or advanced services. Tourism is largely in the hands of foreign operators as is the vital mineral extraction sector. Subsistence economies allow for the survival of the majority of the population, but not the extended reproduction of capital. There is thus a renewal of calls for the reconstruction of society on the basis of self-reliance outside the tentacles of globalisation. Whether delinking is possible in the era of globalisation is a moot point, it certainly was not in the 1970s when calls for delinking through the likes of Samir Amin (Amin 1990) were at their highest level. But is this picture of globalisation excluding sectors of the population and even whole countries actually correct and is delinking a viable alternative?

These structural Marxist perspectives of Castells and others on the exclusion of some countries and whole populations from a useful contribution to development, have been contested from a more post-structuralist optic as exemplified by James Ferguson. The 'black hole' analogy is sees by Ferguson as "a negative characterisation [that] risks ignoring the social, political and institutional specificity of Africa and reinventing Africa as a twenty-first century 'dark continent'" (Ferguson 2006, 29). Africa cannot be seen as a simple 'development failure' or defined by what it is not. In many ways, the African experience under globalisation highlights what globalisation is not. As Ferguson puts it 'the global, as seen from Africa, is not a seamless, shiny, round and all-encompassing totality (as the word seems to imply)' (Ferguson 2006, 48). We see, rather a large amount of connectivity in some domains and sharp breaks, inequalities and exclusion in others. Put simply, uneven development deepens with globalisation; we are not moving into a flat or smooth world.

Development III had as a major plank the 'rolling back' of the state to allow full play of market forces undisturbed by any controls. It was meant to usher in a moment of liberation as human enterprise and creativity was freed from the 'dead hand' of the state. In most of Africa this did not lead to less state interference and inefficiency but rather, as Ferguson puts it 'simply less order, less peace, and less security' (Ferguson 2006, 39). Selective integration into the new world order for resources is matched by disconnection in other domains. Globally networked enclose economies—like those of the nineteenth century—exist within territories characterised by marginalisation and subsistence. No amount of mobile phones in the hands of agriculturalists and petty commodity entrepreneurs can suture this gap between the promises of globalisation and the reality.

In Latin America, as the twenty-first century dawned, it seemed as though globalisation offered a new paradigm for social-economic development and political democratisation. Where once we spoke of 'dependency' now we accepted the natural state of 'interdependence'. Latin America's growing internationalisation since the 1980s—though the economic, social and cultural processes that became known as globalisation—seemed to signal a new cultural political economy for the region. A novel political language emerged around terms such as civil society, empowerment, capacity-building and active citizenship that sat uneasily with the previous language of the national poplar and anti-imperialism. Reactions from the progressive camp varied, with some taking a firm anti-globalisation perspective and a return to the previous nationalist discourse of dependency, others began to explore whether globalisation was more complex and left open some avenues for a new development politics.

For many authors globalisation was simply the latest manifestation of US imperialism and did not usher on a qualitatively different framework for development. It was not seen as a novel condition on a continent where powerful external forces had shaped the political economy from the days of the Conquest. For Atilio Borón globalisation had simply 'caused the new Latin American democracies to surrender important margins of national sovereignty and self-determination' (Borón 1998, 10). Part of Borón's argument parallels that of the globalisation sceptics (like Wood) in stating that its impact has been exaggerated. The main argument, however, is political and simply promotes the older ideologies of developmentalism and the role of the state in countering the deleterious effects of economic internationalisation under the aegis of neoliberalism. This amounts to a 'business as usual' recipe for the left and a refusal to pander, as they would see it, to the culturalist reading of globalisation as hybridity (see Chapter 8).

On the other hand, authors such as Antonio Negri (in this case writing with Cocco) postulated a radical rupture being caused by globalisation, Basically, 'the world market is no longer external and conflicts cut across it at all levels: between the centre and periphery, clearly of course but also within the centre and periphery' (Negri and Cocco 2016, 491). There can thus be no return to the national development paradigm and the temptation of isolationist or rhetorical anti-imperialist rhetoric. They turn to the social forces of the 'multitude' as the engine for social transformation, a project that resonated with the rise of the new social movements after 2000. They advocate a radical Foucaultian-style biopolitcs to confront the new power bloc to contest rationality which takes the administration of life and populations as its subject. In a way, we could argue that these authors see globalisation opening as many pathways to social transformation as it closes in its attack on the nation state and developmentalism.

A third position was articulated by F.H. Cardoso, one time progenitor of the dependency framework, then-President of Brazil and managing the country's integration into the new world order. For Cardoso, as dependency theorist and as state manager, globalisation was simply a game changer. Interestingly he argued that his own 'new dependency' analysis of the late 1970s was in retrospect, actually referring to globalisation *avant la lettre* as it were. This provides an element of continuity in terms of internationalisation preceding full globalisation after the end of the cold war and collapse of actually existing socialism in 1990. Cardoso was cognisant of the way Development III closed off much of the room for manoeuvre for developing nation states such as Brazil. He notes that 'the South is in double jeopardy – seemingly able neither to integrate itself, pursuing its own best interests, nor to avoid 'being integrated" as servants of the rich countries' (Cardoso 1993, 156). However, he continued to stress a less necessitarian reading of the structural historical framework of dependency/globalisation which did not preclude national (and regional) decision-making power.

In conclusion, neither Sub-Saharan Africa nor Latin America can be described as 'black holes' in terms of development. They have been incorporated through globalisation into the Development III project. Globalisation was always going to be uneven and selective in its impact. As Mc Michael puts it 'although the globalization project replaces the development project [my Development II), "development" has not lost its currency' (Mc Michael 1996, 150). To its overarching objective of 'liberalisation'—that is giving unlimited access for the market to all human activities—it was added a social wing as it were through the support for the plethora of non-governmental organisations (NGOs) that seek to fill the vacuum left by the developmental state long since anguished. The globalisation project was powerful while it could avoid its contradictions. From 1990 to 2007 we can talk about the 'easy' phase of globalisation, since the Great Financial Crisis the many contradictions have come home to roost.

While the unregulated nature of financial capital is perhaps the major contradiction of globalisation its tendency to generate marginalisation is also a long-term problem. The legitimacy of the nation state suffers when large swathes of the country form part of transnational criminal enterprise. The erosion of state infrastructure and all forms of social safety nets deepens that sense of illegitimacy. Development III's tendency towards marginalisation also deepens the informalisation of labour and life itself. Precarious work and informal labour relations create instability and make it hard to achieve stable bourgeois rule. The whole notion of citizenship becomes problematic in this context. Society does react back against untrammelled market dominance and its corrosive social effects, but this can be inchoate and will as likely take reactionary forms as pose progressive options.

Development Futures

The mythology of global development portrays it as a consensual affair and minimises the level of violence that is at its core. It is thus appropriate to begin this final section with a reminder of the role of force. Thus, Marx and Engels were not just using a rhetorical turn when, in the Communist Manifesto, they referred to how 'The cheap price of commodities are the heavy artillery with which [the bourgeoisie] batters down all Chinese walls' (Marx and Engels 1970, 56). Marx went further when discussing the opium wars in China to show how 'brute force' might be necessary if its artillery of commodities failed: 'force is the midwife of every old society which is pregnant with a new one' (Marx 1976, 916). As Arrighi puts it in relation to these passages on the state and market, East and West, 'military force was indeed the key to the subjection of East Asia to the West. What is more, its use was a direct result of the incapability of British merchants to penetrate the Chinese market by legal means' (Arrighi 2008, 338).

In terms of global development today capitalism, in its globalised, financialised and informationalised mode, has huge resources at its disposal. Force is used continuously both overtly and covertly, in new colonial wars, economic sanctions and aggressive foreign policies. Rosa Luxemburg comes to mind (see Chapter 6) but we can also mention the neglected work of Friedrich Engels on the importance of warfare and the growth of the state development, in particular, after the death of Marx. Wolfgang Streck goes as far as to argue that 'Engels can thus be seen as opening up an additional line of historical-materialist research, in which, the means of destruction exist alongside the means of production, and state formation frames and overlaps with class formation' (Streeck 2020, 86). The 'means of destruction' have never been far from the frontline as globalisation imposed itself on the world as a new form of domination from 1990 onwards. And the state has not, of course, left the scene just because neoliberalism said it should.

Neither globalisation theory nor the various post-development theories have much to say about the role of the state and, specifically, the democratic development state of the twentieth century that managed to create an effective alliance with industrial capital. The rise of the East Asian Tigers in the 1970s from 'underdeveloped' to 'developed' in less than two generations is a testament to its effectiveness. We witnessed accelerated economic growth, productive synergies between agriculture and industry and later, high value-added services. A developmental state for the twenty-first century would need to look beyond an industrial elite and address a much broader cross-section of society. As Peter Evans puts it even though, as he admits, 'it will not be easy. Shared interests in capability expansion are broad and deep but articulating them is a very politically demanding task. 'Civil society' is a complicated beast…' (Evans 2010, 49). Nevertheless, without the engagement of civil society (and I do not mean just the NGOts) democratic development will not be possible.

Development in the twenty-first century will not be a reprise of development in the twentieth century, let alone the nineteenth century. Globalisation has effectively changed the parameters of the game and its possibilities (García Canclini 1999, 50). Globalisation did not deliver a 'level playing field' and it is not 'the tide that lifts all boats'. It has been uneven, producing unprecedented levels of growth and wealth while exacerbating inequalities, particularly between countries. However, a simple Manichean nationalist response will have little purchase in this contest and will certainly not deliver sustained growth and social inclusion. At best, regional strategies for development will be possible as in Europe but also in Latin America, Africa and, of course, a China-led coalition in East Asia.

It is the development of a market economy in China under the disciplines of a strong state that is probably the main event in international development since the 1980s. While China is the undoubted lead in this process it is worth noting that the global South's of world manufactured exports rose from 7% in 1975 to 23% in 1998. What is most noticeable is that the rise of a market economy in China was achieved under the aegis of a developmental state and not through the adoption of neoliberal policies. Also, following Arrighi, its success was due in large part the 'accumulation by dispossession' characteristic of primitive accumulation elsewhere: 'where the African peasantry has long been dispossessed of the means of production without a corresponding creation of the demand conditions for its absorption in wage employment- much of Chinese economic growth can be traced to the contribution that TVEs [Township and Village Enterprises] have made to the reinvestment and redistribution of industrial profits within local circuits' (Arrighi 2008, 364).

Taking a broader look at global development, we can note that U.S. hegemony after the Second World War failed to produce a global state and it has found itself on the defensive globally ever since its defeat in Vietnam in 1975. It was, however, able to produce a global market as the cold war and communist rule collapsed in 1990. Yet China was ranked No 2 in the world by the IMF in 2020 in terms of nominal Gross Domestic Product (GDP) and if measured in terms of Purchasing Power Party (PPP) that takes into account cost of living differences between countries it is now No1 globally. This is due to its particular model of market-based but state-led development with an overwhelming emphasis on human capital, that is people, rather than capital. The separation of producers from the means of production has been the result of this process, not its precondition as Marx had argued in his account of primitive accumulation. The international development debate needs to examine much more closely the Chinese experience that cannot just be described as capitalist development. Its impact across the global South is, of course, considerable and growing.

One lesson we learn from the dramatic development of China since the 1990s is about the nature of social struggles around development. The classic Marxist perspective was that the proletariat—waged workers without access to means of production were the privileged agents of historical change. Harvey may be going too far but he has a point when he says that 'struggles against accumulation by dispossession were considered irrelevant' (Harvey 2003, 171). Certainly, there is a tradition of 'metropolitan Marxism' that considered only the industrial workers of the global North to be a true proletarian vanguard on a worldwide scale. This was countered in the 1960s by Chinese inspired notions of 'proletarian nations' and the whole tradition of Third worldism which posited national liberation as the only path to socialism. Today we have moved beyond such futile counterpositions and with Harvey would accept that the anti-capitalist and anti-imperialist dynamics are conjoined and that 'if the two forms of struggle are organically linked within the historical geography of capitalism, then the left was not only disempowering itself but was also crippling its analytical and programmatic powers by totally ignoring a side of this duality' (Harvey 2003, 171).

What this means in terms of the practice of social movements and the political programmes of the left is that we need to see a dialectical relationship between anti-capitalist and anti-dispossession struggles. So, in China we see what Beverly Silver calls 'Polanyi-type waves of labour unrest from workers whose established ways of life and livelihood have been overturned' (Silver 2003, 167). The failure of Development 2 in the 1970s, the debt crisis and austerity policies, also fuelled a Polanyi-type societal reaction against the depreciation of the unregulated market. Yet across the world—and not least in China—more classic 'Marxist' responses have been seen as organised groups of workers establish collective organisations and struggle against exploitation (see Munck 2018). To argue for a conjoint Marx + Polanyi lenses is the same as to say that the struggles against exploitation and dispossession are two sides of the same coin.

In this chapter, we have reviewed the evidence as to whether globalisation has produced a 'flat world' where we would see a convergence between poor and rich countries. While we found that uneven development has continued, and indeed deepened, we recognise that globalisation is not just the current incarnation of nineteenth-century imperialism. Global development has changed the parameters of what is possible. National development paths have become more problematic and the effective developmental state of the twentieth century would need to be translated into one much more engaged with civil society and the social movements. All regions of the world have been sucked into the vortex of global development and we find little evidence of 'black holes' even if some integration notion global economy (e.g. criminal or extractive networks) are extremely prejudicial.

As to the future of development, it is clearly constrained by the emerging climate crisis. It is simply impossible to imagine even one-quarter of the populations of China, India and Brazil can attain the living standards of the wealthy countries. That does not mean that a 'soft' sustainable development that would continue with the present model is a credible answer. What we need to develop is a measure for national resources that is not determined solely by market criteria, such as carbon credits. From a Marxist perspective, we would seek mechanisms to subordinate all social activity to use value and not exchange value. As Jean-Marie Harribey puts it 'the international dimension for anticapitalist struggle finds a natural extension in the universal demand for a habitable planet for all living beings' (Harribey 2009, 207). In this task, Marxists can, of course, learn from the various versions of post-development theory, not least the indigenous development philosophy and practice.

Development, especially in its Development III (globalisation) guise. Is prone to utopian thinking: spatial barriers will tumble, poverty and inequality will evaporate and the new information technologies will take us into a post-capitalist future effortlessly. Manuel Castells (once an influential Marxist) wrote recently (with Kekka Himanen) that 'development, from our perspective, is the self-defined social process by which humans enhance their wellbeing and assert their dignity while creating the structural conditions for sustainability of the process of development itself' (Castells and Himanen 2014, 7). It is very little in this somewhat circular definition that situates development on the sphere of political economy or even hints at the division of the world into rich and poor. Instead, we have a discourse that posits a universal 'human development' strategy that takes the 'Silicone Valley Model' as the template that must be applied across the world with Finland now the promised land under Development III much as the United States was under Development II.

So, for example, we find Castells (with Fernando Calderón) arguing that Pinochet's military monetarism laid the basis for Chile to become, after 1990 'a relatively successful democratic model of economic development combined with enhanced human development in a fully democratic state based on freedom and a system of industrial relation' (Castells and Calderón 2014, 180). Chile's post-Pinochet elected governments (under the dictatorship's constitution) maintained the market-based export-oriented model of the dictatorship. This continued to generate huge inequalities and finally exploded in a mass uprising in 2019. Integration with the world economy is seen by Castells the same way as the economic mainstream, as unambiguously positive as his (and Calderón's) earlier commitment to a dependency perspective was set aside. The future—utopian or dystopian—is for Latin America (and the global South more generally) to integrate further into the capital circuits of the global economy by adapting to the new mode of capitalist development they identify as 'informationalism' that will put Latin America on a path to becoming the Finland of the South.

Our analysis in this chapter lends no support to such wishful thinking. That does not mean, however, that the Marxist perspective(s) on development represent a clear and self-sufficient lens to grasp the complexity and contradictions of development today. There is still a strong tension between those Marxists who stress the development of capitalism as a driver of human progress and those for whom 'underdevelopemnt'—practically a new mode of production—is the enduring characteristic of the Third World, global South or postcolonial world. There are Marxists who still stress the crucial role of industrialisation for development and those for whom services or the informal sector are key. There are those Marxist-influenced currents such as dependency, post-development and indigenous development that bring a non-Eurocentric perspective to bear. One way or another 'a certain spirit of Marxism' will remain at the core of our efforts to rethink development in the twenty-first century.

I would, for myself, wish to add in a utopian element or vision to a renewed critical Marxist theory and practice of development. The orthodox or, rather, institutional Marxist tradition was always hostile to what it called 'utopian socialism' seen as an ideal without the necessary pathways to achieve it drawn out in a plausible way. But there has always been a subterranean Marxist current with a strong utopian element from the time of Ernst Bloch and Walter Benjamin to the politics of the Zapatistas and Buen Vivir. A transformative Marxist interpretation of development arguably needs to build on these perspectives and incorporate a utopian element into its discourse. It also needs to build closer relations with the utopian vision of the early anti-colonial movements and the postcolonial theorising.

Marxism is not necessarily opposed to all utopian thinking, a simple materialist political economy as it were. As Karl Marx wrote 'the capitalist mode of production is in fact a transitional form which by its own organism must lead to a higher, to a cooperative mode of production, to socialism' (cited in Hudis 2012, 206). As Hudis comments on this passage, it is clear that 'for Marx it is the development of capitalism in and of itself, that creates the forces of liberation that will lead to the reconstruction of society' (Hudis 2012, 206). The struggle for 'development', and that includes the anti-development school of thought which still operates within its paradigm while critiquing it- brings to the fore a range of social, political and cultural forces that are seeking a better life beyond capitalism. Capitalist development—as Marx and the recent global financial crisis equally testify—carries within it basic contradictions that can only be resolved through a transition to another type of socio-economic order, whether we call it socialism or something else. This is a very grounded utopia to put it that way and one that will be necessary to develop concretely if the current impasse—of the old being dead but the new not yet born—is to be superseded.

Utopian thinking can, of course, be deeply idealist and a block on the politico-strategic work that needs to be undertaken to move into a new non-capitalist development order. To counter this tendency Jameson tells us that 'the desire called Utopia must be concrete and ongoing without being defeatist or incapacitating' (Jameson 2007, 233). Utopian thinking has helped us realise how false the dictum of neoliberal globalisation that *There is No Alternative* was. It is utopia, we might argue, that best 'expresses our relationship to a genuinely political future' (Jameson 2007, 232) compared to many of the current programmes of action that circulate. Development utopias like *Buen Vivir* take us beyond the limitations of the current failed development models and allow us to imagine an (other) development. We need to articulate this utopian break with the failed *status quo*, with the concrete practical and political challenges of the conjuncture in particular places and spaces.

References

Amin, Samir. 1990. *Delinking*. London: Zed Books.

Arrighi, Giovanni. 2008. *Adam Smith in Beijing. Lineages of the Twenty First Century*. London: Verso.

Bárcena, Alicia. 2020. América Latina ha perdido dos trenes: el de la política industrial y el de la innovación. *El País* (7 February). https://elpais.com/economia/2020/02/05/actualidad/1580921046_527634.html.

Borón, Atilio. 1998. Globalization: a Latin American Perspective. *Estudos Sociedade a Agricultra* (October): 164–180.

Borón, Atilio. 2012. *América Latina en la geopolítica del imperialismo*. Buenos Aires: Ediciones. Luxemburg.

Calderón, Fernando, and Manuel Castells. 2014. Development, Democracy and Social Change in Chile. In *Reconceptualizing Development in the Global Information Age*, ed. Manuel Castells and Pekka Himanen. Oxford: Oxford University Press.

Cardoso, Fernando Henrique. 1993. North South Relations in the Present Context: A New Dependency. In *The New Global Economy in the Information Age*, ed. Martin Carnoy et al. University Park, PA: Pennsylvania State University Press.

Castells, Manuel, and Pekka Himanen. 2014. Modes of Development in the Global Information Age: Constructing an Analytical Framework. In *Reconceptualizing Development in the Global Information Age*, ed. Manuel Castells and Pekka Himanen. Oxford: Oxford University Press.

Castells, Manuel. 1998. *The Information Age Volume III. End of Millennium*. Oxford: Blackwell.

Dollar, David, and Aart Kraay. 2002. Spreading the Wealth. *Foreign Affairs* (January/February): 120–133.

Evans, Peter. 2010. Constructing the 21st Century Development State: Potentialities and Pitfalls. In *Constructing a Democratic Developmental State in South Africa*, ed. Omano Edigheji. Cape Town: HSRC Press.

Ferguson, James. 2006. *Global Shadows. Africa in the Neoliberal World Order*. Durham and London: Duke University Press.

Friedman, Thomas. 2007. *The World Is Flat. A Brief History of the Twenty First Century*. New York: Farrar and Strauss.

García Canclini, Néstor. 1999. *La Globalización Imaginada*. Buenos Aires: Paidós.

Hardt, Michael, and Antonio Negri. 2000. *Empire*. Harvard: Harvard University Press.

Harribey, Jean-Marie. 2009. Ecological Marxism or Marxian Political Ecology? In *Critical Companion to Contemporary Marxism*, ed. Jacques Bidet and Stathis Kouvelakis. Chicago: Haymarket.

Harvey, David. 1989. *The Condition of Postmodernity*. Oxford: Blackwell.

Harvey, David. 2003. *The New Imperialism*. London: Verso.

Held, David, and Antony McGrew. 2003. The Great Globalization Debate: An Introduction. In *The Global Transformations Reader*, ed. David Held and Antony McGrew. London: Polity.

Hudis, Peter. 2012. *Marx's Concept of the Alternative to Capitalism*. Chicago: Haymarket Books.

Jameson, Fredric. 2007. *Archaeologies of the Future, the Desire Called Utopia and other Science Fictions*. London: Verso.

Kenny, Charles, and David Williams. 2001. "What Do We Know About Economic Growth" or, Why Don't We Know Very Much? *World Development* 29 (1): 1–22.
Leadbeater, Charles. 2002. *Up the Down Escalator*. Why the Global Pessimists Are Wrong. London: Viking.
Marx, Karl, and Frederick Engels. 1970. *"The Manifesto of the Communist Party" The Revolution of 1848*. Harmondswork: Penguin.
Marx, Karl. 1976. *Capital Vol. 1 A Critiue of Political Economy*. Harmondsworth: Penguin Books
McMichael, Philip. 1996. *Development and Social Change. A Global Perspective*. London: Pine Forge Press.
Milanovic, Branko. 2012. Global Inequality: From Class to Location, From Proletarians to Migrants. *Global Policy* 3 (2): 125–134.
Munck, Ronaldo. 2018. *Rethinking Global Labour: After Neoliberalism*. Newcastle: Agenda Publishing.
Nederveen Pieterse, Jan. 2001. *Development Theory. Deconstructions/Reconstructions*. London: Sage.
Negri, Antonio, and Giuseppe Cocco. 2016. *Global: Biopoder y luchas en una América Latina globalizada*. Buenos Aires: Paidós.
Silver, Beverly. 2003. *Forces of Labour, Workers' Movements and Globalization Since 1870*. Cambridge: Cambridge University Press.
Streeck, Wolfgang. 2020. Engels's Second Theory. *New Left Review* 123 (May–June).
United Nations. 2020. Rising Inequality Affecting More Than Two Thirds of the Globe. https://news.un.org/en/story/2020/01/1055681.
Wolf, Martin. 2004. *Why Globalization Works*. Yale: Yale University Press.
Wolf, Martin. 2014. *The Shifts and the Shocks: What We've Learnt-and Still have to Learn—From the Financial Crisis*. Harmondswork: Penguin.
Wood, Ellen Meiksins. 2005. *Empire of Capital*. London: Verso.
World Bank. 2020. Fragility and Conflict: On the Front Lines of the Fight Against Poverty. https://www.worldbank.org/en/topic/poverty/publication/fragility-conflict-on-the-front-lines-fight-against-poverty.

Index

R. Munck, *Rethinking Development*, Marx, Engels, and Marxisms,
https://doi.org/10.1007/978-3-030-73811-2

T

U

W